ADVANCES IN OBJECT RECOGNITION SYSTEMS

Edited by **Ioannis Kypraios**

Advances in Object Recognition Systems
Edited by Ioannis Kypraios

Published by InTech

Janeza Trdine 9, 51000 Rijeka, Croatia

Publishing Process Manager Sasa Leporic

Technical Editor Teodora Smiljanic

Cover Designer InTech Design Team

Additional hard copies can be obtained from orders@intechopen.com

Advances in Object Recognition Systems, Edited by Ioannis Kypraios
p. cm.
ISBN 978-953-51-0598-5

For EU product safety concerns:
IN TECH d.o.o., Prolaz Marije Krucifikse Kozulić 3, 51000 Rijeka, Croatia, info@intechopen.com or visit our website at intechopen.com.

Meet the editor

Dr Ioannis Kypraios received his BEng in Computer Systems Engineering with first class honours. He has an MSc in Modern Digital communication Systems with distinction. He was awarded an EU Bursary and in 2004 he completed his Doctorate at University of Sussex in Fully-Robust Object Recognition Systems. He is the author of over 30 submitted and/or published papers in high quality refereed International conferences and journals, including IEEE Proceedings, IET Sussex Network Special Presentation Series, Optical Society of America (OSA) Applied Optics Journal and SPRINGER Special Series, over 20 Technical Reports and he has presented his research results at several public exhibitions and invited seminars. In 2008, Dr. Kypraios became a full-time Research Fellow (Research Assist. Prof.-USA level) at University of Sussex. In January 2011, he became Senior Lecturer at Department of Engineering and IT, ICTM, London, and in April 2012 he joined the APEM Computing Labs (Remote Sensing and R&D Division) at Begbroke Science Park of University of Oxford, UK. Dr. Kypraios is a full member of several processional bodies including the IET and IEEE, and he is a registered FP7 Expert/Reviewer and a registered IEEE Expert Spokesperson. In February 2012, he was appointed as an IEEE Computational Intelligence Society (CIS) GOLD Subcommittee panel member.

Contents

Preface

An invariant object recognition system needs to be able to recognise the object under any usual *a priori* defined distortions such as translation, scaling and in-plane and out-of-plane rotation. Ideally, the system should be able to recognise (detect and classify) any complex scene of objects even within background clutter noise. This problem is a very complex and difficult one. In this book, we present recent advances towards achieving fully-robust object recognition. In the book's chapters' cutting edge recent research is discussed in details for all the readers with a core or wider interest in this area.

In section 1, the relation and importance of object recognition in the cognitive processes of humans and animals is described as well as how human- and animal-like cognitive processes can be used for the design of biologically-inspired object recognition systems. Chapter 1 discusses about the neurophysiopathology of attention, learning and memory. Then, it discusses about object recognition, and a novel object recognition test and its role in building an experimental model of Alzheimer's disease. Chapter 2 discusses about episodic human memory and episodic-like animal memory. Then, it discusses about object recognition and a novel object recognition task which can be used as an experimental tool for investigating full episodic memory in different animal species. Chapter 3 presents the performance analysis of the biologically-inspired modified-hybrid optical neural network object recognition system within cluttered scenes. The system's biologically-inspired hybrid design is analysed and is shown to combine a knowledge representation unit being the optical correlator block with a knowledge learning unit being the NNET block. Several experiments were conducted for testing the system's problem solving abilities as well as its performance in recognising multiple objects of the same or different classes within cluttered scenes.

In section 2, we discuss about colour processing and how it can be used to improve object recognition. Chapter 4 reviews the current state-of-the-art research about the specific role of colour information in object recognition. Then, it investigates the role of colour in the recognition of colour and non-colour diagnostic objects at different levels of the brain's visual processing.

In literature, we can identify two main categories of object recognition systems. The first category consists of linear combinatorial type filters. The second category consists of pure neural modelling approaches. In section 3, we discuss about those two categories of optical correlators and of artificial neural networks, respectively. Chapter 5 presents an iterative approach for synthesizing adaptive composite correlation filters for object recognition. The approach can be used for improving the quality of a simple composite filter in terms of quality metrics using all available information about the true-class object to be recognised and false-class objects to be rejected such as the background. Two different filters employing this iterative approach are described. First, an adaptive constrained filter is described which optimises its class discrimination properties, and, second, an adaptive unconstrained composite filter is described which optimises its properties with respect to the average correlation height (ACH), average correlation energy (ACE) and average similarity measure (ASM). Chapter 6 presents a method of integrating image features from the object's contour, its type of curvature or topographical surface information and depth information from a stereo camera, and then after being concatenated form an invariant vector descriptor which is input to a Fuzzy ARTMAP artificial neural network for learning and recognition purposes. Experimental results are discussed when using a single contour vector description (BOF), a combination of surface information vector (SFS) with BOF, and the full concatenated vector of BOF+SFS+Depth.

In section 4, we present two different applications of object recognition with still images and with video sequences. Chapter 7 presents an application of object recognition for the discrimination of modern coins into several hundreds of different classes, and the identification of hand-made ancient coins. Modern coins are acquired by a machine vision system for coin sorting but for ancient coins a scanner and camera devices are considered. In particularly, the use of a 3D acquisition device and 3D models of ancient coins are discussed. Different methods of segmentation are discussed for modern and ancient coins. Two main methods for classification are compared, one based on matching edge features in log-polar space and a second method based on an eigenspace representation. For the identification of coins features extracted from the edge of a coin and from the Fourier domain representation of the coin contour are used, and a Bayesian fusion of coin sides is studied. Improvement by 3D analysis and modelling is also presented. Results are discussed for all considered datasets and methods. Chapter 8 presents an application of non-rigid objects recognition in video sequences. An approach for recognising human action using spatiotemporal interest points (STIPs) is described. The STIPs are detected by employing different detectors. Several motion analysis techniques are presented, such as activity function, human body interest regions, and spatiotemporal boxes. Those techniques can be applied on a set of detected STIPs as an effective way of action representation. Several motion classification algorithms are discussed, such as support vector machines (SVM), probabilistic latent semantic analysis (pLSA) and others, and a proposed by the authors algorithm based on unsupervised k-means clustering algorithm. The proposed algorithm is compared with existing algorithms by being tested with the KTH human action database.

The Editor would like to acknowledge everyone that supported and actively or with their Prayers helped the successful completion of the book's publishing process stages. Special thanks to Ms Sasa Leporic InTech 's Publishing Process Manager for her unceasingly support and great help throughout the publication process.

Ioannis Kypraios
APEM Computing Labs (Remote Sensing –R&D Division), Centre for Innovation & Enterprise, Oxford University, Begbroke Science Park, Begbroke Hill, Oxfordshire, UK

Dept. of Engineering and IT, at ICTM, London, UK

School of Engineering and Design, University of Sussex, Falmer, Brighton, UK

Section 1

Cognition, and Biologically-Inspired Systems

1

Neural Basis of Object Recognition

R. Marra[1], D. Rotiroti[2] and V. Rispoli[2,*]
[1]Institute for Neurological Sciences, Pharmacological Section, National Council of Researches, Catanzaro,
[2]Laboratory for Preclinical Researches in Neuropharmacology and Neurodegenerative Diseases, Department of Pharmacological Sciences, University Magna Græcia of Catanzaro, Italy

1. Introduction

Interaction between environment and human beings, as well as each living organism, is essential for survival. Indeed, in nature every interaction among different living species is not possible without the integrity of central nervous system (CNS), which generates brain activity such as arousal, attention, learning and memory. Moreover, face perception and recognition of face are fundamental brain processes for human relationship. The ability to hold objects in memory is essential to intelligent behavior, but its neural basis still remains poorly understood.

Many studies running in the last decades in neuroscience researches have contributed to clarify the intricate puzzle about brain recognizes objects [Ungerleider and Haxby, 1994].

Now, questioning is: "How does brain recognize? What is the neural basis of objects recognition?".

Here, we briefly review neuroanatomical substrates and neurophysiological correlates which could explain the neural basis of object recognition; we also describe our contribution in this field of neuroscience reporting own pharmacological data.

2. Neurophysiopathology of attention, learning and memory

What is knowledge? How is knowledge acquired? How do we know what we know?

Starting from these essential questions, much of the epistemological debate has focused on analyzing the neurophilosophical and neuropsychological nature of knowledge in living species and how it relates to connected neurobiological aspects.

Thinking about neural basis of recognition memory it means to imagine how biological systems integrate functional information that provide reference knowledge for successive recognition.

---

*Corresponding Author

In brain, recognition of objects depends from interaction between visual system and cognitive processes such as attention and learning [Desimone and Duncan, 1995].

It is well known that there is not learning without attention as well as there is no learning without memory. Prefrontal cortex (PFC) in brain is an important area known to be involved in attention and action recognition-dependent behaviour. It also is central to active short-term memory maintenance too [Warden and Miller, 2010]. In fact, PFC, promoting attention mechanism, allows learning and memory.

The terms *Attention, Learning* and *Working Memory*, respectively, refer to systems that provide for selective prioritization for processing of information, short-term maintenance and manipulation of information necessary for performance of complex tasks.

Although there is still little direct evidence how brain remembers and discriminates objects, most neurophysiological researches on memory suggest that multiple items may be held in memory by oscillatory activity across neuronal populations. Neuronal activity, recorded from the prefrontal cortices of primate remembering two visual objects over a brief interval, has shown that oscillatory neuronal synchronization mediates a phase-dependent coding of memorized objects in the prefrontal cortex. [Funahashi et al., 1989; Buschman and Miller, 2009; Fries et al., 2007]. Moreover, neuronal information about two objects held in short-term memory is enhanced at specific phases of underlying oscillatory population activity in hippocampus.

With the advent of modern brain imaging techniques, considerable progress has been made in understanding the organization of the human brain. Above all, the further development of functional brain imaging, including PET (positron emission tomography) and fMRI (functional magnetic resonance imaging), has given great impulse and fervor to map the functional organization of the human brain with far greater precision than is possible both in physiological conditions and in humans subjected to brain injury.

The neural system, responsible for working memory, involves a large number of brain regions, but abundant neurophysiological evidence and lesion studies in nonhuman primates indicate that prefrontal cortex is a critical component [Fuster 1990; Goldman-Rakic 1990].

In fact, brain-imaging studies, using PET and fMRI, have also demonstrated that the human prefrontal cortex is implicated in working memory [Jonides et al. 1993; Petrides et al. 1993; Cohen et al. 1994; McCarthy et al. 1994; Ungerleider and Haxby, 1994; Ungerleider, 1995; D'Esposito et al. 1995, 1998; Fiez et al. 1996; Owen, 1997; Courtney et al. 1997].

Although, some questions and some dispute, about the functional organization of the human prefrontal cortex and its exact role in working memory, still remain, at present day, computational neuroscience suggests that in recognition tasks two main learning processes can be distinguished: identification and categorization. Therefore, object perception and recognition are strongly related with experience and learning.

In human studies, event-related potentials (ERPs) have been enlightening for understanding the neural basis of object recognition. Results of these researches indicate that an early ERP component, the N170 wave, is significantly larger when subjects view image with face than when they view other objects [Allison et al., 1999; Eimer, 2000]. On the contrary, patients with prosopagnosia, who have lost the ability to recognize faces, fail to demonstrate an enhanced N170 [Eimer and McCarthy, 1999].

The prefrontal area, studied by fMRI, demonstrates neuronal activity during a face recognition memory. Many findings suggest that the prefrontal attention/working memory systems are already impaired in Alzheimer's disease.

3. Alzheimer's disease

Alzheimer's disease (AD) is a neurodegenerative disorder clinically characterized by progressive decline in memory and cognitive functions. AD is associated with a dramatic loss of cholinergic neurons in the basal forebrain; specifically, those emerging from the nucleus basalis magnocellularis (NBM) [Whitehouse et al., 1981, 1982]; that causes a marked hypofunction in cholinergic transmission mainly innervating the neocortex and, in a lesser degree, the hippocampus (Fig. 1) [Mesulam et al., 1983; Coyle et al., 1983; Francis et al., 1999]. As a consequence of loss of cholinergic neurotransmission, impairment of attention, learning and memory function is produced and, furthermore, many other behavioural and cognitive capacities are also affected [Bartus et al., 1982; Collerton, 1986; Everitt and Robbins, 1997; Mufson et al., 2003].

A correct input from NBM to neocortex is essential for brain mechanisms such as arousal, attention, learning as well as working memory; whereas input from septal cholinergic neurons to hippocampus results important in memory processes such as spatial navigation.

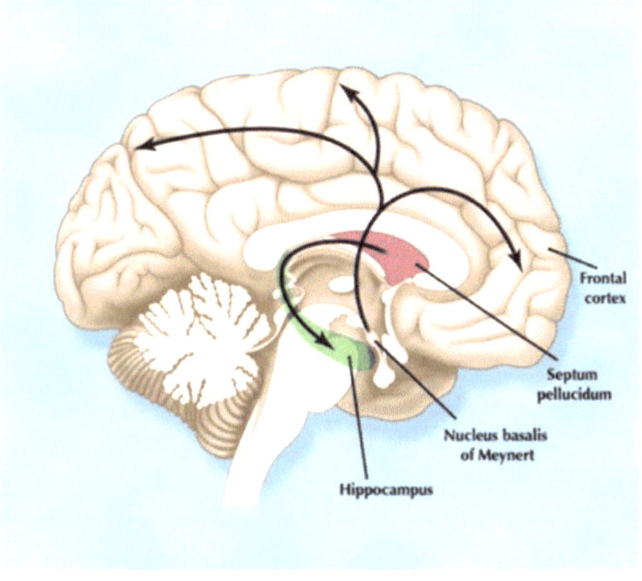

Fig. 1. Cholinergic transmission in brain.

From electrophysiological viewpoint, it is well known that basal cholinergic neurons can generate a spontaneous firing rate to control neocortical neurons; then neocortical activation generates desynchronization of electroencephalogram (EEG) and behavioural states related to alertness and attention [Rasmusson et al., 1994].

In patients with AD, the profound cognitive deficits, following loss of basal cholinergic neurons, is likely due to disrupted cortex-hippocampus neuronal network [Whitehouse e al., 1981; Coyle et al., 1983; Davies et al., 1987].

Although in the last decades there has been considerable progress in understanding the molecular and cellular changes associated with Alzheimer's disease, to date, treatment of AD is merely palliative. In fact, medication with cholinergic drugs can only alleviate clinical symptoms, even if recent fMRI studies have shown the importance of cholinesterase inhibitors (AChEIs) in treating AD [Miettinen et al., 2011].

The recent understanding in AD pathogenesis has resulted in identification of a large number of new possible drug targets. These targets include therapies that aim to prevent production or remove the amyloid-β protein that accumulates in neuritic plaques, to prevent the hyperphosphorylation and aggregation into paired helical filaments of the microtubule-associated protein tau and, finally, to keep neurons alive and functioning normally.

On which basis can we build an experimental model of Alzheimer's disease?

Experimental approach to pathophysiological comprehension of human disease, as well as to new therapeutics, has ethical limitations in medicine. For this reason, design and development of acceptable *in vivo* experimental animal models is important in research.

However, many different experimental approaches and behavioral testing have been suggested to study learning and memory. In particular, neuropharmacological research, involved in discovery of new antidementia agents, needs good experimental models of disease as well as good behavioral tests, which are important to validate pharmacological activity of drugs.

3.1 EEG and EP

Several quantitative electroencephalography (qEEG) studies have reported a progressive slowing of EEG and significant increased power in lower frequencies (delta and theta) in patients with AD [Prichep et al., 1994; van der Hiele et al., 2007]. In normal brain, correct performance in cognitive tasks implicate high levels of alertness and attention [Sala and Courtney, 2009], both dependent on the occurrence of fast EEG rhythms [Steriade, 2000, 2006].

EEG architecture shows great similarities across species. As above described, alertness is associated with fast frequencies in the EEG (e.g., beta activity), whereas non-REM sleep and drowsiness are characterized by slower waves (synchronized firing of cortical neurons).

Many experimental works have shown that drugs affect EEG characteristics in humans and rodents in a similar manner [Dimpfel et al., 1992; Jongsma et al., 1998a,b Coenen and Van Luijtelaar, 2003; Dimpfel, 2005]. In addition, a substantial body of studies suggest a relation between memory performance and EEG. For example, scopolamine decreases arousal level, which in turn increases EEG theta activity and impairs cognitive performance in object recognition in rodents. On the contrary, cholinergic agonists are able to decrease theta power and increase arousal.

Moreover, evoked potentials (EPs) show great correspondence between different species. In fact, auditory stimuli reveal a strong correspondence between rats and humans [Sambeth et al., 2003, 2004]. In both species, the short latency EP components are related to the processing of the physical properties of a stimulus, whereas the later components are associated with more endogenous processing (e.g., the psychological processes involved in the stimulus event) [Sambeth et al., 2003].

A particular aspect fascinate researchers: how does brain encode novel experiences, which are the intricate neural basis of learning and memory?

3.2 Theta oscillation underlies hippocampal novelty detection and learning

Although brain imaging has given important functional information about brain learning and memory, it cannot reveal how the brain works at level of individual neurons.

However, understanding of object recognition and its neural basis, it necessarily means to focus on a first-order question: how individual neurons represent individual memories. This has led to theoretical models of short-term memory such as sustained spiking activity by single neurons that typically reflects a single memorandum [Fuster and Alexander, 1971; Fuster and Jervey, 1982; Hopfield, 1995]. In other words, there is increasing evidence that information encoding may also depend on the temporal dynamics between neurons; for example, from relative spikes to rhythmic activity across the neural population generating local field potential (LFP) [Metha et al., 2002; Ninokura et al., 2003; Warden and Miller, 2007; Siegel et al., 2009; Kayser et al., 2009; Warden and Miller, 2010].

It is well documented that central cholinergic system plays a crucial role in cognitive functions; therefore, from an electrophysiological and neurochemical point of view, the integrity of the frontal cortex and hippocampus circuitry is essential for brain cognitive processes. In fact, it is well known that neuronal loss, following basal cholinergic degeneration, shows a close correlation with neuronal death in another vulnerable region of the brain such as the hippocampus.

Hippocampus is another brain area important for learning and memory and it exhibits relevant theta (4-7 Hz) frequency oscillations *in vivo* during behavioural activity. In fact, neural action can vary during different cognitive processes, becoming rhythmic during such a brain activity; in particular, in brain, hippocampal theta rhythmicity could contribute to learning and memory [Lee et al., 2005]. In rat, spatial memory is supported by interaction between hippocampus and cortical areas, frontal cortex mainly, which is critically involved in attention and learning [O'Keefe and Recce , 1993; Morris, 2001; Monosov et al., 2010].

Different studies indicate that hippocampus plays an essential role in novelty detection. These researches show that an important electrophysiological mechanism, by which hippocampus learn and discriminate objects in novelty detection, is the hippocampal theta activity [König et al., 1995]. Recently, new findings offer an insight into the mechanisms underlying hippocampal novelty detection stimulating new questions within the debate: theta peak or theta power?

It was proposed a link between the hippocampal theta and the detection of novel contexts. Some authors reported that in rats, exposed to familiar and novel environments, the peak hippocampal theta frequency dropped (by about 0.6 Hz) when the rats were tested in a novel environment [Jeewajee et al., 2008]. This change in theta frequency might function as a novelty signal because hippocampal theta frequency is the same in the whole hippocampus [Buzsaki, 2002], and they suggested that the reduction in theta frequency would have implications for memory encoding. The authors speculate that novelty leads a low-frequency theta depending on acetylcholine release. In fact, it is well known that new experience and novel environment induces in brain increase in cholinergic input to the hippocampus and increase in ACh release which affects hippocampal theta activity [Givens and Olton, 1994, 1995; Podol'skii et al., 2001]. On the other hand, other authors did not find any change in peak theta frequency when animals were stimulated by a novel environment; they instead reported a change in theta power that differentiated active from passive behavior, with novelty increasing power at both levels of activity [Sambeth et al., 2009].

Nevertheless, taken together both findings suggest that theta oscillations in hippocampus are affected by novelty, and that this probably gives reasons for hippocampal learning.

3.3 Novelty-induced realese of acetylcholine

Historically, ACh has been implicated in cognitive functions such as learning and short-term memory, as well as dysfunction in central cholinergic transmission was linked to learning and memory impairment present in patients with Alzheimer's disease and other forms of dementia [Bartus et al., 1982; Bartus et al., 1985; Coyle et al., 1983; Collerton, 1986; Davies et al., 1987; Blokland, 1995; Muir, 1997; Francis et al., 1999].

However, brain areas, which are supposingly most important for attentional processing in both animals and humans, appear to be the prefrontal, parietal and somatosensory (especially visual) regions, where ACh plays an essential role in the control of attentional orienting and stimulus discrimination. In addition, cholinergic signaling in the septohippocampal system is suggested to be involved in memory processes.

Trait d'union between cortical areas and hippocampus in attention and cognition is the *basal forebrain cholinergic system* [Mesulam et al., 1983]. To this purpose a lot of studies have been carried out in animals and humans, investigating the role of ACh in attention and cognition. Animal behavioral studies have been performed both in intact and in compromised brain cholinergic transmission, such as in animals subjected to specific cholinergic lesions by toxins or pharmacologically induced amnesia using muscarinic or nicotinic antagonists [Dunnett et al., 1990]. Human studies, which can give some indication on the link between central cholinergic signaling and cognition, are obviously confined to less invasive imaging methods such as fMRI.

Therefore, a large body of researches has contributed to elucidate better the role of ACh in cognitive functions. In contrast to a general role in learning and memory, recent insights have refined the function of cortical ACh more specifically in attentional effort and orienting, and detection of behavioral significant stimuli [Sarter and Bruno, 1997].

Since both ACh release and theta oscillations are affected by a range of factors, testing animals in more settings may be needed to elucidate the nature of novelty effects on hippocampal theta oscillations and phasic ACh release.

In conclusion, some indications can be given. Prefrontal cortex regions are involved in short-term memory and object discrimination. Cholinergic signaling, coming from basal forebrain to frontal cortex, septum and hippocampus, are implicated in short-term memory; in addition, the hippocampus could be important for discrimination processes in cognition.

3.4 The object recognition test

In laboratory, cognitive tasks have shown a good reliability in many experimental models of human neurodegenerative diseases. Specifically, a lot of laboratory studies have shown that the object recognition task in rodents is highly sensitive to psychoactive drug. For example, this is the case of drugs such as acetylcholinesterase inhibitors (AChEIs) which can improve object memory performance in rats [Prickaerts et al., 2002; Hornick et al., 2008; Goh et al., 2009]. In fact, in rats these ACh enhancers can reverse drug-induced memory impairments [Bejar et al., 1999; van der Staay and Bouger, 2005; Yamada et al., 2005]. This has encouraged researchers that such drugs may also be useful in treating memory impairments in patients with dementia. On the other hand, to date, clear evidence for a reliable memory enhancing effect of these drugs in humans is lacking and controversial [Snyder et al., 2005; Wezenberg et al., 2005]; that might probably be related to the discrepancy between the large numbers of animal studies and only a limited number of human studies showing memory enhancing effects of these drugs.

Object discrimination requires the integrity of cortical cholinergic system; in rodents the cortex-hippocampus circuitry consents to distinguish individual objects such as different shapes [Hauser et al., 2009].

The novel object test or object recognition test (ORT) was first described by Ennaceur and Delacour (1988). Rats or mice are exposed first to two identical objects and then one of the objects is replaced by a new object. The time spent exploring each of the objects is measured. The test has become popular for assessing the effects of amnesic drugs in rodents in general and, after that, to test new compounds enhancing attention and memory [Bartolini et al., 1996]. The test is based on spontaneous behavior with no reinforcement such as food or shock. Non-amnesic animals will spend more time exploring the novel object than the familiar one. An absence of any difference in exploration time can be interpreted as a memory defect or, in case an amnesic drug is tested, a non-effective drug.

Although the novel object recognition task has shown high sensibility and it can be a simple approach to test new potential antidementia drugs, researchers need a stronger experimental tools to test *in vivo* pharmacological activity before clinical trials. From our point of view, an electrophysiological approach together with novel object recognition task can probably be useful.

3.5 An experimental model of AD

Discovering the cause of Alzheimer's disease should imply the ultimate hope of developing safe and effective pharmacological treatments [Francis et al., 1999].

Most researches on working memory, carried out in experimental models of AD, have been modelled on those conducted in physiological studies of monkeys.

On basis of these data, in the last decades many attempts have been done to alter central cholinergic neurotransmission. The two major approaches contemplate substances pharmacologically altering central cholinergic neurotransmission or toxins, directly injected in brain and disrupting cholinergic system. Commonly, the aim is to produce highly selective lesions of cholinergic neurons with none or marginal effects on other neurons [Torres et al., 1994; Perry et al., 2001].

Our group is involved in preclinical research investigating new therapeutical approaches to AD (Fig. 2). To this purpose, in the last decade, we developed an experimental model of Alzheimer's disease to investigate the pharmacological effects of drugs with putative antidementia activity. Original compounds, likely thought to enhance central cholinergic activity, were designed, synthesized and firstly studied in our molecular modeling laboratory; after that, their pharmacological properties on both EEG brain activity and novelty object recognition were tested; finally, the relation between the EEG architecture and performance measures was studied too.

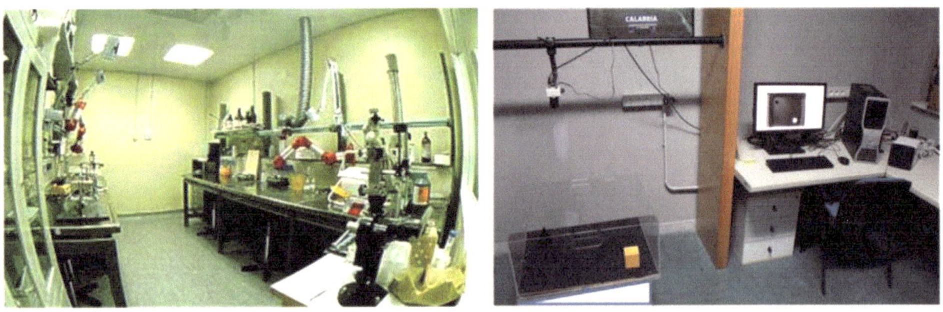

Fig. 2. Laboratory for Preclinical Researches in Neuropharmacology and Neurodegenerative Diseases at the Department of Pharmacological Sciences, University *Magna Græcia* of Catanzaro. Surgery room (left) and Behavioural Lab (right) with Noldus Ethovision® XT 8.0 apparatus for novel object recognition are here depicted.

In this AD model, we selectively damaged portion of NBM which targets the frontal cortex, producing in rat a significant deficit in attention and working memory (Fig. 3), [Rispoli et al., 2004a,b, 2006, 2008]. Further, in this experimental model, attention, learning and working memory can be evaluated monitoring cortico-hippocampal qEEG activity during object recognition task [Rispoli et al., 2011, data in progress].

The brain lesion produces a significant reduction of cholinergic neuronal population in the NBM (45%; $p<0.01$ vs control; Fig. 3, panel B). Immunohistochemistry was performed to quantify the neuronal loss in the NBM by ChAT immunoreactive neurons. Quantitative analysis of ChAT-positive neurons in NBM was carried out using a computerized image analysis system (Axiophot Zeiss microscope equipped with a Vidas Kontron system). Notably no spontaneous recovering of ChAT immunoreactive neurons has been found by us, not even after several weeks post NBM lesion.

To validate our AD model, we compared it with other well validated experimental models producing dysfunction in cognitive processes: the scopolamine-induced amnesia, a classical pharmacological model of amnesia, and that in which cholinergic neurons in the basal forebrain are subjected to immunolesion by IgG-saporin.

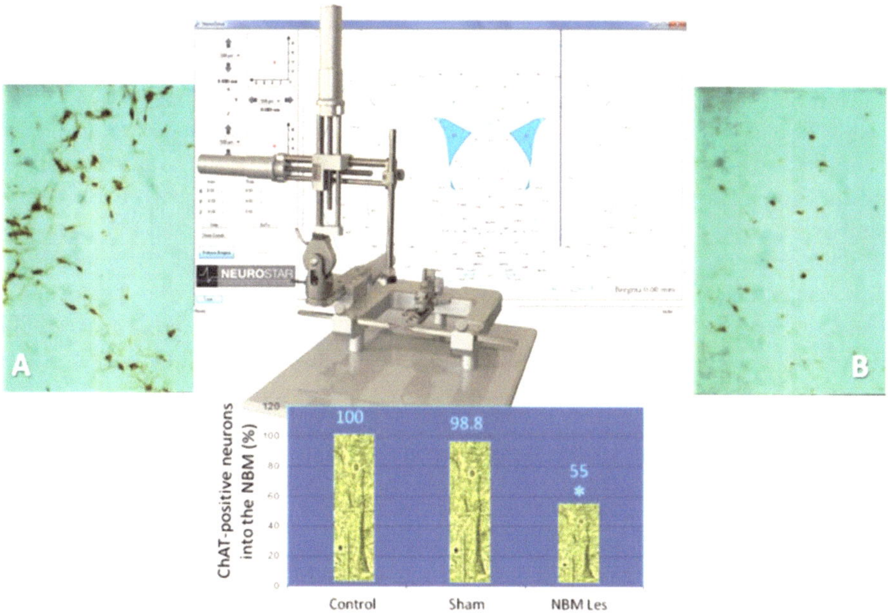

Fig. 3. Stereotaxic lesion of the Nucleus Basalis of Meynert.

Scopolamine impairs object recognition and increases theta frequency in the EEG. In this experimental model it is suggested that scopolamine likely caused a decrement in arousal. However, the effects of scopolamine on mnemonic paradigms can be characterized as disrupting acquisition and encoding information rather than retrieval processes. Most experiments used a relatively low dose of scopolamine (ranging 0.1 to 0.2 mg/kg). In fact, it must be noted that high doses of the muscarinic antagonist may not only have an effect on the muscarinic receptors, but also on the nicotinic receptors [Schmeller et al., 1994,1995]. Methyl-scopolamine, which only differs from scopolamine in that it does not cross the blood brain barrier, is generally used as a control.

Therefore, to target this aim an *in vivo* study, using our model of AD, was designed to test pharmacological properties of new compounds. With this purpose, a set of experiments was planned to evaluate them on cortex- and hippocampus-dependent memory. Attention, learning and working memory, with respect to cortical and hippocampal EEG theta rhythm, recorded during novel object recognition task in animals with lesion,of the nucleus basalis of Meynert, were studied. In NBM-lesioned animals, compared with control, an increased theta power in the cortex and a reduced theta rhythm oscillation in the hippocampus was found. These EEG changes were correlated with a worse performance in learning and memory tasks. In rats with damaged NBM, novel compounds were able to restore EEG architecture, producing cortical desynchronization and reduction in theta power [Rispoli et al., 2004a, 2006, 2008], while in the hippocampus the drugs increased theta oscillation and reduced the impairment in attention/working memory in the behavioural tasks [Rispoli et al., 2011, data in progress].

Here, we report data supporting this experimental model of AD in testing nwe compounds as putative antidementia drugs.

3.6 Novel object recognition test

The current studies investigated attention/memory for novel object recognition, according to Ennaceur and Delacour [1988] and Bartolini and coll. [1996]. Rats, placed in a white arena (70 X 60 X 30 cm) were trained to discriminate objects of different shapes (cubes, pyramids and cylinders). The day before testing, animals were placed in the arena and allowed to explore for 2min. The day after, rats were tested on a task involving two exploratory trials for 5 min with a 60-min delay between each sessions. In the first trial (T1) two identical objects were presented in two opposite corners of the arena and rats were left there until criterion was reached. Exploration was defined as directing the nose at a distance < 2cm to the object and/or touching it with the nose. Following, the second exploratory trial (T2) was conducted where the rat was presented with one object from the first exploratory trial and one novel object (Fig. 4). The time spent exploring the familiar (F) and the novel object (N) was recorded separately and the difference between the two exploration times was taken as the discrimination index (DI, a measure of novelty preference).

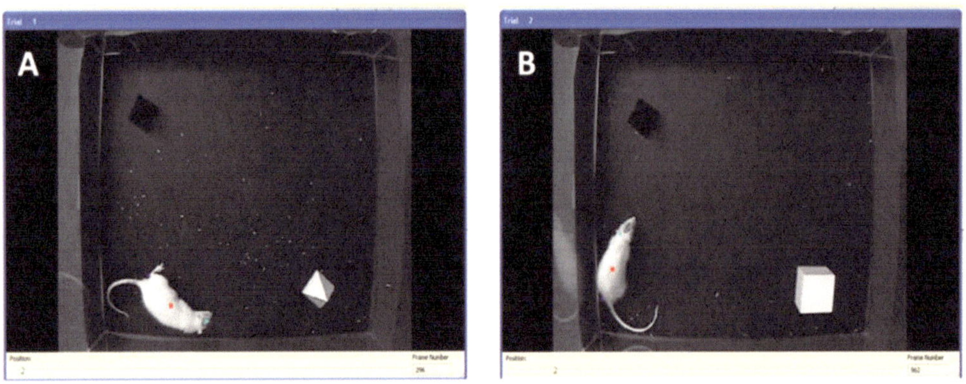

Fig. 4. Novel Object Recognition Test. A. Trial 1; B. Trial 2 (see text for details).

Intact rats, as well as sham-operated, were able to discriminate between the familial and novel object (DI = 0.33 and 0.29 respectively). In NBM-lesioned animals, values of DI were significantly lower than those in intact rats (DI = 0.07; $p<0.001$ vs intact and sham). Administration of our compounds, as well as cholinergic drugs, established discrimination in lesioned animals again, and they displayed a larger DI when compared with NBM-lesioned and saline-treated group. EEG activity in neocortex and hippocampus correlated directly with DI. Ability in novel object discrimination was evaluated as large DI, decreased theta power in neocortex and increased theta oscillation in hippocampus.

Results from the exploratory trials showed a significant impairment in exploration and discrimination in novel object in NBM-lesioned animals when compared with sham and intact group (Fig. 5). The test demonstrated that NBM-lesioned rats spent significantly less time exploring the novel object compared to familial object, indicating that lesioned rats showed disturbed attention and memory. However, NBM-lesioned rats showed no preference for novel object and spent a relatively equal amount of time exploring novel and familial objects. The results suggest that changes in attention and recent memory declines were a result of NBM-related neuronal loss and disruption in cholinergic central neurotransmission in the rodent brain. The findings also may reflect differences in attraction to objects in NBM-lesioned animals. These differences were not due to decreased exploration, motivation, or locomotion, but they likely were due to decresed cholinergic transmission arising from the NBM.

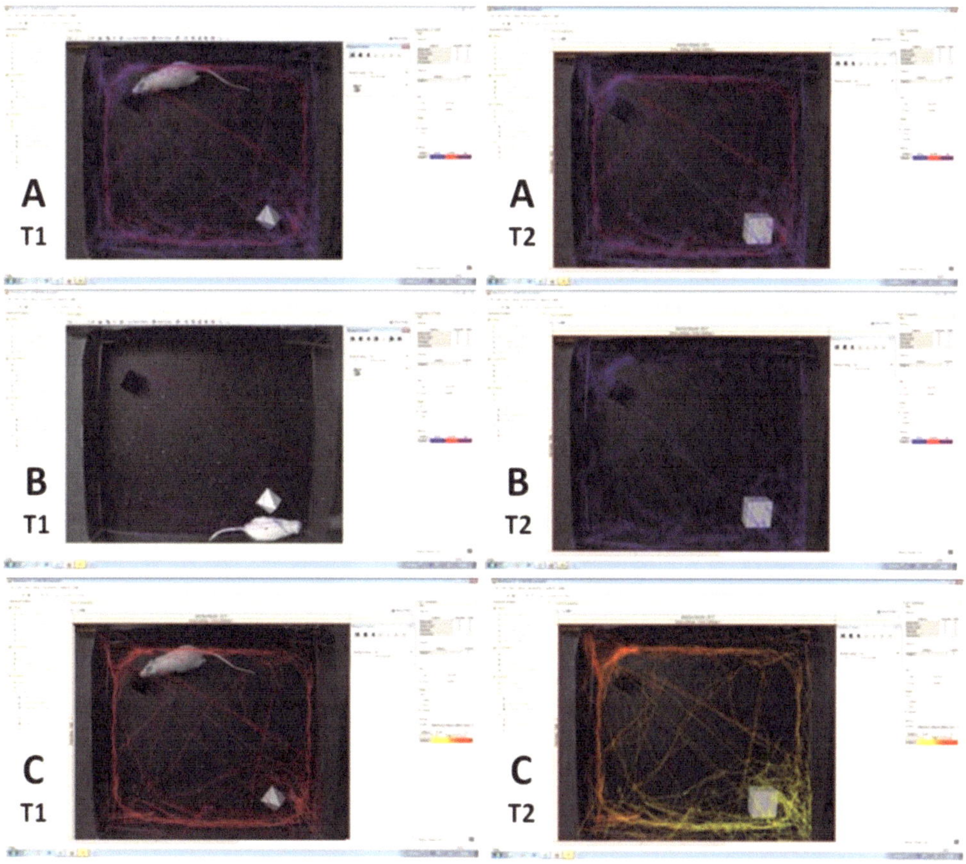

Fig. 5. Typical example of video tracking showing performance of rat with NBM lesion in novel object recognition (Noldus Ethovision® XT 8.0).

Performance in **A.** control animal (intact and sham-operated); **B.** NBM lesioned rat and **C.** NBM lesioned animal treated with AC1. Note the increased traces in T2 around the novel object in control (A) and NBM lesioned and AC1 treated animal (C).

3.7 EEG recording

Rats were equipped with neocortical electrodes to record EEG from cerebral cortex while an other electrode was implanted into the dorsal hippocampus to register hippocampal theta activity, since previous work has shown the last brain area to be involved in object recognition [Prickaerts et al., 2002; Broadbent et al., 2004].

In intact as well as in NBM-lesioned rats, EEG activity, derived from neocortex and hippocampus, was continuously monitored and recorded when animals were exposed to familiar and novel environments.

For statistical purpose, bipolar signals, derived from each neocortical area in both brain hemispheres as well as in the hippocampus, were analysed. qEEG analysis was performed on the theta range both in the hippocampus and on the whole EEG spectrum in the cerebral cortex. Five artifact-free epochs, of 10 s each, selected from EEG baseline and that recorded during the performance in behavioural tasks, were processed using Fast Fourier Transform (FFT) as previously described [Rispoli et al., 2004b]. Statistical analysis of the data was performed on the EEG signal amplitude (μV).

Neocortical EEG architecture and hippocampal theta activity was dramatically changed in NBM-lesioned rats when compared with sham-operated and intact animals. In NBM-lesioned animals, EEG baseline activity resulted significantly increased in total power (Fig. 6); in detail, quantitative analysis of EEG spectrum showed a marked raise in theta power; while neocortical high voltage spindle (HVS) appeared. No significant EEG difference was reported in sham group when compared with intact control one. No significant EEG change was also reported in lesioned animals during behavioural performance.

In NBM lesioned animals, during object recognition performance, our compounds produced desynchronisation and evidenced a marked decrease in the energy of the whole EEG power; a further analysis of the EEG spectrum showed a significant reduction of theta energy (Fig. 7). Incidence of HVS activity was also significantly reduced in NBM-lesioned animals. Moreover, in this AD model statistical analysis revealed very significant correlation between EEG changes and ORT performance.

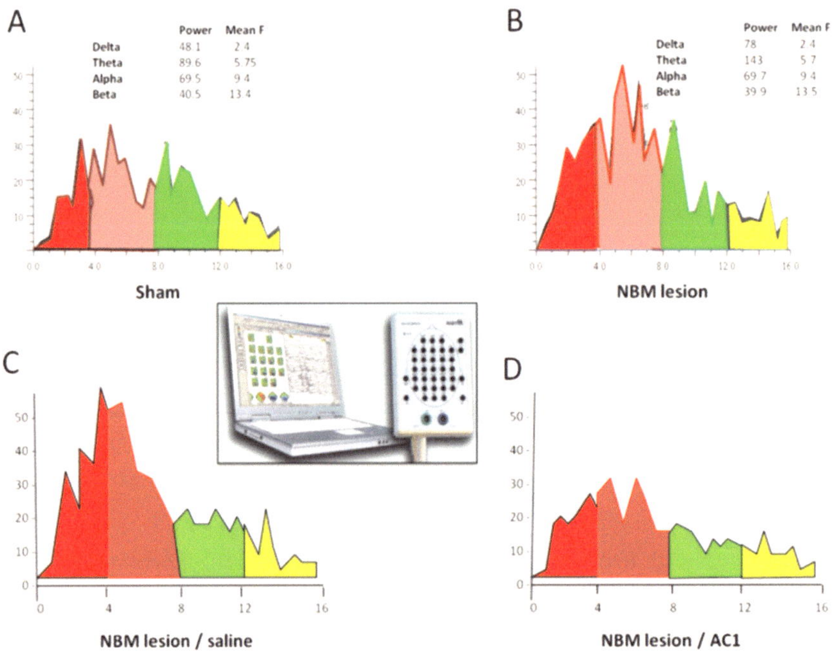

Fig. 6. Quantitative EEG and Spectral Analysis.

A typical example of neocortical EEG activity recorded in sham-operated (**A**) and NBM-lesioned animals (**B**). In NBM-lesioned animals, EEG architecture was altered; in fact, qEEG analysis showed a strong increase in total as well as delta and theta power ($p<0.001$ vs sham). **C.** and **D.** depict EEG spectrum power recorded in NBM lesioned animal after systemic administration of saline (C) or AC1 (D). The cholinergic agonist dramatically modified EEG power when compared with EEG baseline activity. A significant ($p<0.001$) fall in total voltage power, as well as in the power of lower frequency bands (0.25-3 and 4-7 Hz) is here highlighted. No EEG effect was reported after saline administration. Sham group showed no significant difference in EEG activity when compared with intact animals (data not shown). Each experiment. n =7. AC1 (12.5 mg/kg i.p.), saline (2 ml i.p.). Ordinates show the voltage power expressed in arbitrary values, abscissae show the frequency range (0.25-16 Hz).

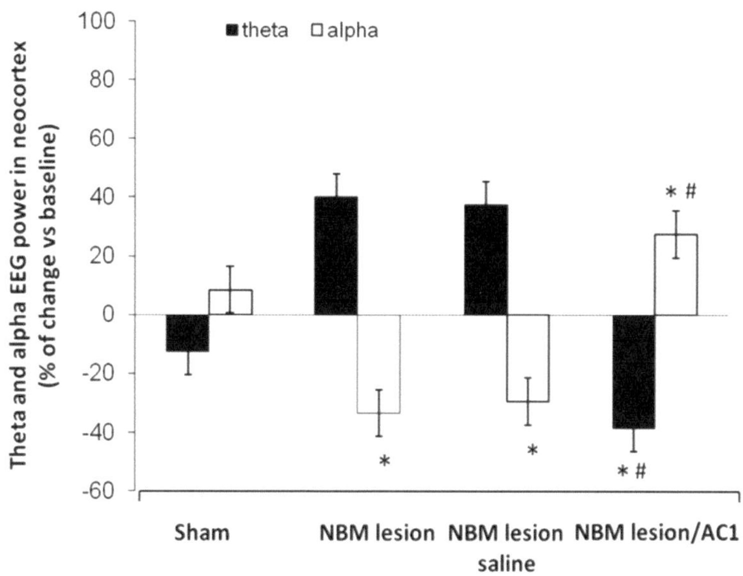

Fig. 7. Theta and alpha EEG power recorded in neocortex of rat subjected to lesion of the NBM during ORT performance.

In NBM lesioned animals, theta power resulted dramatically increased while alpha power was reduced (*$p<0.001$ vs sham). Treatment with AC1 was able to reverse the neocortical EEG activity producing a significant increase in alpha power and a marked reduction in theta power (*$p<0.001$ vs NBM lesion; #p<0.001 vs baseline). Values in mean $\pm$ SEM.

3.8 Hippocampal activity and ORT

The effects of these new compounds on learning and memory consolidation were investigated by hippocampal activity and in novel object recognition. Using the spectral analysis of the EEG, theta band (4-7 Hz) was directly recorded in rats by hippocampal depth electrode (Fig. 8). Theta oscillation was continuously monitored and recorded before and during exploration. In control animals, exploratory behaviour was correlated with an increase in hippocampal theta oscillation activity. In NBM-lesioned rats, no change in hippocampal theta frequency oscillations was observed during familial and novel recognition (Fig. 9).

The hippocampal theta oscillation, recorded in NBM-lesioned animals during the task, increased after drug treatment. In fact, compared to NBM-lesioned and not treated group, NBM-lesioned animals, which received the cholinomimetics, showed a significant increase in the duration and number of episodes of hippocampal theta activity (increase in frequency of theta rhythm) (Fig. 8).

The amount in hippocampal theta oscillations was correlated to performance in novel exploration (Fig. 10).

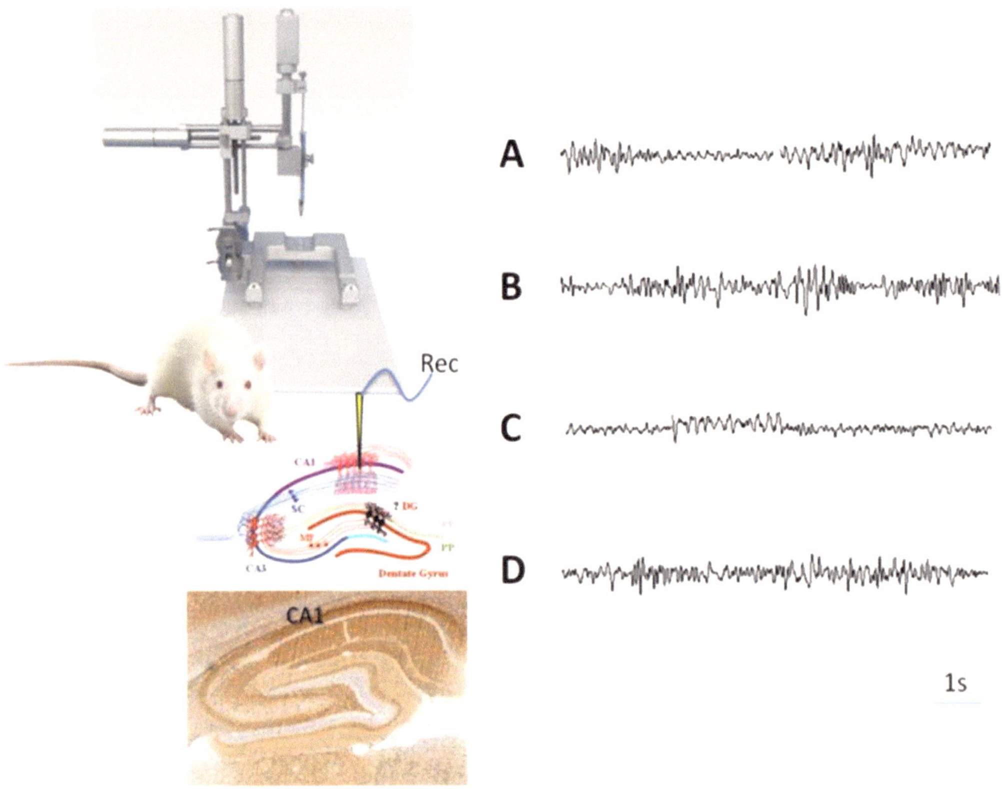

Fig. 8. Hippocampal Theta Oscillation in rats during exploration in ORT.

A bipolar electrode, stereotaxically implanted, was directly inserted into the CA1 area of the hippocampus to permit EEG recording. Theta rhythm was recorded during exploration in ORT and oscillatory activity (frequency) was studied. **A.** Control rat (intact and sham operated); **B.** Intact rat treated with AC1; **C.** Rat with lesion of the NBM and **D.** NBM lesioned rat injected with AC1. AC1 (12,5 mg/kg i.p.); seven animals for each experiment.

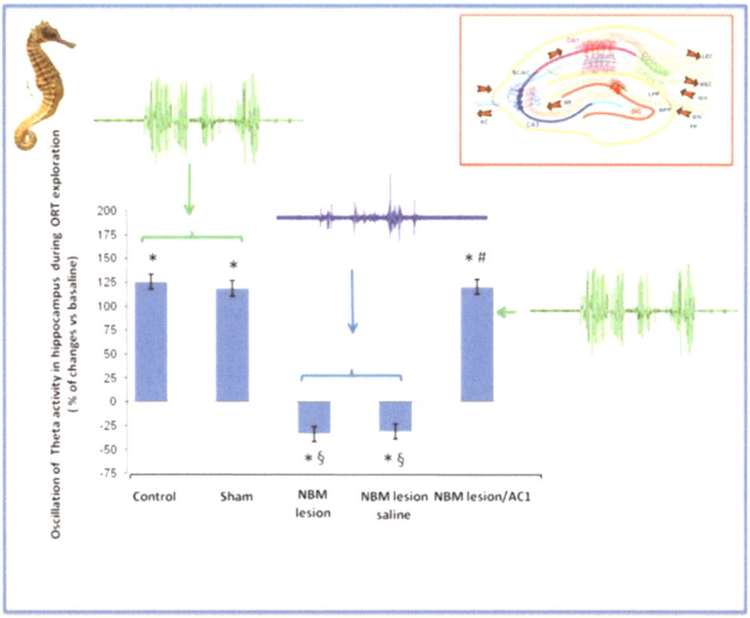

Fig. 9. Quantitative changes in hippocampal theta (3 -7 Hz) activity (frequency in theta oscillations) recorded during ORT exploration in rat with NBM lesion.

Theta activity in hippocampus was significantly reduced in animals with disrupted NBM. Theta oscillation, in this group of rats, was restored after intraperitoneal injection of AC1 (12.5 mg i.p.). Data are expressed as percent change (mean $\pm$ SEM); *$p<0.0001$ vs baseline; ; §$p<0.0001$vs control and sham; #$p<0.0001$ vs NBM lesion and NBM lesion/saline.

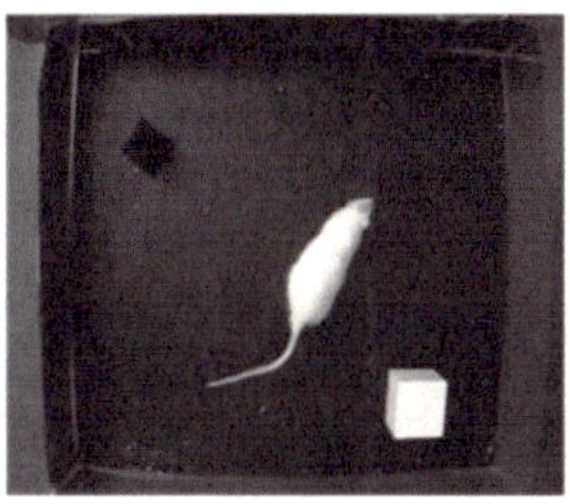

A

	Trial T2		D
	Familial (s + SEM)	*Novel* (s + SEM)	
Control (intact)	5.2 ± 1.6	10.0 ± 1.3*	0.31
Sham	6.0 ± 1.5	12.5 ± 2.3*	0.29
Lesion	12.6 ± 2.6	11.6 ± 1.5	0.06†
Not treated	10,5 ± 1.9	8.6 ± 2.9	0.09†
Saline	12.0 ± 1.6	12.6 ± 1.9	0.03†
AC1	7.2 ± 1.3	13.5 ± 2.3**	0.32"

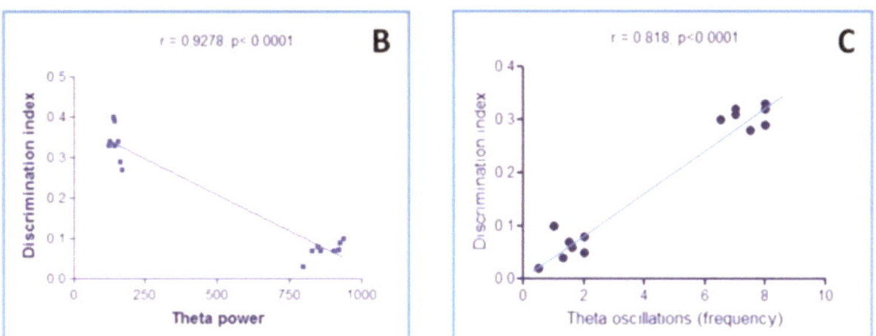

Fig. 10. Correlation between ORT performance and Theta activity in neocortex and hippocampus in rat subjected to NBM lesion.

A. Table reporting data on performance of rats in novel object recognition. NBM lesioned animals lost the ability to discriminate between the object getting a lower discrimination index (DI) than control group. **B.** Correlation between EEG theta power, recorded from neocortex in NBM-lesioned rats, and learning performance in ORT task. Damage of the cholinergic area caused a robust increase in theta power and a lower DI. AC1, in this group of animals, produced a reduction in theta power correlated with a higher DI. There was an extremely significant correlation ($r = 0.9278$, $p<0.0001$) between theta power and DI. **C.** Correlation between performance in novel object recognition and hippocampal theta oscillation (frequency) in rat with NBM lesion. The frequency of theta activity correlates to cognitive deficits in NBM-lesioned animals. Animals subjected to NBM-lesion scored a lower DI than control and showed reduced frequency in theta oscillation. AC1 administration was able to reduce the impairment in novel object recognition and restore the hippocampal theta rhythm during ORT. Theta oscillation correlates with DI ($r = 0.818$; $p<0,0001$). ORT. Spearman correlation between theta power and oscillation activity during object exploration performance evaluated as DI. Data are expressed as mean $\pm$ SEM (time (s) in object exploration). *p<0.01 N vs F (two-tailed Student's *t*-test). $^{+}$p<0.001 vs intact-control and sham. $^{\#}$p<0.001 vs lesioned and not-treated and saline-treated (Tukey-Kramer test for multiple comparison). T2 = exploration session, DI = Discrimination index (N-F/N+F). F = exploration time. AC1 (12.5 mg/kg i.p.). In each set of experiments 7 animals were used.

In conclusion, this Alzheimer's model, likely to other models, in animals produced memory deficit, worsening in behavioural performance and failing discrimination in novel object; moreover, changes in the architecture of EEG is also generated, such a significant increase in EEG theta power. Another interesting finding, coming from such an approach, was that selective cholinergic lesions of the nucleus basalis impaired spatial learning in the Morris water escape task [Rispoli et al., 2004, 2006, 2008]. The deficit in attention, learning and memory, highlighted in this experimental AD, shows a close correlation between changes in cortex-hippocampus neuronal network and novelty recognition of objects. Indeed, like AD, in this experimental model, produced by selective bilateral lesion of the NBM, normal EEG activity and cognitive function are progressively restored after administration of drugs enhancing central cholinergic transmission.

In conclusion, taken together, the present data suggest that these new drugs are able to restore the cholinergic cortico-hippocampal functional connectivity.

4. Conclusions

In brain, working memory selectively maintains a limited amount of currently relevant information in an active state to influence future perceptual processing, thought and behavior. The representation of information held in working memory is still unknown. In action recognition, distinguishing individual objects in a scene is so important for living organism because it can allow survival.

Although at present our knowledge about the precise neurobiological, neurophysiological and neuropsychological mechanisms of object recognition is not yet whole complete, many evidence indicate that the framework for investigating the neural system underlying awareness of stimuli, memories and knowledge can not be pictured without the cholinergic basal forebrain →cerebral cortex → hippocampus neural circuitry. In fact, object memory deficits point to the frontal cortex and hippocampus as early targets of functional disruption following loss of cholinergic neurons in the basal forebrain.

Alzheimer's disease is a progressive neurodegenerative disease for which no cure exists. Accordingly, there is a substantial need for new therapies that offer improved symptomatic benefit and disease-slowing capabilities. Therefore, although no cure for Alzheimer's disease are available presently, a large number of potential therapeutic interventions have emerged, designed to correct loss of cholinergic function. A few of these compounds have confirmed efficacy in delaying the deterioration of symptoms of Alzheimer's disease.

Indeed, we addressed the question of how we could contribute to alleviate cognitive decline in Alzheimer's disease.

Because human brain imaging cannot reveal the work of any brain structure at the level of individual neurons, EEG characteristics in animals may be used to predict central activity of drugs in humans. Clearly, such an approach can also be used if first a relation between EEG and memory performance can be found in animals.

In our opinion, EEG and object recognition well interface each other to study cognitive function in brain such as recognition and discrimination memory. To date, according to our experience, EEG and object recognition task still remain the best experimental approach to test pharmacological activity of potential new antidementia drugs.

The animal model of AD here presented was designed for assessing the pharmacological efficacy of original compounds, thought enhancing central cholinergic transmission, on object recognition task combined with the EEG study of neocortical and hippocampal activity. On basis of the data obtained, we believe that this Alzheimer's disease model could be reliable because a significant disturbance in attention was produced. Furthermore, results from qEEG and object recognition correlation confirm that. Moreover, cholinergic drug treatment recovered functionality in that saliency-based brain region.

Although we limit our experiments to a particular attention system, we believe that our results can be generalized to other system configurations. If this is indeed the case, more experimental testing would be required to verify this speculation, for example, a tools for measuring phasic ACh release in the hippocampus.

In conclusion, some remarks can be drown. First, we have considered the relationship between prefrontal cortex, important for working memory, and hippocampus processing information associated with object recognition. We then presented, evidence from electrophysiological, pharmacological and brain-imaging studies demonstrating that prefrontal cortex shows sustained activity during acquisition of information in working memory tasks; that indicates that this area maintains on-line representations of stimuli after they are removed. Furthermore, we discussed the possibility that the cholinergic basal forebrain → cortex → hippocampus network plays an essential role in working memory during the acquisition and maintenance of information, monitoring and manipulating the engaged novelty. Finally, we also proposed an innovative experimental model of AD which might be used to test new antidementia drugs; moreover, we reported data from our pilot study in which evidence for a contribute in this field of research have been produced.

5. Acknowledgement

Funding for this project was provided by National Council of Researches. A special thank to Dr. G.B. Politi and Dr. A. Leo for their professional competence, skill and passion in carrying out the experiments.

6. References

Allison T, Puce A, Spencer DD, McCarthy G. Electrophysiological studies of human face perception. I: Potentials generated in occipitotemporal cortex by face and non-face stimuli. Cereb. Cortex 1999; 9: 415-30.

Bartolini L, Casamenti F, Pepeu G. Aniracetam restores object recognition impaired by age, scopolamine, and nucleus basalis lesions. Pharmacol. Biochem. Behav. 1996; 53: 277-83.

Bartus RT, Dean III RL, Beer B, Lippa AS. The cholinergic hypothesis of geriatric memory dysfunction. Science 1982; 217: 408-417.

Bartus RT, Dean RL, Pontecorvo MJ, Flicker C. The cholinergic hypothesis: a historical overview, current perspective, and future directions. Ann. N. Y. Acad. Sci. 1985; 444: 332–58.

Bejar C, Wang RH, Weinstock M. Effect of rivastigmine on scopolamine induced memory impairment in rats. Eur. J. Pharmacol. 1999; 383: 231–240.

Blokland A. Acetylcholine: a neurotransmitter for learning and memory? Brain Res. Rev. 1995; 21: 285–300.

Broadbent NJ, Squire LR, Clark RE. Spatial memory, recognition memory, and the hippocampus. Proc. Natl. Acad. Sci. USA 2004; 101: 14515-20.

Buschman TJ, Miller EK. Serial, covert shifts of attention during visual search are reflected by the frontal eye fields and correlated with population oscillations. Neuron 2009; 63: 386–396.

Buzsaki G. Theta oscillations in the hippocampus. Neuron 2002; 33: 325–340.

Coenen AM, Van Luijtelaar EL. Genetic animal models for absence epilepsy: a review of theWAG/Rij strain of rats. Behav. Genet. 2003; 33: 635–655.

Cohen JD, Forman SD, Braver TS, Casey BJ, Servan-Schreiver D & Noll DC. Activation of the prefrontal cortex in a nonspatial working memory task with functional MRI. Hum. Brain Mapp. 1994; 1: 293-304.

Collerton D. Cholinergic function and intellectual decline in Alzheimer's disease. Neuroscience 1986; 19: 1-28.

Courtney SM, Ungerleider LG, Maisog JM & Haxby JV. Differences in transient fMRI responses during face encoding and recognition in a working memory task. Soc. Neurosci. Abstr. 1997; 23, 1679.

Coyle JT, Price DL, DeLong MR. Alzheimer's disease: a disorder of cortical cholinergic innervation. Science 1983; 219: 1184-90. Review.

Davies CA, Mann DM, Sumpter PQ, Yates PO. A quantitative morphometric analysis of the neuronal and synaptic content of the frontal and temporal cortex in patients with Alzheimer's disease. J Neurol. Sci. 1987; 78: 151-64.

Desimone R. and Duncan J. Neural mechanisms of selective visual-attention. Annu. Rev. Neurosci. 1995; 18: 193–222.

D'Esposito M, Detre JA, Alsop DC, Shin RK, Atlas S. & Grossman M. The neural basis of the central executive system of working memory. Nature 1995; 378: 279-281.

D'Esposito M, Aguirre G K, Zarahn E, Ballard D, Shin R K & Lease J. Functional MRI studies of spatial and non-spatial working memory. Cogn. Brain Res. 1998; 7: 1-13.

Dimpfel W. Pharmacological modulation of cholinergic brain activity and its reflection in special EEG frequency ranges from various brain areas in the freely moving rat (Tele-Stereo-EEG). Eur. Neuropsychopharmacol. 2005; 15: 673–682.

Dimpfel W., Spuler M., Wessel K. Different neuroleptics show common dose and time dependent effects in quantitative field potential analysis in freely moving rats. Psychopharmacology 1992; 107: 195–202.

Dunnett SB, Wareham AT, Torres EM. Cholinergic blockade in prefrontal cortex and hippocampus disrupts short-term memory in rats. Neuroreport 1990; 1: 61–4.

Eimer M, McCarthy RA. Prosopagnosia and structural encoding of faces: evidence from event-related potentials. Neuroreport 1999; 10: 255-9.

Eimer M. The face-specific N170 component reflects late stages in the structural encoding of faces. Neuroreport 2000; 11: 2319-24.

Ennaceur A. and Delacour J. A new one trial test for neurobiological studies of memory in rats. I: Behavioural data. Behav. Brain Res. 1988; 31: 47-59.

Everitt BJ, Robbins TW. Central cholinergic system and cognition. Ann. Rev. Psychol. 1997; 48: 649-684.

Fiez JA, Raife EA, Balota DA, Schwarz JP, Raichle ME & Petersen SE. A positron emission tomography study of the short-term maintenance of verbal information. J. Neurosci. 1996; 16: 808-822.

Francis PT, Palmer AM, Snape M, Wilcock GK. The cholinergic hypothesis of Alzheimer's disease, a review of progress. J Neurol. Neurosurg. PS 1999; 66: 137-147.

Fries P, Nikolic´ D, Singer W. The gamma cycle. Trends Neurosci. 2007; 30: 309–316.

Funahashi S, Bruce CJ, Goldman-Rakic PS. Mnemonic coding of visual space in the monkey's dorsolateral prefrontal cortex. J Neurophysiol. 1989; 61: 331–349.

Fuster JM and Alexander GE Neuron activity related to short-term memory. Science 1971; 173: 652–654.

Fuster JM and Jervey JP. Neuronal firing in the inferotemporal cortex of the monkey in a visual memory task. J Neurosci. 1982; 2: 361–375.

Fuster JM. Behavioral electrophysiology of the prefrontal cortex of the primate. In *Progress in brain research* (ed. HBM. Uylings, JPC.Van Eden, MA De Bruin, MA Corner & MGP. Feenstra), Elsevier Amsterdam 1990; pp. 313-323.

Givens B and Olton DS. Local modulation of basal forebrain: Effects on working and reference memory. J. Neurosci. 1994; 14: 3578– 3587.

Givens B and Olton DS. Bidirectional modulation of scopolamine induced working memory impairments by muscarinic activation of the medial septal area. Neurobiol. Learn. Mem. 1995; 63: 269–276.

Goldman-Rakic PS. Cellular and circuit basis of working memory in prefrontal cortex of nonhuman primates. In *Progress in brain research* (ed. HBM. Uylings, JPC. Van Eden, MA. De Bruin, MA. Corner & MGP Feenstra), Elsevier Amsterdam, 1990; pp. 325-336.

Goh DP, Neo AH, Goh CW, Aw CC, New LS, Chen WS, Atcha Z, Browne ER, Chan EC. Metabolic profiling of rat brain and cognitive behavioral tasks: potential complementary strategies in preclinical cognition enhancement research. J Proteome Res. 2009; 8: 5679-90.

Hauser E, Tolentino JC, Pirogovsky E, Weston E, Gilbert PE. The effects of aging on memory for sequentially presented objects in rats. Behav. Neurosci. 2009; 123: 1339-45.

Hopfield JJ. Pattern recognition computation using action potential timing for stimulus representation. Nature 1995; 376: 33–36.

Hornick A, Schwaiger S, Rollinger JM, Vo NP, Prast H, Stuppner H. Extracts and constituents of Leontopodium alpinum enhance cholinergic transmission: brain ACh increasing and memory improving properties. Biochem. Pharmacol. 2008; 76: 236-48.

Jeewajee A, Lever C, Burton S, O'Keefe J, Burgess N. Environmental novelty is signaled by reduction of the hippocampal theta frequency. Hippocampus 2008; 18: 340–348.

Jongsma ML., Van Rijn CM., De Bruin EA., Dirksen R, Coenen AM. Time course of chronic diazepam effects on the auditory evoked potential of the rat. Eur. J Pharmacol. 1998a; 341: 153–160.

Jongsma ML., Van Rijn CM, Setz A, Smit A, Berben I, Dirksen R, Coenen AM. Effects of diazepam on auditory evoked potentials (AEPs) and omission evoked potentials (OEPs) in rats and students. Sleep-Wake Res. Neth. 1998b; 9: 65–72.

Jonides J, Smith EE, Koeppe RA, Awh E, Minoshima S. & Mintun MA. Spatial working memory in humans as revealed by PET. Nature 1993; 363: 623-625.

Kayser C, Montemurro MA, Logothetis NK, Panzeri S. Spike-phase coding boosts and stabilizes information carried by spatial and temporal spike patterns. Neuron 2009; 61: 597–608.

König P, Engel AK, Roelfsema PR, Singer W. How precise is neuronal synchronization? Neural Comput. 1995; 7: 469–485.

Lee H, Simpson GV, Logothetis NK, Rainer G. Phase locking of single neuron activity to theta oscillations during working memory in monkey extrastriate visual cortex. Neuron 2005; 45:147–156.

McCarthy G, Blamire AM, Puce A, Nobre AC, Bloch G, Hyder F, Goldman-Rakic P & Shulman RG. Functional magnetic resonance imaging of human prefrontal cortex activation during a spatial working memory task. Proc. Natn. Acad. Sci. USA 1994; 91: 8690-8694.

Mehta MR, Lee AK, Wilson MA. Role of experience and oscillations in transforming a rate code into a temporal code. Nature 2002; 417: 741–746.

Mesulam MM, Mufson EJ, Levey QI, Wainer BH. Cholinergic innervation of Cortex by the Basal forebrain: Cytochemistry and Cortical connections of the Septal Area Diagonal Band Nuclei; Nucleus Basalis, Substantia Innominata, and Hypotalamus in the Rhesus monkey. J Com. Neurol. 1983; 214: 170-197.

Miettinen PS, Pihlajamäki M, Jauhiainen AM, Tarkka IM, Gröhn H, Niskanen E, Hänninen T, Vanninen R, Soininen H. Effect of Cholinergic Stimulation in Early Alzheimer's Disease - Functional Imaging During a Recognition Memory Task. Curr. Alzheimer Res. 2011; May 18. [Epub ahead of print].

Monosov IE, Sheinberg DL, Thompson KG. Paired neuron recordings in the prefrontal and inferotemporal cortices reveal that spatial selection precedes object identification during visual search. Proc. Natl. Acad. Sci. USA. 2010; 107: 13105-10.

Morris RG. Episodic-like memory in animals: psychological criteria, neural mechanisms and the value of episodic-like tasks to investigate animal models of neurodegenerative disease. Philosophical Transaction of the Royal Society of London: Biological Sciences 2001; 356: 1453-65.

Mufson EJ, Ginsberg SD, Ikonomovic MD, DeKosky ST. Human cholinergic basal forebrain: chemoanatomy and neurologic dysfunction. J Chem. Neuroanat. 2003; 26: 233–242.

Muir JL. Acetylcholine, aging, and Alzheimer's disease. Pharmacol. Biochem. Behav. 1997; 56: 687–96.

Ninokura Y, Mushiake H, Tanji J. Representation of the temporal order of visual objects in the primate lateral prefrontal cortex. J Neurophysiol. 2003; 89: 2868–2873.

O'Keefe J, Recce ML. Phase relationship between hippocampal place units and the EEG theta rhythm. *Hippocampus* 1993, 3:317–330.

Owen AM. The functional organization of working memory processes within human lateral frontal cortex: the contribution of functional neuroimaging. Eur. J. Neurosci. 1997; 9: 1329-1339.

Perry T, Hodges H, Gray JA. Behavioural, histological and immunocytochemical consequences following 192 IgG-saporin immunolesions of the basal forebrain cholinergic system. Brain Res. Bull. 2001; 29–48.

Petrides M, Alivisatos B, Meyer E & Evans AC. Functional activation of the human frontal cortex during the performance of verbal working memory tasks. Proc. Natn. Acad. Sci. USA 1993; 90: 878-882.

Podol'skii I.Y., Vorob'ev V.V., Belova N.A. Long-term changes in hippocampus and neocortex EEG spectra in response to pharmacological treatments affecting the cholinergic system. Neurosci. Behav. Physiol. 2001; 31: 589–595.

Prichep LS, John ER, Ferris SH, Reisberg B, Almas M, Alper K, Cancro R. Quantitative EEG correlates of cognitive deterioration in the elderly. Neurobiol. Aging 1994; 15: 85-90.

Prickaerts J, de Vente J, Honig W, Steinbusch HW, Blokland A. cGMP, but not cAMP, in rat hippocampus is involved in early stages of object memory consolidation. Eur. J Pharmacol. 2002; 436: 83-7.

Rasmusson DD, Clow K, Szerb JC. Modification of neocortical acetylcholine release and electroencephalogram desynchronization due to brainstem stimulation by drugs applied to the basal forebrain. Neuroscience 1994; 60: 665-77.

Rispoli V, Rotiroti D, Carelli V, Liberatore F, Scipione L, Marra R, Tortorella S, Di Rienzo B. Electroencephalographic effects induced by choline pivaloyl esters in scopolamine treated or nucleus basalis magnocellularis lesioned rats. Pharmacol. Biochem. Behav. 2004b; 78: 667-73.

Rispoli V, Rotiroti D, Carelli V, Liberatore F, Scipione L, Marra R, Giorgioni G, Di Stefano A. Choline pivaloyl esters improve in rats cognitive and memory performances impaired by scopolamine treatment or lesions of the nucleus basalis of Meynert. Neurosci. Lett. 2004a; 356: 199-202.

Rispoli V, Marra R, Costa N, Scipione L, Rotiroti D, De Vita D, Liberatore F, Carelli V. Choline pivaloyl ester strengthened the benefit effects of Tacrine and Galantamine onelectroencephalographic and cognitive performances in nucleus basalis magnocellularis lesioned and aged rats. Pharmacol. Biochem. Behav. 2006; 84: 453-67.

Rispoli V, Marra R, Costa N, Rotiroti D, Tirassa P, Scipione L, De Vita D, Liberatore F, and Carelli V. Choline pivaloyl ester enhances brain expression of both nerve growth factor and high-affinity receptor TrkA, and reverses memory and cognitive deficits, in rats with excitotoxic lesion of nucleus basalis magnocellularis. Behav. Brain Res. 2008; 190: 22-32.

Sala JB and Courtney SM. Flexible working memory representation of the relationship between an object and its location as revealed by interactions with attention. Atten Percept Psychophys 2009;71: 1525-33.

Sambeth A, Maes JH, Van Luijtelaar G, Molenkamp IB, Jongsma ML, Van Rijn CM. Auditory event-related potentials in humans and rats: effects of task manipulation. Psychophysiology 2003; 40: 60–68.

Sambeth A, Maes JH, Quian Quiroga R, Coenen AM. Effects of stimulus repetitions on the event-related potential of humans and rats. Int. J Psychophysiol. 2004; 53: 197–205.

Sambeth A, Meeter M, Blokland A. Hippocampal Theta Frequency and Novelty. Hippocampus 2009; 19: 407–408.

Sarter M and Bruno JP. Cognitive functions of cortical acetylcholine: toward a unifying hypothesis. Brain Res. Rev. 1997; 23: 28–46.

Schmeller T, Sauerwein M, Sporer F, Wink M, Müller WE. Binding of quinolizidine alkaloids to nicotinic and muscarinic acetylcholine receptors. J Nat. Prod. 1994; 57: 1316-9.

Schmeller T, Sporer F, Sauerwein M, Wink M. Binding of tropane alkaloids to nicotinic and muscarinic acetylcholine receptors. Pharmazie 1995; 50: 493-5.

Siegel M, Warden MR, Miller EK. Phase-dependent neuronal coding of objects in short-term memory. Proc. Natl. Acad. Sci. USA 2009; 106: 21341-6.

Snyder P., Bednar M., Cromer J., Maruff P. Reversal of scopolamineinduced deficits with a single dose of donepezil, an acetylcholinesterase inhibitor. Alz. Dem. 2005; 1: 126–135.

Steriade M. Corticothalamic resonance, states of vigilance and mentation. Neuroscience 2000; 101: 243-76. Review.

Steriade M. Grouping of brain rhythms in corticothalamic systems. Neuroscience 2006; 137:1087-106. Review.

Torres EM, Perry TA, Blokland A, Wilkinson LS, Wiley RG, Lappi DA., et al. Behavioural, histochemical and biochemical consequences of selective immunolesions in discrete regions of the basal forebrain cholinergic system. Neuroscience 1994; 63: 95–122.

Ungerleider L and Haxby J. 'What' and 'where' in the human brain. Curr. Op. Neurobiol. 1994; 4: 157–165.

Ungerleider LG. Functional brain imaging studies of cortical mechanisms for memory. Science 1995; 270: 769-775.

van der Hiele K, Vein AA, Reijntjes RH, Westendorp RG, Bollen EL, van Buchem MA, van Dijk JG, Middelkoop HA. EEG correlates in the spectrum of cognitive decline. Clin. Neurophysiol. 2007; 118: 1931-9.

van der Staay FJ and Bouger PC. Effects of the cholinesterase inhibitors donepezil and metrifonate on scopolamine-induced impairments in the spatial cone field orientation task in rats. Behav. Brain Res. 2005; 156: 1–10.

Warden MR and Miller EK. The representation of multiple objects in prefrontal neuronal delay activity. Cereb. Cortex 2007; 17: 41–50.

Warden MR and Miller EK. Task-dependent changes in short-term memory in the prefrontal cortex. J Neurosci. 2010; 30: 15801-10.

Wezenberg E, Verkes RJ, Sabbe BG, Ruigt GS, Hulstijn W. Modulation of memory and visuospatial processes by biperiden and rivastigmine in elderly healthy subjects. Psychopharmacology 2005; 181: 582–594.

Whitehouse PJ, Price DL, Clark AW, Coyle JT, DeLong MR. Alzheimer's disease: evidence for selective loss of cholinergic neurons in the nucleus basalis. Ann Neurol., 1981; 10: 122-126.

Whitehouse PJ, Struble RG, Clark AW, Price DL. Alzheimer's disease: plaques, tangles, and the basal forebrain. Ann Neurol. 1982; 12: 494-XX.

Yamada K, Takayanagi M, Kamei H, Nagai T, Dohniwa M, Kobayashi K, Yoshida S, Ohhara T. Takuma K, Nabeshima T. Effects of memantine and donepezil on amyloid beta-induced memory impairment in a delayed-matching to position task in rats. Behav. Brain Res. 2005; 162: 191–199.

2

Spontaneous Object Recognition in Animals: A Test of Episodic Memory

Amy-Lee Kouwenberg, Gerard M. Martin, Darlene M. Skinner, Christina M. Thorpe and Carolyn J. Walsh
Memorial University of Newfoundland
Canada

1. Introduction

Episodic memory is characterized by Tulving (1983, 2002) as a discrete form of memory that involves mentally re-enacting previously experienced events. Traditionally, the investigation of episodic memory has been restricted to human subjects because the ability to mentally re-enact past experiences suggests that it requires self-consciousness and the ability to mentally travel forward and backward in time (Tulving, 1983, 2002). Because of the difficulty of demonstrating these abilities without the use of complex verbal language, many believed that episodic memory could not be studied in non-humans. However, through a series of elegant experiments, Clayton, Dickinson and their colleagues (e.g., Clayton & Dickinson, 1998) have developed a paradigm that allows researchers to model some aspects of episodic memory in non-humans. In particular, they focus on the abilities of food-caching birds to represent the "what/where/when" of an event into a single tripartite code. While this model has opened up the field of episodic memory to testing in non-humans, it is not easily applied to non-caching species. More recently, Eacott and Norman (2004) have developed a paradigm using object recognition that allows researchers to model episodic memory in a wider variety of non-human animals. Their paradigm involves altering the "what/where/*when*" code of Clayton and Dickinson to a tripartite code consisting of "what/where/*which*."

In this chapter, we make the argument that this use of object recognition is a better paradigm for studying episodic memory in non-humans. We begin with a description of episodic memory and the paradigms used to study it in non-human animals. We then describe studies of object recognition in non-human animals and studies that use object recognition to test episodic-like memory in rodents and pigs. And finally, we discuss how this research complements the growing field of episodic-like memory in non-human animals.

2. Episodic memory

Episodic memory has been characterized as a discrete form of memory that involves mentally re-enacting previously experienced events (Tulving 1983, 2002). Specifically, this type of memory requires the integrated recall of the "what, where and when" circumstances of an event, the ability to recognize subjective time, and autonoetic consciousness (knowledge of self; Tulving, 1983, 2002). The main distinction between episodic memory and other forms of recall involves the recreation of a personally experienced event. Simple retrieval of discrete facts (e.g., Marconi received a wireless transmission at Signal Hill in 1901), does not require the self-consciousness nor the ability to mentally travel forward and backward in time that are indicative of episodic memory (e.g., I was on Signal Hill yesterday and read a sign about Marconi). Despite the acceptance of episodic memory in humans, its presence in non-human animals is controversial.

In the absence of a measure of consciousness in non-human animals, it has not been possible to demonstrate episodic memory that is equivalent to humans. However, by studying food caching (Clayton & Dickinson, 1998), food finding (Babb & Crystal, 2006), fear conditioning (O'Brien & Sutherland, 2007), and object exploration (Eacott & Norman, 2004), researchers claim to have demonstrated a form of episodic memory in scrub jays (Clayton & Dickinson, 1998), pigeons (Zentall et al., 2001), mice (Dere et al., 2005), rats (Eacott & Norman, 2004; O'Brien & Sutherland, 2007), gorillas (Schwartz & Evans, 2001), rhesus monkeys (Hoffman et al., 2009), and chimpanzees/bonobos (Menzel, 1999; Martin-Ordas et al., 2010).

The interpretation of such studies is often controversial because there is no consensus regarding a definition of non-human episodic memory (Hampton & Schwartz, 2004). Schwartz, Hoffman and Evans (2005) outlined five operational definitions of non-human episodic memory including: (1) the demonstration of what/where/when memory (Clayton & Dickinson, 1998; Babb & Crystal, 2006), (2) the demonstration of what/where/which memory (Eacott & Norman, 2004), (3) the demonstration of spontaneous recall (Menzel, 1999), (4) the ability to recall an event when not expecting a test (Zentall et al., 2001), and (5) the ability to report on past events over a long term (Schwartz & Evans, 2001). Unfortunately, these definitions tend to be species-specific. For example, definitions of episodic memory based on research with food-caching birds (Clayton & Dickinson, 1998) often do not fare well when applied to non-caching species (Bird et al., 2003; Hampton et al., 2005). Consequently, alternative methods and definitions have been developed for rodents, primates, and non-caching birds.

3. What/where/when memory in western scrub jays

Clayton and Dickinson (1998) have been largely responsible for introducing and developing the concept of episodic memory in non-humans. They have demonstrated that Western scrub jays form integrated memories of what, where and when information in the context of caching and recovering food. Furthermore, they suggest that the types of caching behaviour shown by the scrub jays requires them to mentally travel forward and backward in time, which is a component of human episodic memory (Clayton et al., 2003a). However, because Clayton, Dickinson and their colleagues have not been able to demonstrate autonoetic consciousness (i.e., a sense of self) in scrub jays, they have stopped short of declaring that scrub jays have human-equivalent episodic memory. Instead, they have opted to conclude that scrub jays possess "episodic-like memory." This type of memory shares some characteristics with the definition of human episodic memory (Tulving, 1983), but avoids the currently impossible task of demonstrating consciousness without the use of verbal language (Clayton et al., 2003b).

Clayton and Dickinson (1998) took advantage of the scrub jays' natural food-storing behaviours and allowed each bird to cache both perishable, but preferred, worms and non-perishable peanuts in opposite sides of an ice-cube tray filled with sand. Initially, the scrub jays demonstrated the ability to recall the location ("where") in which they cached each type of food ("what"), and consequently retrieved the preferred food, worms, before peanuts. In subsequent trials, the researchers replaced freshly cached worms with decayed worms if worms were cached first (124 h before retrieval) and peanuts cached second (4 h before retrieval). In contrast, fresh worms were left in their cached locations if peanuts were cached first (124 h before retrieval) and worms cached second (4 h before retrieval). Remarkably, the scrub jays quickly learned to retrieve peanuts if worms were cached first (since decayed worms are unpalatable) and to retrieve worms if peanuts were cached first. A similar result, although less compelling, was found when jays were taught that worms were removed (pilfered) if they were cached 124 h before retrieval.

In numerous subsequent studies, Clayton and Dickinson further developed their case for episodic-like memory in scrub jays. Specifically, through allowing jays to cache peanuts and dog kibble and then recover these items on successive trials, they demonstrated that scrub jays update their memories about which cache sites contain food (Clayton & Dickinson, 1999). Furthermore, by making one food less preferable than another through pre-feeding, they found that jays successfully identified food caches that were both non-recovered and contained preferable food. Clayton and Dickinson (1999) argue that this ability indicates that scrub jays form episodic-like memories that integrate the type of food in a cache, the location of that cache, the last activity at that cache (recovery or caching) and how long ago food was stored. Clayton et al., (2005) have also shown that scrub jays use novel information about the decay of a food source to reverse their strategies for recovery, since jays cache more non-perishable food items if their caches are consistently degraded on recovery. Emery and Clayton (2001) found that scrub jays who have previously raided the food cache of a conspecific will re-cache food if they are observed during their own caching process. Recently, Cheke and Clayton (2011) examined caching in the Eurasian jay and demonstrated that birds distinguish between their current food preference (created by pre-feeding a specific food) and their future needs. This was evidenced by the birds overcoming motivation to cache currently desired food and instead caching currently non-preferred foods according to their future value. Taken together, these findings provide preliminary evidence that caching scrub and Eurasian jays make decisions based on past episodes and anticipated future needs. Because these results suggest that episodic-like memory includes aspects of the mental time travel involved in human episodic memory, further study in this area, including research on non-caching species, such as ant-following birds, is suggested (Clayton et al., 2003c; Logan et al., 2011).

4. What/where/when memory in other species

Many researchers have used the basic what/where/when criteria proposed by Clayton and Dickinson (1998) in their attempts to demonstrate episodic-like memory in species such as pigeons (Skov-Raquette et al., 2006), primates (Hoffman et al., 2009; Martin-Ordas et al., 2010), mice (Dere et al., 2005), and rats (Babb & Crystal, 2006; Fortin et al., 2002; Kart-Teke et al., 2006; O'Brien & Sullivan, 2007). The majority of studies have been conducted using mice and rats, which has led to the development of several different testing paradigms.

Babb and Crystal (2006) developed a radial maze task that required rats to remember the type of food contained in different maze arms at different times. They showed that rats were able to integrate what/where/when memories to obtain preferred foods, and that rats changed their preferences if these preferred foods were devalued. Fortin et al. (2002) developed a task in which rats were required to remember a series of odour cues to obtain food from sand-filled cups. The rats were able to remember the odour and whether it occurred before or after another odour in the sequence. However, Clayton et al., (2003a) argued that rats may have solved this task using internal interval timing, and that this task does not demonstrate integrated memory for "where." O'Brien and Sutherland (2007) took advantage of the observation that rats need exposure to a context to form context-shock associations (Faneslow, 1990) and that the associations formed can be based solely on the memory of the context (Rudy et al., 2002). They (O'Brien & Sutherland, 2007) exposed rats to two distinctive boxes, one in the morning and the other in the evening. After the exposure, rats were exposed to a third box that was an amalgam of the morning and evening box. They were shocked in this box in either the morning or the evening session. Tests of freezing at an intermediate time interval in either the morning or the evening box demonstrated freezing to the box congruent with the time of day the shock had been received. This finding indicated that the rats had formed a time-place memory and that this memory had been updated at the time the shock had been administered. A recent study with chimpanzees, bonobos and orangutans adapted the methods of Clayton and Dickinson (1998) and showed that apes integrate what/where/when memories to choose between frozen juice (the preferred food after a 5 min rest interval, but not after a 1h rest interval because it melts and becomes unavailable) and a grape (the preferred food after a 1h rest interval because the juice is unavailable) (Martin-Ordas et al., 2010).

Although not exhaustive, the above list illustrates the main testing strategies that have been used to demonstrate what/where/when memory in non-caching species. The absence of caching behaviour in many species is a serious hindrance to replicating the results found in scrub jays (Bird et al., 2003; Hampton et al., 2005). Although numerous clever methods have been developed to test the what/where/when criteria, many of these cannot avoid alternate, more parsimonious explanations for results. With the possible exception of O'Brian and Sutherland (2007), this is particularly true for the "when" component of episodic-like memory. Even studies that have gone so far as to show that memories are flexible (i.e., a rat's change in food preference shown by Babb & Crystal 2006) are confounded by the possibility of relative memory strengths and internal time intervals experienced by subjects.

The problematic nature of the "when" aspect of memory is also demonstrated by distinct but related research in daily Time-Place Learning. In daily Time-Place learning tasks, animals are trained that a food reward is available in one location in morning sessions and in another location in afternoon sessions (Thorpe & Wilkie, 2006). This task is different from episodic tasks in that the subjects require repeated training prior to restricting their searches to the appropriate locations at the correct times of day. To solve this task, an animal must learn to associate event/place/time or what/where/when information in a single code. Paralleling the results in the episodic-like literature, pigeons learn this task relatively easily (Saksida & Wilkie, 1994); however, both fish (e.g., Barreto et al., 2006) and rats (e.g., Thorpe et al., 2003) have much more difficulty acquiring the task. Research has shown, however, that rats quickly learn to restrict their searches to the locations that provide food indicating that they have learned the bipartite what/where code (Thorpe, et al., 2003). It is also known that rats can learn when in the day that they will receive food - or the bipartite what/when code (Means et al., 2000; Thorpe et al., 2003). However, it is only under certain conditions that rats combine these three components into a tripartite what/where/when code and successfully solve the task. For example, in situations in which there is a high cost of making a mistake, either in effort or in time, rats are more likely to solve the task (Widman et al., 2000). Given these findings, animals may be able to learn temporal information, but it may not reflect the natural way events are encoded.

5. What/where/which episodic-like memory

In an attempt to avoid some of the confounds and problems involved in demonstrating "when" memory, Eacott and Norman (2004) used *context* to replace time as the "when" component of episodic-like memory, which broadens the definition of episodic-like memory to include integration of the "what, where, and *which*" details of an event. They argue that the function of the "when" aspect of episodic memory is simply to mark an event as being unique. Therefore, requiring animals to remember the discrete time at which an event occurred (e.g., 1 hour ago or 24 hours ago) is the same as having animals discriminate the context in which an event occurred (e.g., white-walled room vs. black-walled room; Eacott & Gaffan, 2005; Eacott & Norman 2004;). Either chronological time or context can serve as the reference point that identifies a specific event and allows it to be recalled. This idea is further supported by the fact that time does not appear to be an essential part of human episodic memory. Humans tend to use background cues that are present during an event, rather than time, to distinguish it from other similar events (Friedman, 1993).

6. Novel object recognition task

The paradigm used most often to assess what/where/which memory is the novel object recognition task. This clever but simple task takes advantage of a predisposition in many species to explore novel objects over familiar ones. Ennaceur and Delacour (1988) first reported the object recognition task, in which rats were exposed to objects during an acquisition trial and then tested on their ability to discriminate between familiar and novel objects, as a test of working memory. The object recognition test has been used to show that rats are sensitive to the location of objects (Dix & Aggleton, 1999; Ennaceur et al., 1997; Poucet, 1989), to the topological relationship between objects (Dix & Aggleton, 1999; Goodrich-Hunsaker et al., 2008; Harley et al., 2001; Lemon et al., 2009), to changes in the distance between objects (Goodrich-Hunsaker et al., 2008), to the context in which objects have been experienced (Dix & Aggleton, 1999; Eacott & Norman, 2004), and to changes in object compounds (Norman & Eacott, 2004).

In addition to the innovative what/where/which definition, Eacott and Norman's (2004) unique method of testing episodic-like memory meets the requirements of spontaneous recall (Menzel, 1999) and recall during an unexpected test (Zentall et al., 2001). Eacott & Norman (2004) found that rats can integrate memories of a specific object (what), its spatial location (where) and the context in which it occurs (which) to discriminate the more novel of two object/location/context combinations. Rats explored the locations (left or right) of each of the objects (A or B) in each of the two contexts (1 or 2). During the test, the rat was placed in one of the contexts with two copies of the same object (e.g., A and A), and the amount of time the rat spent exploring each object was recorded. Since identifying the more novel of two configurations requires the simultaneous recall of what, where and which (object/location/context) information, Eacott and her colleagues argued that novel object recognition tasks test episodic-like memory (Eacott et al., 2005; Kart-Teke et al., 2006). In fact, they argued that object recognition is superior to other methods because it requires very little training before subjects are tested, which reduces potential confounds caused by reinforced learning (Eacott & Norman, 2004). Furthermore, since exploring novelty is a natural response for many species, recall of the more novel object/location/context appears to be spontaneous, which meets Menzel's (1999) criterion for episodic-like memory. As well, explicit cues or rewards are not needed to prompt memories, which meets Zentall et al.'s (2001) criterion that episodic-like memory tests must be unexpected.

Similarly, others have shown that rats (Kart-Teke et al., 2006) and mice (Dere, et al., 2005) integrate what and where information with the order in which stimuli are presented. An object recognition task was used that required the animals to discriminate more novel objects based on a combination of the objects' locations and the order in which they were presented. The animals spent more time exploring a less recently presented object compared to a more recently presented object, which indicates that they had integrated "what and when" memory. The authors found that "what and when" memory was integrated with "where" because the animals responded differently to displacement of more recent and less recent objects. When presented with two more recently experienced objects, the animals spent more time with the object that had been displaced to an unfamiliar location as compared to the object in a familiar location. In contrast, when presented with two less recent objects, the animals spent more time with the object in the familiar location than with the object in an unfamiliar location. They concluded that these findings provided evidence for integration of what/where/when memories into a single tripartite code because they show that these three dimensions are not encoded, stored and retrieved independently (Dere, et al., 2005; Kart-Teke et al., 2006). As well, they argue that animals could not use relative memory strengths to discriminate whether an object was displaced because spatial information was obtained on a single trial.

The use of object recognition/preference to study episodic memory has also been extended to the study of recall of information without the stimuli being re-presented in the test phase (Eacott et al., 2005). Rats were trained to explore an E-shaped maze with two objects, followed by exposure to a different E-shaped maze with the same objects in opposite locations. After the two exposures, the rats were placed in a different context with one of the objects for a habituation session. When the rats were placed back into one of the E-shaped mazes, they tended to go to the non-habituated object, which was not visible from the middle stem of the E. In order to explore the more novel (non-habituated) object, the rats must remember which of the two objects (what) is in each arm (where) in which context. This recollection task, like the caching task used with scrub jays, 'asks' rats about objects that they cannot see and is more akin to the types of recall used in human measures of episodic memory.

7. Episodic-like memory in pigs

Eacott and Norman's (2004) successful demonstration of what/where/which memory in rats has led to an interest in applying this definition and method to other species. Similar to rats, pigs naturally tend to explore novel aspects of their environment (Wood-Gush & Vestergaard, 1991). Pigs also have good spatial memory abilities and they are able to learn tasks quickly (e.g., Croney, 1999; Held et al., 2002; Held et al., 2005; Puppe et al., 2007; reviewed in Gieling et al., 2011). As well, wild and feral pigs have a life history in which memory is valuable; particularly because they live socially, have large foraging ranges, and have foraging habits/movement patterns/nesting sites that change with season and food availability (Graves, 1984). Since domestic pigs have retained many natural behaviours despite the domestication process, particularly in foraging (Gustafsson et al., 1999), it is reasonable to speculate that domestic pigs retain the memory abilities possessed by their wild ancestors. These factors indicate that episodic-like memory in pigs may be more developed than in some other species.

The physiological similarity between humans and pigs is likely responsible for the recent increased popularity of pigs as biomedical models of human disease and cognition (for reviews, see Gieling et al., 2011; Kornum & Knudsen, 2011; Lind et al., 2007). Accordingly, pigs may also provide a more effective comparison than other species between human episodic memory and episodic-like memory in animals. Specifically, the pig brain is more similar to the human brain in structure (gyration), myelination and electrical activity than are the brains of rodents and other small laboratory animals (Dickerson & Dobbing, 1966; Pond et al., 2000). Also similar to humans, the pig brain develops perinatally, with a growth spurt extending from mid-gestation to about 40 days after birth (Dickerson & Dobbing, 1966; Dobbing & Sands, 1973; Pond et al., 2000). Such similar physiological brain development may be particularly valuable in studies of changes in memory with age.

Prior to our work (Kouwenberg et al., 2009), the existence of episodic-like memory in pigs remained virtually unexplored. However, there were several studies that demonstrated pigs can perform spontaneous object recognition, using modifications of the Ennaceur and Delacour (1988) protocol (Gifford et al., 2007; Kornum et al., 2007; Moustgaard et al., 2002). We explored episodic-like memory in pigs by examining their ability to discriminate between objects according to the location and context in which they occurred (Figures 1 and 2). On each trial, a pig was confined to a holding pen for 2 min prior to a 10 min exposure to one context containing two objects (e.g., Context 1 with Object A on the right and Object B on the left). After an additional 5 min in the holding pen, the pig was given a 10 min exposure to another context containing the same objects but in opposite locations (i.e., Context 2 with Object A now on the left and Object B on the right). The test trial was administered after another 5 min in the holding pen, and consisted of a 10 min exposure to one of the contexts with two identical objects (e.g., Context 2 with two copies of Object A). If the pigs remembered the location and context in which each object occurred during the two exposure phases, they should allocate their exploration time differentially, based on the familiarity of the object/location/context configurations during the test phase.

Pigs spent more time with the less familiar object/location/context during the test phases of the episodic-like memory trials, indicating that they were able to simultaneously recall memories of what (object), where (location) and which (context). Since the separate aspects (object, location, and context) of each object/location/context configuration are equally familiar, it is only the combination of all three aspects that makes one configuration less familiar than another. Therefore, the pigs' significant preference for the *less* familiar configuration cannot be attributed to object preference alone, location preference alone, or

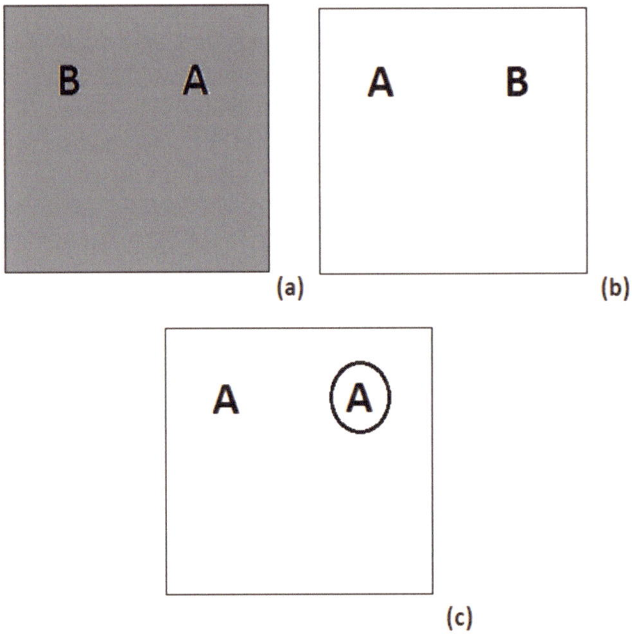

Fig. 1. A diagram of the episodic-like memory trial used in our study. An example of a possible configuration for the first exposure phase (a), second exposure phase (b), and test phase (c). Shading indicates a different floor colour (i.e., different context). The black circle indicates the novel object/location/context in the test phase of this trial.

Fig. 2. A pig interacting with an object during episodic-like memory test.

context preference alone. Objects in the test phase were identical, pigs had been equally exposed to both locations before the test phase, and pigs had been equally exposed to both contexts before the test phase. Furthermore, the preference for the less familiar object/location/context could not be attributed to object and location alone because objects and locations were counterbalanced for each pig. Thus, each pig received an episodic-like memory trial with two objects "A" in the test phase and a trial with two objects "B" in the test phase. If pigs were ignoring context and making decisions based solely on object and location, half of the time pigs would spend more time with the left-hand object and the other half of the time the pig would spend more time with the right-hand object. This would have resulted in no significant overall preference for either object/location/context. Our data indicate that this is not the case, leading to the conclusion that pigs formed integrated memories of what/where/which information. Whether pigs can also do the recollection task used by Eacott et al. (2005) remains to be determined.

8. Conclusion

The above findings indicate that the formation of a tripartite code of either "what/where/when" or "what/where/which" seems to be within the compass of animals when species-typical preferences are taken into account. While the what/where/when model of Clayton and Dickinson (1998) is an elegant demonstration of episodic-like memory, its usefulness may be restricted due to the limited number of animals that cache food. While some researchers, notably Babb and Crystal (2006), have attempted to modify this task with rodents it requires a significant amount of pre-training because it does not use behaviours that naturally exist within the repertoire of some species. The recent findings from object exploration indicate that this may be a powerful way to study the formation of a tripartite code in animals. The paradigm allows for the testing of a tripartite code of what/where/which but not what/where/when memory (Eacott & Norman, 2004). It takes advantage of the tendency to explore novel objects, seen in many species, to demonstrate spontaneous recall (Menzel, 1999). It tests an animal's recall of an event when the test is not expected (Zentall et al., 2001) and may even allow for a test of past events over a long period of time (Schwartz & Evans, 2001) although no such long term tests have yet been carried out.

While a model of episodic memory based on object recognition is applicable to a greater variety of animals than a model based on food caching behaviour, we acknowledge that many of the criticisms that have been lodged against the what/where/when model (e.g., Suddendorf & Busby, 2003) also apply to the what/where/which model. For example, evidence for future planning and mental time travel would greatly improve both models of episodic-like memory. Clayton et al., (2003a) have recognized that their basic what/where/when criteria no longer adequately define the evolving concept of episodic-like memory. In response, they have refined their definition of episodic-like memory to include three particular behavioural criteria. Specifically, they state that a solid demonstration of episodic-like memory requires *content* (what/where/when details of a specific past event), *structure* (integration of the what/where/when details into a consolidated memory), and *flexibility* (ability to change how information gained from an episodic-like memory is used). Eacott et al. (2005) have argued that these three criteria are also met in their modified task examining recall of objects.

If we are willing to accept that the what/where/which model of episodic memory is a *model* of human episodic memory, and therefore, concede that it does not encompass the human characteristics of consciousness and mental time travel, then we can use this model to investigate the tripartite what/where/which code. One of the main strengths of this model is that it allows for episodic-like memory to be studied in a wide range of species. Comparative work should focus on the ability of other animals, including pigs, to recall information without the stimuli being re-presented on test (similar to that of Eacott et al., 2005) and to determine if this ability is long-lasting.

9. Acknowledgement

This chapter reflects research supported by individual NSERC Discovery Grants to G. Martin, D. Skinner, C. Thorpe, and C. Walsh, and by a NSERC Canadian Graduate Scholarship (CGS-D) to A-L. Kouwenberg.

10. References

Babb, S. J. & Crystal, J.D. (2006). Episodic-like memory in the rat. *Current Biology*, Vol.16, No.30, pp. 1317-1321, ISSN 09609822

Barreto, R. E., Rodrigues, P., Luchiari, A.C., & Delicio, H.C. (2006). Time-place learning in individually reared angelfish, but not in pearl cichlid. *Behavioural Processes*, Vol.73, No.3, pp. 367-372, ISSN 03766357

Bird, R., Roberts, W.A., Abroms, B., Kit, K.A., & Crupi, C. (2003). Spatial memory for hidden food by rats (*Rattus norvegicus*) on the radial maze: Studies of memory for where, what, and when. *Journal of Comparative Psychology*, Vol.117, No.2, pp. 176-187, ISSN 07357036

Cheke, L.G. & Clayton, N.S. (2011). Eurasian jays (Garrulus glandarius) overcome their current desires to anticipate two distinct future needs and plan for them appropriately. *Biology Letters,* doi:10.1098/rsbl.2011.0909.

Clayton, N.S., Bussey, T.J., & Dickinson, A. (2003b). Can animals recall the past and plan for the future? *Nature Reviews Neuroscience*, Vol.4, No. 8, pp. 685-691, ISSN 14710048

Clayton, N. S., Bussey, T. J., Emery, N. J., Dickinson, A., Suddendorf, T., & Busby, J. (2003c). Prometheus to Proust: The case for behavioural criteria for 'mental time travel'. *Trends in Cognitive Sciences*, Vol.7, No.10, pp. 436-438, ISSN 13646613

Clayton, N. S., Dally, J., Gilbert, J., & Dickinson, A. (2005). Food caching by Western scrub-jays (*Aphelocoma californica*) is sensitive to the conditions at recovery. *Journal of Experimental Psychology: Animal Behavior Processes,* Vol.31, No.2, pp. 115-124, ISSN 00977403

Clayton, N. S. & Dickinson, A. (1998). Episodic-like memory during cache recovery in scrub jays. *Nature*, Vol.395, No.6699, pp. 272-274, ISSN 00280836

Clayton, N.S., & Dickinson, A.D. (1999). Memory for the content of caches by scrub jays. *Journal of Experimental Psychology: Animal Behavior Processes*, Vol.25, No.1, pp. 82-91, ISSN 00977403

Clayton, N. S., Yu, K. S., & Dickinson, A. (2003a). Interacting Cache Memories: Evidence for Flexible Memory Use by Western Scrub-Jays (*Aphelocoma californica*). *Journal of Experimental Psychology: Animal Behavior Processes*, Vol.29, No.1, pp. 14-22, ISSN 00977403

Croney, C., (1999). Cognitive abilities of domestic pigs (*Sus scrofa*). Ph.D. Dissertation, The Pennsylvania State University, University Park, Pennsylvania.

Dere, E., Huston, J. P., & De Souza Silva, M. A. (2005). Integrated memory for objects, places and temporal order: Evidence for episodic-like memory in mice. *Neurobiology of Learning and Memory*, Vol.84, No.3, pp. 214-221, ISSN 10747427

Dickerson, J. W. T. & Dobbing, J. (1967). Prenatal and postnatal growth and development of the central nervous system of the pig. *Proceedings of the Royal Society of London B Biological Science*, Vol.166, No.1005, pp. 384-395, ISSN 14712954

Dix, S.L., & Aggleton, J.P. (1999). Extending the spontaneous preference test of recognition: Evidence of object-location and object-context recognition. *Behavioural Brain Research*, Vol.99, No.2, pp. 191-200, ISSN 01664328

Dobbing, J. & Sands, J. (1973). Quantitative growth and development of human brain. *Archives of Disease in Childhood*, Vol.48, pp. 757-767, ISSN 14682044

Eacott, M. J., Easton, A. & Zinkivskay, A. (2005). Recollection in an episodic-like memory task in the rat. *Learning and Memory*, Vol.12, No.3, pp. 221-223, ISSN 10720502

Eacott, M.J., & Gaffan, E.A. (2005). The roles of perirhinal cortex, postrhinal cortex and the fornix in memory for objects, contexts and events in the rat. *Quarterly Journal of Experimental Psychology Section B*, Vol.58, No.3-4, pp. 202-217, ISSN 02724995

Eacott, M. J., & Norman, G. (2004). Integrated memory for object, place and context in rats: A possible model of episodic-like memory? *Journal of Neuroscience*, Vol.24, No.8, pp. 1948-1953, ISSN 02706474

Emery, N. J. & Clayton, N. S. (2001). Effects of experience and social context on prospective caching strategies in scrub jays. *Nature*, Vol.414, No.6862, pp. 443-446, ISSN 00280836

Ennaceur, A., & Delacour, J. (1988). A new one-trial test for neurobiological studies of memory in rats. 1. Behavioural data. *Behavioural Brain Research*, Vol.31, No.1, pp. 47-59, ISSN 01664328

Ennaceur, A., Neave, N., and Aggleton, J.P. (1997). Spontaneous object recognition and object location memory in rats: the effects of lesions of the cingulated contices, the medial prefrontal cortex, the cingulum bundle and the fornix. *Experimental Brain Research*, Vol.113, No.3, pp. 509-519, ISSN 00144819

Fanselow, M.S. (1990). Factors governing one-trial contextual conditioning. *AnimalLearning & Behavior*, Vol.18, No.3, pp. 264-270, ISSN 15434494

Fortin, N. J., Agster, K. L., & Eichenbaum, H. B. (2002). Critical role of the hippocampus in memory for sequences of events. *Nature Neuroscience*, Vol.5, No.5, pp. 458-462, ISSN 10976256

Friedman, W.J. (1993). Memory for the time of past events. *Psychological Bulletin*, Vol.113, No.1, pp. 44-66, ISSN 00332909

Gieling, E.T., Nordquist, R.E., & van der Staay, F.J. (2011). Assessing learning and memory in pigs. *Animal Cognition*, Vol.14, No. 2, pp. 151-173, ISSN 14359448

Gifford, A.K., Cloutier, S., & Newberry, R.C. (2007). Objects as enrichment: effects of object exposure time and delay interval on object recognition memory of the domestic pig. *Applied Animal Behaviour Science*, Vol.107, No.3-4, pp. 206-217, ISSN 01681591

Goodrich-Hunsaker, N.J., Hunsaker, M.R., Kesner, R.P. (2008). The interactions and dissociations of the dorsal hippocampus subregions: How the Dentate Gyrus, CA3,

CA1 process spatial information. *Behavioral Neuroscience*, Vol.122, No.1, pp. 16-26, ISSN 07357044

Graves, H.B. (1984). Behaviour and ecology of wild and feral swine (*Sus scrofa*). *Journal of Animal Science*, Vol.58, No.2, pp. 483-492, ISSN 00218812

Gustafsson, M., Jensen, P., de Jonge, F., & Schuurman, T. (1999). Domestication effects on foraging strategies in pigs (*Sus scrofa*). *Applied Animal Behaviour Science*, Vol.62, No.4, pp. 305-317, ISSN 01681591

Hampton, R. R., Hampstead, B.M., & Murray, E.A. (2005). Rhesus monkey (*Macaca mulatta*) demonstrate robust memory for what and where, but not when, in an open-field test of memory. *Learning & Motivation*, Vol.36, No.2, pp. 245-259, ISSN 00239690

Hampton, R. R., & Schwartz, B. L. (2004). Episodic memory in nonhumans: What, and where, is when? *Current Opinion in Neurobiology*, Vol.14, No.2, pp. 192-197, ISSN 09594388

Harley, C.W., Martin, G.M., Skinner, D.M., Squires, A. (2001). The moving fire hydrant experiment: Movement of objects to a new location reelicits marking in rats. *Neurobiology of Learning and Memory*, Vol.75, No.3, pp. 303-309, ISSN 10747427

Held, S., Baumgartner, J., KilBride, A., Byrne, R.W., & Mendl, M. (2005). Foraging behaviour in domestic pigs (*Sus scrofa*): remembering and prioritizing food sites of different value. *Animal Cognition*, Vol.8, No.2, pp. 114-121, ISSN 14359448

Held, S., Mendl., M., Laughlin K. & Byrne, R.W. (2002). Cognition studies with pigs: livestock cognition and its implication for production. *Journal of Animal Sc*ience, Vol.80, No.1, pp. 10-17

Hoffman, M.L., Beran, M. J., & Washburn, D. A. (2009). Memory for "what", "where",and "when" information in rhesus monkeys (Macaca mulatta). *Journal of Experimental Psychology: Animal Behavior Processes*, Vol.35, No.2, pp. 143-152, ISSN 00977403

Kart-Teke, E., De Souza Silva, M. A., Huston, J. P., & Dere, E. (2006). Wistar rats show episodic-like memory for unique experiences. *Neurobiology of Learning and Memory*, Vol.85, No.2, pp. 173-182, ISSN 10747427

Kornum B.R., & Knudsen G.M. (2011). Cognitive testing of pigs (*Sus scrofa*) in translational biobehavioral research. *Neuroscience Biobehavioral Review*, Vol.35, No.3, pp. 437-451, ISSN 01497634

Kornum, B.R., Thygesen, K.S., Nielsen, T.R., Knudsen, G.M., & Lind, N.M. (2007). The effect of the inter-phase delay interval in the spontaneous object recognition test for pigs. *Behavioural Brain Research*, Vol.181, No.2, pp. 210-217, ISSN 01664328

Kouwenberg, A.-L., Walsh, C.J., Morgan, B.E., & Martin, G.M. (2009). Episodic-like memory in crossbred Yucatan minipigs (Sus scrofa). *Applied Animal Behaviour Science*, Vol.117, No.3-4, pp. 165-172, ISSN 01681591

Lemon, N., Aydin-Abidin, S., Flunke, K., & Manahan-Vaughan, D. (2009). Locus coeruleus activation facilitates memory encoding and induces hippocampal LTD that depends on ß-adrenergic receptor activation. *Cerebral Cortex*, Vol.19, No.2, pp. 2827-2837, ISSN 10473211

Lind, N. M., Moustgaard, A., Jelsing, J., Vajta, G., Cumming, P., & Hansen, A. K. (2007). The use of pigs in neuroscience: modeling brain disorders. *Neuroscience and Biobehavioral Reviews*, Vol.31, No.2, pp. 728-751, ISSN 01497634

Logan, C.J., O'Donnell, S. & Clayton, N.S. (2011). A case of mental time travel in ant-following birds? *Behavioral Ecology*, doi:10.1093/beheco/arr104

Martin-Ordas, G., Haun, D., Colmenares, F., & Call, J. (2010). Keeping track of time: evidence for episodic-like memory in great apes. *Animal Cognition*, Vol.13, No.2, pp. 331-340, ISSN 14359448

Means, L. W., Arolfo, M. P., Ginn, S. R., Pence, J. D., & Watson, N. P. (2000). Rats more readily acquire a time-of-day go no-go discrimination than a time-of-day choice discrimination. *Behavioural Processes*, Vol.52, No.1, pp. 11-20, ISSN 03766357

Menzel, C. R. (1999). Unprompted recall and reporting of hidden objects by a chimpanzee (*Pan trogolodytes*) after extended delays. *Journal of Comparative Psychology*, Vol.113, No.4, pp. 426-434, ISSN 07357036

Moustgaard, A., Lind, N.M., Hemmingsen, R., & Hansen, A.K. (2002). Spontaneous object recognition in the Gottingen Minipig. *Neural Plasticity*, Vol.9, No.4, pp. 255-259, ISSN 07928483

Norman, G., & Eacott, M.J. (2004). Impaired object recognition with increasing levels of feature ambiguity in rats with prerirhinal cortex lesions. *Behavioural Brain Research*, Vol.148, No.1-2, pp. 79-91, ISSN 01664328

O'Brien, J. & Sutherland, R.J. (2007). Evidence for episodic memory in a Pavlovian conditioning procedure in rats. *Hippocampus*, Vol. 17, No.12, pp. 1149-1152, ISSN 10509631

Pond, W. G., Boleman, S. L., Fiorotto, M. L., Ho, H., Knabe, D. A., Mersmann, H. J., Savell, J. W. & Su, D. R. (2000). Perinatal ontogeny of brain growth in the domestic pig. *Proceedings of the Society for Experimental Biology and Medicine*, Vol.223, No.1, pp. 102-108, ISSN 00379727

Poucet, B. (1989). Object exploration, habituation, and response to spatial change in rats following septal or medial frontal cortical damage. *Behavioral Neuroscience*, Vol.103, No.5, pp. 1009-1016, ISSN 07357044

Puppe, B., Ernst, K., Schon, P.C., & Manteuffel, G. (2007). Cognitive enrichment affects behavioural reactivity in domestic pigs. *Applied Animal Behaviour Science*, Vol.105, No.1-3, pp. 75-86, ISSN 01681591

Rudy, J.W., Barrientos, R.M., & O'Reilly, R.C. (2002). Hippocampal formation supports conditioning to memory of a context. *Behavioral Neuroscience*, Vol.336, No.4, pp. 530-538, ISSN 07357044

Saksida, L. M., & Wilkie, D. M. (1994). Time-of-day discrimination by pigeons *Columba livia*. *Animal Learning & Behavior*, Vol.22, No.2, pp. 143-154, ISSN 00904996

Schwartz, B. L., & Evans, S. (2001). Episodic memory in primates. *American Journal of Primatology*, Vol.55, No.2, pp. 71-85, ISSN 02752565

Schwartz, B. L, Hoffman, M. L., & Evans, S. (2005). Episodic-like memory in a gorilla: A review and new findings. *Learning and Motivation*, Vol.36, No.2, pp. 226-244, ISSN 00239690

Skov-Rackette, S. I., Miller, N. Y. & Shettleworth, S. J. (2006). What-where-when memory in pigeons. *Journal of Experimental Psychology: Animal Behavior Processes*, Vol.32, No.4, pp. 345–358, ISSN 00977403

Suddendorf, T. & Busby, J. (2003). Mental time travel in animals? *Trends in Cognitive Sciences*, Vol.7, No.9, pp. 391-396, ISSN 13646613

Thorpe, C.M., Bates, M.E., & Wilkie, D.M. (2003). Rats have trouble associating all three parts of the time-place-event memory code. *Behavioural Processes*, Vol.63, No.2, pp. 95-110, ISSN 03766357

Thorpe, C. M., & Wilkie, D. M. (2006). Properties of time-place learning, In: *Comparative Cognition: Experimental Explorations of Animal Intelligence,* T. R. Zentall & E. A. Wasserman (Eds.), Oxford University Press, ISBN 0195167651, Oxford, UK

Tulving, E. (1983). *Elements of Episodic Memory.* Clarendon Press, ISBN 0198521022, Oxford, UK

Tulving, E. (2002). Episodic Memory: From mind to brain. *Annual Review of Psychology,* Vol.53, pp. 1-25, ISSN 00664308

Widman, D. R., Gordon, D., & Timberlake, W. (2000). Response cost and time-place discrimination by rats in maze tasks. *Animal learning & Behavior,* Vol.28, No.3, pp. 298-309, ISSN 00904996

Wood-Gush, D. G. M, and Vestergaard, K. (1991). The seeking of novelty and its relation to play. *Animal Behaviour,* Vol.42, No.4, pp. 599-606, ISSN 00033472

Zentall, T., Clement, T., Bhatt, R., & Allen, J. (2001). Episodic-like memory in pigeons. *Psychonomic Bulletin and Review,* Vol.8, No.4, pp. 685-690, ISSN 10699384

3

Performance Analysis of the Modified-Hybrid Optical Neural Network Object Recognition System Within Cluttered Scenes

Ioannis Kypraios
Department of Engineering & Computing, ICTM,
London,
UK

1. Introduction

In literature, we could categorise two broad main approaches for pattern recognition systems. The first category consists of linear combinatorial-type filters (LCFs) (Stamos, 2001) where commonly image analysis is done in the frequency domain with the help of Fourier Transformation (FT) (Lynn & Fuerst, 1998; Proakis & Manolakis, 1998). The second category consists of pure neural modelling methods. (Wood, 1996) has given a brief but clear review of invariant pattern recognition methods. His survey has divided the methods into two further sub-categories of solving the invariant pattern recognition problem. The first sub-category has two distinct stages of separately calculating the features of the training set pattern to be invariant to certain distortions and then classifying the extracted features. The second sub-category, instead of having two separate stages, has a single stage which parameterises the desired invariances and then adapts them. (Wood, 1996) has also described the integral transforms, which fall under the first sub-category of feature extractors. They are based on Fourier analysis, such as the multidimensional Fourier transform, Fourier-Mellin transform, triple correlation (Delopoulos et al., 1994) and others. Part of the first sub-category is also the group of algebraic invariants, such as Zernike moments (Khotanzad & Hong, 1990; Perantonis & Lisboa, 1992), generalised moments (Shvedov et al., 1979) and others. Wood has given examples of the second sub-category, the main representative being based on artificial neural network (NNET) architectures. He has presented the weight-sharing neural networks (LeCun, 1989; LeCun et al. 1990), the high-order neural networks (Giles & Maxwell, 1987; Kanaoka et al. 1992; Perantonis & Lisboa, 1992; Spirkovska & Reid, 1992), the time-delay neural networks (TDNN) (Bottou et al., 1990; Simard & LeCun, 1992; Waibel et al., 1989) and others. Finally, he has included an additional third sub-category with all the methods which cannot be placed under either the feature-extraction feature-classification approach or the parameterised approach. Such methods are image normalisation pre-processing (Yuceer & Oflazer, 1993) methods for achieving invariance to certain distortions. (Dobnikar et al., 1992) have compared the invariant pattern classification (IPC) neural network architecture versus the Fourier Transform method. They used for their comparison black-and-white images. They have proven the generalisation properties and fault-tolerant abilities to input patterns of the artificial neural network architectures.

An alternative approach for a pattern recognition system has been well demonstrated previously with the Generalised Hybrid Optical Neural Network (G-HONN) filter (object recognition system) (Kypraios, 2010; Kypraios et al., 2004a). G-HONN system combines the digital design of a filter by artificial neural network techniques with an optical correlator-type implementation of the resulting non-linear combinatorial correlator type filter (Jamal-Aldin et al., 1998). The motivation for the design and implementation of the G-HONN object recognition system was to achieve the performance advantages of both artificial neural networks (Looney, 1997; Haykin, 1999; Beale & Jackson, 1990) and the optically implemented correlators (Kumar, 1992). Thus, NNETs exhibit non-linear superposition abilities (Kypraios et al., 2002) of the training set pattern images, learning and generalisation abilities (Kypraios et al., 2004a; Kypraios et al., 2003) over the whole set of the input images. Also, optical correlators allow high speed implementation of the algorithms described.

There are two main design blocks in the G-HONN system, the NNET and a non-linear combinatorial-type correlator (filter) block (Jamal-Aldin, 1998; Casasent, 1984; Caulfield, 1980; Caulfield & Maloney, 1969). Briefly, the original input images pass first through the NNET block and, then, the extracted images from the NNET block's output are used to form a non-linear combinatorial-type correlator filter. Thus the output of the correlator block is a composite image of the G-HONN system's output. To test the system, we correlate it with an input image. Before proceeding to analytical descriptions of the general architecture of the G-HONN system and in an effort to keep consistency between the different mathematical symbolism of artificial neural networks and optical correlators we need to unify their representation. We denote the variables names and functions by non-italic letters (except the vector elements written within the vector, which are written in italic, too), the names of the vectors by italic lower case letters and the matrices by italic upper case. The frequency domain vectors, matrices, variable names and functions are represented by bold letters and the space domain vectors, matrices, variables and functions by plain letters.

Let $\boldsymbol{h}(\boldsymbol{k},\boldsymbol{l})$ denote the composite image of the correlator block and $\boldsymbol{x}_i(\boldsymbol{k},\boldsymbol{l})$ denote the training set images, where $\mathrm{i}=1,2,\cdots,\mathrm{N}$ and N is the number of the training images used in the synthesis of a combinatorial-type filter. The basic filter's transfer function, from the weighed linear combination of x_i, is given by:

$$h(k,l)=\sum_{\mathrm{i}=1}^{\mathrm{N}} \mathrm{a}_\mathrm{i}\, x_i(k,l) \qquad (1)$$

where the coefficients $\mathbf{a}_\mathrm{i}$ $(\mathbf{i}=\mathbf{1,2,...,N})$ are to set the constraints on the peak given by ***c***. The a_i values are determined from:

$$a=R^{-1}c \qquad (2)$$

where a is the vector of the coefficients $\mathbf{a}_\mathrm{i}$ $(\mathbf{i}=\mathbf{1,2,...,N})$, R is the correlation matrix of t_i and c is the peak constraint vector. The elements of this are usually set to zeros for false-class objects and to ones for true class objects.

Now, let an image s be the input vector to an artificial neural network's hidden neuron (node), $t_{p\kappa}$ represent the target output for pattern p on node κ and $o_{p\kappa}$ represent the calculated output at that node. The weight from node ι to node κ is represented by $w_{\iota\kappa}$. The activation of each node κ, for pattern p, can be written as:

$$net_{p\kappa} = \sum_{i}\left(w_{\iota\kappa}\, o_{p\kappa} + b_{\iota} \right) \tag{3}$$

i.e. it is the weighted sum of the calculated output from the node ι to node κ. b_{ι} represents the bias vector of unit ι.

We train a novel-designed NNET with N training set images. The network has N neurons in the hidden layer, i.e. equal to the number of training images. There is a single neuron at the output layer to separate two different object classes. (In a multi-class object recognition problem, the increase of the different classes of objects would require more than one neuron at the output layer to correctly separate all the training images.) From Eq. (3) the net input of each of the neurons in the hidden layer is now given by:

$$net_{x_i} = \sum_{\iota=1}^{m\times n} w_{\iota}^{x_i}\, s_{\iota}^{x_i} \tag{4}$$

where *net* is the net input of each of the hidden neurons. $w_{\iota}^{x_i}$ are the input weights from the input layer to the hidden neurons for the training image x_i of size $\left[m\times n \right]$ in matrix form or of size $\left[1\times\left(m\times n \right) \right]$ in vector form. Similarly, for the training image x_N of size $\left[m\times n \right]$ in matrix form ($\left[1\times\left(m\times n \right) \right]$ in vector form) the net input, net_{x_N} is given by:

$$net_{x_N} = \sum_{\iota=1}^{m\times n} w_{\iota}^{x_N}\, s_{\iota}^{x_N} \tag{5}$$

From Eqs.(1) and (3) and (5) there is a direct analogy between the combinatorial-type filter synthesis procedure and the combination of all the layers' weighted input vectors.

There are two possible and equivalent custom designs (The Mathworks, 2008) of NNET architectures which could be used to form the basis of the combinatorial-type filter synthesis. In both of the designs each neuron of the hidden layer is trained with only one of the training set images. In effect, neuron_1 with the training image x_1, neuron_2 with the training image x_2 and so on, ending with neuron_N with the training image x_N. In the first design the number of the input sources is kept constant whereas in the second design the number of the input sources is equal to the number of the training images. In both designs each hidden neuron learns one of the training images. In effect the number of the input weights increases proportionally to the size of the training set:

$$N_{iw} = N\times\left[m\times n \right] \tag{6}$$

where N_{iw} is the number of the input weights, N, is the size of the training set equal to the number of the training images and $\left[m\times n \right]$ is the size of the image of the training set. The latter design would allow parallel implementation, since all the training images could be input through the NNET in parallel due to the parallel input sources. However, to allow easier implementation, we chose the former design of the NNET.

Let assume there are three training images of a car, size $\left[100 \times 100\right]$ ($\left[1 \times \left(100 \times 100\right)\right]$ in vector form), of different angle of view, to pass through the NNET. The chosen first design (see Fig. 1) consists of one input source used for all the training images. The input source consists of 10,000 i.e. $\left[1 \times \left(100 \times 100\right)\right]$ input neurons equal to the size of each training image (in vector form). Each layer needs, by definition, to have the same input connections to each of its hidden neurons. However, Fig. 1 is referred to as of the fourth layer since there are three hidden layers (shown here aligned under each other) and one output layer. The input layer does not contain neurons with activation functions and so is omitted in the numbering of the layers. Each of the hidden layers has only one hidden neuron. Though the network initially is fully connected to the input layer during the training stage, only one hidden layer is connected for each training image presented through the NNET. Fig. 1 is thus not a contiguous three (hidden) layer network during training, which is why the distinction is made.

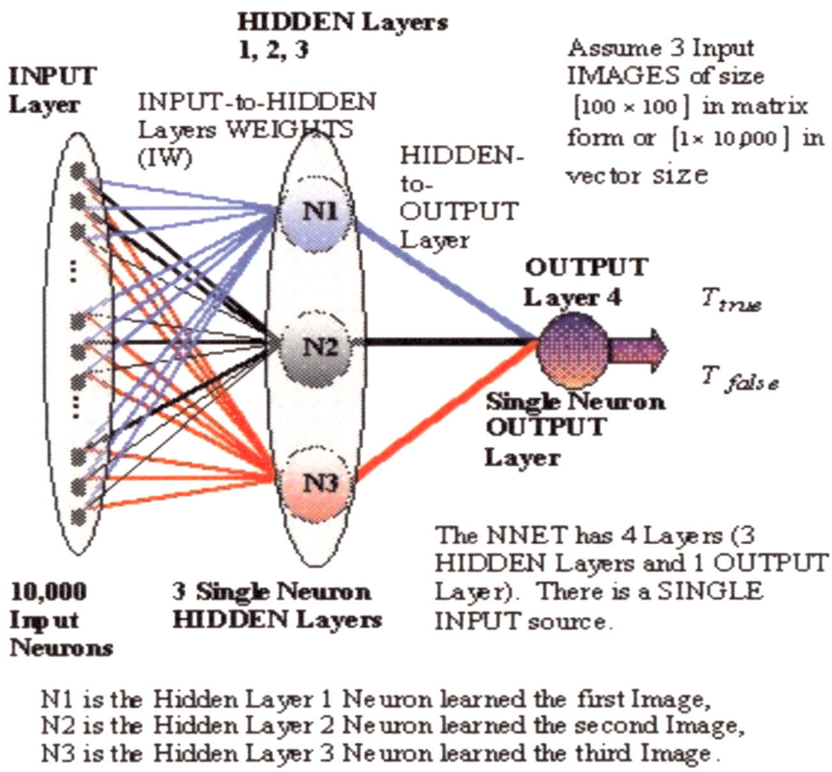

Fig. 1. Architecture of the selected artificial NNET block of the HONN filter.

Next, in section 2 we will give a brief description of the G-HONN system's design and implementation already described with details in the literature. Section 3 describes the M-HONN system. Section 4 focuses on multiple objects recognition and the M-HONN system's design. It describes the augmented design of the NNET block for accommodating multiple objects recognition of different classes. Section 5 discusses about the performance of M-HONN system with respect to peak sharpness and detectability, distortion range and discrimination ability. We discuss about the M-HONN system and biologically-inspired knowledge learning and representation. Finally, we record the series of tests we conducted with M-HONN system for multiple objects recognition of the same class and of different classes within clutter. Section 6 concludes and suggests future work.

2. General HONN filter's design and implementation

The novel design of NNET's architecture of the G-HONN system is implemented as a feedforward multi-layer architecture trained with a backpropagation algorithm. It has a single input source (as explained in the previous section) of input neurons equal to the size of the training image in vector form. In effect, for the training image $x_{i=1...N}$ of size $[m \times n]$, there are $[m \times n]$ input neurons in the single input source. The input weights are fully-connected from the input layer to the hidden layers. There are N_{iw} input weights proportional to the size of the training set. The number of the hidden layers, N_l, is equal to the number of the images of the training set, N :

$$N = 1,2,3,\cdots,i \tag{7}$$

$$N_l = N \tag{8}$$

Each hidden layer consists of a single neuron. The layer weights are fully connected to the output layer. If we set the output layer to have a single output neuron, then the number of the layer's weights, N_{lw} equals the number of the training images N :

$$N_{lw} = N \times N_{opn} \tag{9}$$

where $N_{opn} = 1$ is the number of the output neurons. There are bias connections to each one of the hidden layers:

$$N_b = N_l \tag{10}$$

where N_b is the number of the bias connections. But from Eq. (8), Eq. (10) becomes:

$$N_b = N \tag{11}$$

Assuming there is only a single output neuron in the output layer, then there is only one target connection for that output neuron.

We apply Nguyen-Widrow (Nguyen & Widrow, 1989; Nguyen & Widrow, 1990) initialisation algorithm for setting the initial values of the input weights, the layer weights and the biases. The transfer function of the hidden layers is set as the Log-Sigmoidal function. When a new training image is presented to the NNET we leave connected the input weights of only one of the hidden neurons. In order not to upset any previous learning of the rest of the hidden layer neurons we do not alter their weights when the new image is input to the NNET. It is emphasised that there is no separate feature extraction stage (The Mathworks, 2008; Talukder & Casasent, 1999; Casasent et al., 1998) applied to the training set images. To achieve faster learning we used a modified steepest descent (Looney, 1997; The Mathworks, 2008) back propagation algorithm based on heuristic techniques. This adaptive training algorithm updates the weights and bias values according to the gradient descent momentum and an adaptive learning rate:

$$\Delta w(i,i+1) = \mu \times \Delta w(i-1,i) + \alpha \times \mu \times \frac{\Delta P_f}{\Delta w(i+1,i)} \tag{12}$$

$$\Delta b(i,i+1) = \mu \times \Delta b(i-1,i) + \alpha \times \mu \times \frac{\Delta P_f}{\Delta b(i+1,i)} \tag{13}$$

$$\alpha = \begin{Bmatrix} \alpha = \alpha + \varepsilon \quad \text{if } \Delta P_f < 0 \\ \alpha = \text{no change} \quad \text{if } 0 < \Delta P_f \;\&\&\; \Delta P_f > \max(P_f) \\ \alpha = \alpha - \varepsilon \quad \text{if } \Delta P_f > \max(P_f) \end{Bmatrix} \tag{14}$$

where now variable i is the iteration index of the network and is updated every time all the training set images pass through the NNET. Δw is the update function of the input and layer weights, Δb is the update function of the biases of the layers and μ is the momentum constant. The momentum (Looney, 1997; Haykin, 1999; Beale & Jackson, 1990; The Mathworks, 2008) allows the network to respond not only to the local gradient, but also to recent trends in the error surface. Thus, it acts like a low-pass filter by removing the small features in the error surface of the NNET. The employment of momentum in the training algorithm allows the network not to get stuck in a shallow local minimum, but to slide through such a minimum. P_f is the performance function, usually set as being the mean square error (mse) (Looney, 1997; Haykin, 1999) and ΔP_f is the derivative of the performance function. The learning rate is indicated with the letter α. It adapts iteratively based on the derivative of the performance function ΔP_f. In effect, if there is a decrease in the ΔP_f, then the learning rate is increased by the constant ε. If ΔP_f increases but the derivative does not take a value higher than the maximum allowed value of the performance function, $\max(P_f)$, then the learning rate does not change. If ΔP_f increases more than $\max(P_f)$, then the learning rate decreases by the constant ε. The layer weights remain connected with all the hidden layers for all the training set and throughout all the training session.

Hence, now that we have described the design and implementation of the G-HONN filter (object recognition system) we can proceed with a detailed description of the modified-HONN filter.

3. Modified-HONN system implementation

We can make the following qualitatively observations for the G-HONN system. Though the combinatorial-type filters (Samos, 2001) contain no information on non-reference objects in the training set used during their synthesis, the NNET includes information for reference and non-reference images of the true-class object. That can be explained due to the NNET interpolating non-linearly (Kypraios et al.,2002) between the reference images included in the training set and forcing all the non-reference images to follow the activation graph. Moreover the NNET generalizes between all the reference and non-reference images. Quantitatively, we could demonstrate the above observations as follows. The average training set image $\bar{x}$ in the space domain of the combinatorial-type filters is given by:

$$\bar{x} = \frac{1}{N}\sum_{i=1}^{N} x_i \tag{15}$$

In the frequency domain Eq. (15) is written as:

$$\bar{\mathbf{x}} = \frac{1}{\mathbf{N}}\sum_{i=1}^{N} \mathbf{x}_i \tag{16}$$

The non-linear activation function of each hidden neuron of an artificial neural network with a non-linear activation function such as the sigmoidal function $f_s(\ )$ can take the form:

$$f_s(x) = \alpha\frac{1-\exp(\beta x)}{1+\exp(\beta x)} \tag{17}$$

where α and β shift the graph of the function with respect the x-axis and y-axis and are called the saturation level and slope. It can be shown (Kypraios et al., 2009) that the output y_N of an artificial neural network with a non-linear activation function corresponding to an input s_i for $i=1,\ldots,N$ (where N is the number of the training set images) is written as:

$$f\left(\sum_{i=1}^{N} s_i g_i - \theta\right) = \\ = \alpha\frac{1-k\exp(\beta s_1 g_1)\exp(\beta s_2 g_2)\exp(\beta s_3 g_3)\cdots\exp(\beta s_{N-1} g_{N-1})\exp(\beta s_N g_N)}{1+k\exp(\beta s_1 g_1)\exp(\beta s_2 g_2)\exp(\beta s_3 g_3)\cdots\exp(\beta s_{N-1} g_{N-1})\exp(\beta s_N g_N)} \tag{18}$$

where $k=\exp(-\beta\theta)$ takes a constant value (and g_i the neural network node' weights). Therefore from Eq. (16) and Eq. (18) it is shown that any artificial neural network with a non-linear activation function can non-linearly interpolate through the different training set views of the true-class object. Thus, the average training set image $\bar{x}$ in the space domain of the NNET is given by:

$$\bar{x} = \frac{1}{N} f_\kappa(x_i) \tag{19}$$

where $f_\kappa(\ )$ is the activation function of node κ in the space domain. Eq. (19) is written in the frequency domain as:

$$\bar{\mathbf{x}} = \frac{1}{\mathbf{N}} \mathbf{f}_\kappa(\mathbf{x}_i) \tag{20}$$

The activation function $f_\kappa(\ )$ of node κ against the training set images x_i is plotted in Fig. 2. On the activation function graph the true-class object values (which is similar for the false-class object) are marked with + . Now, if we mark on the plot the activation function values for the training image at 30° and 40° degrees object poses, then the activation function for the training image at 35° degrees will be located on the graph between the values of the activation function for the 30° and 40° degree inputs. The actual activation function values for the training set images of x_{30}, x_{40} and x_{35} are located in the area included under the graph for activation function values greater or equal to the pre-specified true-class object classification level, in this case shown we assume it is set at +40.

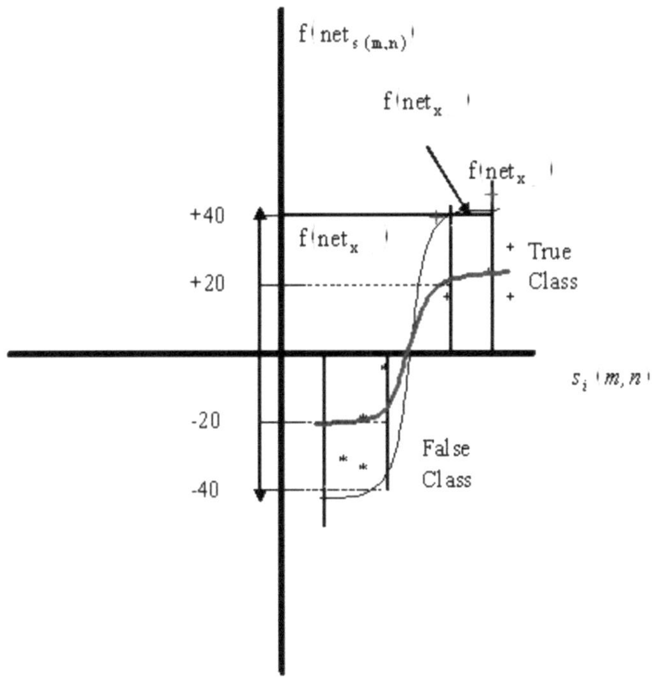

Fig. 2. It shows the activation function graph of node κ against the training set images x_i .

Motivated by these observations, we apply an optical mask to the filter's input (see Fig. 3). The mask is constructed by the weight connections of the reference images of the true-class object and is applied to all the tested images. Modified-HONN (M-HONN) system is described as follows:

$$\Gamma_c = W^{x_c} \times L^{x_c} = \begin{bmatrix} w_{11}^{x_c} & w_{12}^{x_c} & L & w_{1n-1}^{x_c} & w_{1n}^{x_c} \\ w_{21}^{x_c} & w_{22}^{x_c} & L & w_{2n-1}^{x_c} & w_{2n}^{x_c} \\ \\ w_{m1}^{x_c} & w_{m2}^{x_c} & L & w_{mn-1}^{x_c} & w_{mn}^{x_c} \end{bmatrix} \times \begin{bmatrix} l_{11}^{x_c} \; L \; l_{1q}^{x_c} \\ l_{21}^{x_c} \; L \; l_{2q}^{x_c} \\ \\ l_{n1}^{x_c} \; L \; l_{nq}^{x_c} \end{bmatrix} \tag{21}$$

where W^{x_c} and L^{x_c} are the input and layer weights from the input neuron of the input vector element at row m and column n to the associated hidden layer for the training image $x_c(m,n)$. $l_{mn}^{x_c}$ are the input and layer weights from the hidden neuron of the layer vector element at row m and column n to the associated output neuron q. This time, instead of multiplying each training image with the corresponding weight connections as for the G-HONN system's implementation, we keep constant the weight connection values, setting

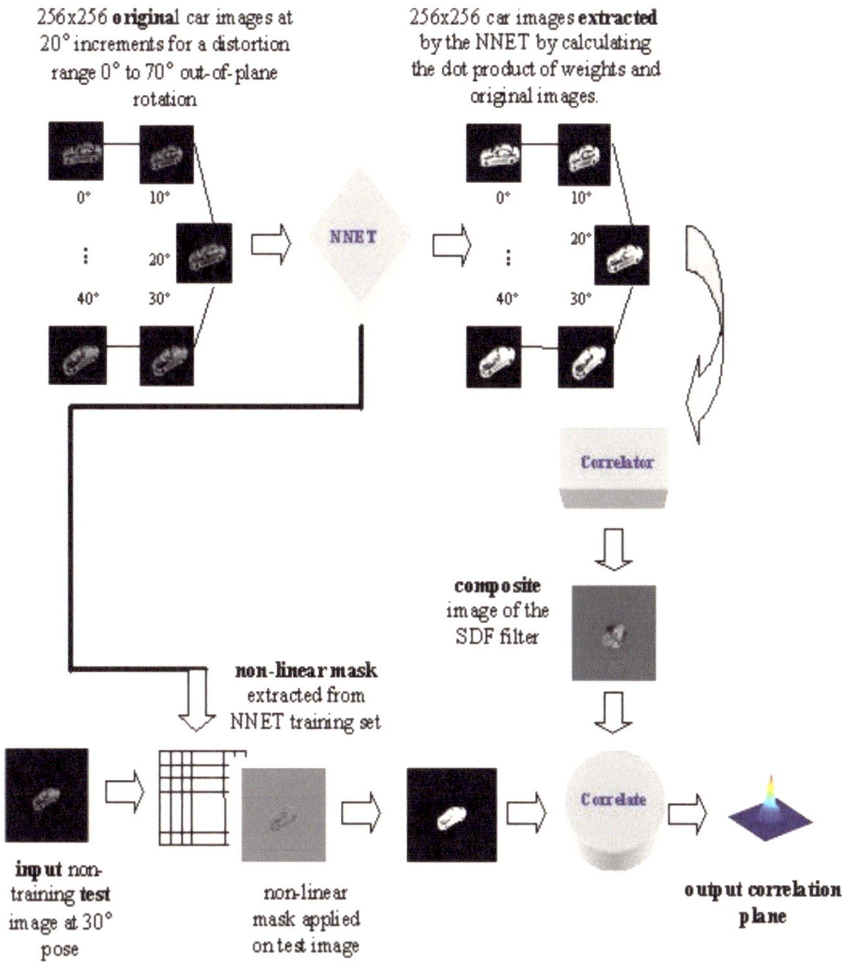

Fig. 3. M-HONN system block diagram.

them to be equal with a randomly chosen image included in the training set $x_c(m,n)$. The matrix Γ_c is used for creating the optical mask for the M-HONN system's implementation. The transformed image $S_{i=1\cdots N}(m,n)$ calculated from the dot product of the matrix elements of Γ_c with the corresponding training image matrix elements of $X_{i=1\cdots N}(m,n)$ is given by:

$$S_{i=1\cdots N} = \Gamma_c \cdot X_{i=1\cdots N}(m,n) \tag{22}$$

Thus, the M-HONN system's transfer function is formulated as follows:

$$M-HONN = \sum_{i=1\cdots N}^{N} a_i \cdot S_i(m,n) \tag{23}$$

In Eq. (23) we have chosen to constrain the correlation peak height values as we did with the constrained-HONN (C-HONN) system's implementation, but we can also easily re-write the system's transfer equation for the case of the unconstrained peak height values as with the unconstrained-HONN (U-HONN) system's implementation (Mahalanobis, 1994; Kypraios et al., 2004b).

4. Multiple objects recognition

Multiple objects of the same class can be accommodated by the G-HONN type filters to be recognised within an input cluttered image due to the shift invariance properties inherited by its correlator unit. Thus, in the M-HONN system all the training set images pass through the NNET unit. This time, instead of multiplying each training image with the corresponding weight connections (mask) as for the C-HONN filter, we keep constant the weight connection values, setting them to be equal with a randomly chosen image included in the training set. All the test set images are multiplied with the same randomly chosen image's weight connection values. Then, the training set images, after being transformed (masked) through the NNET unit by being multiplied with the mask, pass through the correlator unit where they are correlated with the masked test set images. In effect, the cross-correlation of each masked test set image with the transformed training set images (reference kernel) returns an output correlation plane peak value for each cross-correlation step. Hence, the maximum peak height values of the output correlation plane correspond to the recognised true-class objects.

4.1 Modified NNET block architecture for multiple objects of different classes recognition

As for all the HONN-type systems (Kypraios et al., 2004; Kypraios et al., 2003; Kypraios et al., 2009), in the M-HONN system's NNET block (unit) there is a single input source used for all the input data. Assuming we have N = 3 input still images or video frames of size 256×256 in pixels, then the input source consists of 65.536 i.e. [1(256×256)] input neurons equal to the size of each training image or frame (in vector form). Each layer needs, by definition (Hagan et al., 1996), to have the same input connections to each of its hidden neurons. Therefore, the shown NNET architecture is referred to as N+1 = 3+1 = 4, four-layered since there are, N = 3, three hidden neurons (though shown here aligned under each other, they do not belong in the same hidden layer but rather create three separate hidden layers each of a single hidden neuron) and one output layer. Each of the hidden layers consist of only one hidden neuron. The input layer does not contain neurons with activation functions and so is omitted in the numbering of the layers. Though the network initially is fully connected to the input layer during the training stage, only one hidden layer is connected for each training image presented through the NNET. NNET is thus not a contiguous three layer network during training, which is why the distinction is made. In effect, neuron_1 is trained with the training still image or video frame x_1, neuron_2 is trained with the training still image or video frame x_2 and so on, ending with neuron_N being trained with the training still image or video frame x_N. Thus, the number of the input weights increases proportionally to the size of the training set:

$$N_{iw} = N \times [m \times n] \tag{24}$$

where N_{iw} is the number of the input weights, N, is the size of the training set equal to the number of the training images and [m×n] is the size of the image of the training set.

Fig. 4 shows the modified NNET block architecture for accommodating multiple objects for more than one class recognition. As for all the family of G-HONN filters, NNET is implemented as a feedforward multi-layer architecture trained with a backpropagation algorithm. It has a single input source of input neurons equal to the size of the training image or video frame in vector form. In effect, for the training still image or video frame $x_{i=1...N}$ of size [m×n], there are [m×n] input neurons in the single input source. The input weight are fully connected from the input layer to the hidden layers. There are N_{iw} input weights proportional to the size of the training set. The number of the hidden layers, N_l is equal to the number of the images or video frames of the training set N:

$$N = 1,2,3,\cdots,i \quad \text{and} \quad N_l = N \tag{25}$$

We have set to each hidden layer to contain a single neuron. The layer weights are fully connected to the output layer. Now, the number of the layer weights N_{lw} is equal to:

$$N_{lw} = N \times N_{opn} \quad \text{and} \quad N_{opn} = N_{classes} \tag{26}$$

where N_{opn} is the number of the output neurons and $N_{classes}$ is the number of the different classes. In effect, we have augmented the output layer by adding more output neurons, one for each different class. On Fig. 4 we assume $N_{classes} = 2$. Thus:

$$N_{opn} = N_{classes} = 2 \quad \text{so, there are} \quad N_{lw} = N \times 2 \tag{27}$$

and

$$N_{class1\ lw} = N \ , \ N_{class2\ lw} = N \tag{28}$$

where $N_{class1\ lw}$ and $N_{class2\ lw}$ are the layer weights corresponding to object class 1 and object class 2, respectively. There are bias connections to each one of the hidden layers:

$$N_b = N \tag{29}$$

where N_b is the number of the bias connections. There are $N_{target\ w}$ target connections from the N_{opn} output neurons of the output layer:

$$N_{target\ w} = N_{opn} \tag{30}$$

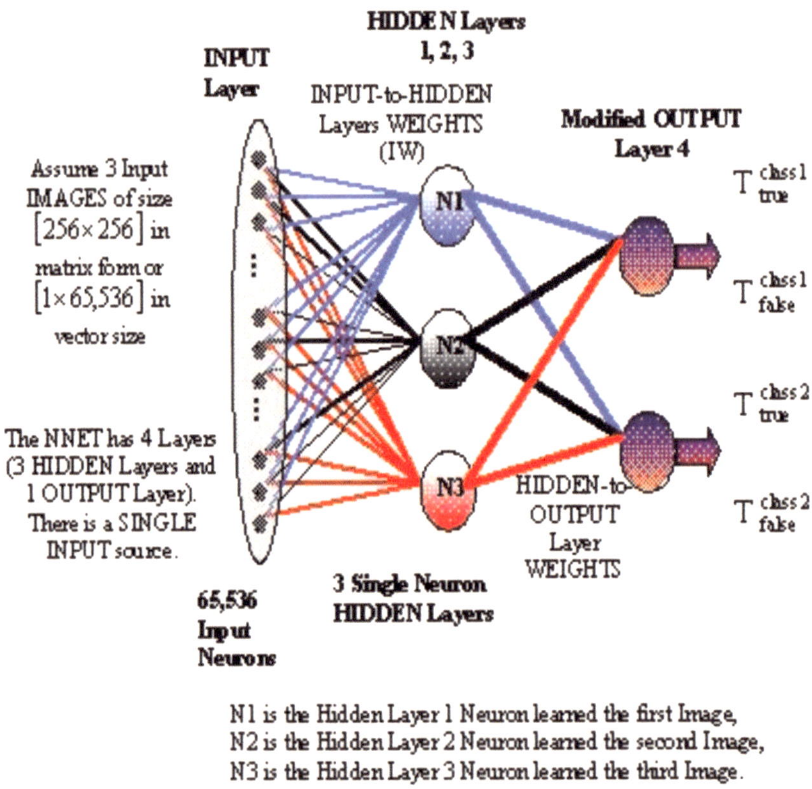

Fig. 4. Modified NNET block of the M-HONN system for multiple objects recognition of different classes

Thus, now for $N_{classes} = 2$ there will be N transformed images being created for class 1 and N transformed images being created for class 2. Then, both sets of transformed images are used for the synthesis of the system's composite image. M-HONN system for multiple objects recognition of different class objects is written as follows:

$$M\text{-}HONN = \sum_{i=1 L N_{classes}\times N}^{N_{classes}\times N} a_i \cdot S_i^{class}(m,n)$$
$$= a_1 \cdot \left(\Gamma_c^{class} \times X_1(m,n)\right) + a_2 \cdot \left(\Gamma_c^{class} \times X_2(m,n)\right) + L + \tag{31}$$
$$+ \cdots a_N \cdot \left(\Gamma_c^{class} \times X_N(m,n)\right)$$

or in the frequency domain the above equation is re-written as:

$$\boldsymbol{M\text{-}HONN} = \sum_{i=1 L N_{class}\times N}^{N_{class}\times N} a_i \cdot S_i^{class}(m,n) \tag{32}$$

The above Eq. (31) in spatial domain, and Eq. (32) in frequency domain describe the M-HONN system's transfer function for multiple objects recognition (where the upper script *class* is used for the class index, i.e. for Fig. 4 we have *class* = *class1, class2*). Thus, the M-HONN filter (robust object recognition system) is composed of a non-linear space domain superposition of the training set images or from the video frames of the training set video sequences. As for all the HONN-type systems, the multiplying coefficient now becomes a non-linear function of the input weights and the layer weights, rather than a simple linear multiplying constant as used in a constrained linear combinatorial-type filter synthesis procedure. The non-linear M-HONN system is inherently shift invariant and it may be employed in an optical correlator as would a linear superposition constrained-type filter, such as the synthetic discriminant function (SDF) -type (Bahri & Kumar, 1988) filters. It may be used as a space domain function in a joint transform correlator architecture or be Fourier transformed and used as Fourier domain filter in a 4-f Vander Lugt (Vander Lugt, 1964) type optical correlator.

5. Performance analysis

We have constructed a data set of input images of an S-type Jaguar car model at 10° increments of out-of-plane rotation at an elevation angle of approximately 45° to be used for the M-HONN system. A second set of images was constructed for the Police car model Mazda Efini RX-7 at the same elevation angle to serve as the out-of-class data for discrimination tests (see Fig. 5). A third data set was created of the background images of typical car parks (see Fig. 6) and the images of the S-type car model and the Mazda RX-7 car model added in the background scene. The size of all the images was $\left[256\times256\right]$ and all the images are in grey-scale bitmap format. All the input training images (and all the input test set images) for M-HONN system are concatenated row-by-row into a vector of size $\left[1\times\left(256\times256\right)\right]$ prior to input to the NNET block. Normally this size of image is impossibly large for

processing by any artificial neural network architecture, since to be implemented by enough input and layer weights:

$$\begin{aligned} N_{iw} &= 10\times\left[256\times256\right] \\ &= 10\times65,536 \\ &= 655,360 \end{aligned} \tag{33}$$

Thus, for a training set of $N=10$ individual vectors of size $\left[256\times256\right]$, there would, in total, be more than half-a-million input weight connections needed. Thus the selective weight connection architecture is employed to overcome this problem. To overcome this problem we developed a novel selective weight connection architecture (see Section 2). Also, applying the heuristic training algorithm with momentum and an adaptive learning rate into the NNET training session (Nguyen & Widrow, 1989; Nguyen & Widrow, 1990), has speeded up the learning phase and reduced the memory size needed to complete fully the training session. Here, it worth mentioning that the NNET block and, in overall, M-HONN system is able to process input still images and video frames for all the test series in few a msec with a Dual Core CPU at 2.4 GHz with 4.0GB RAM. Additionally, due to the generalization properties exhibited by a NNET architecture, the number of the training images decreases, in comparison to the typical number of images required for the training set of linear combinatorial filters (such as the SDF filter).

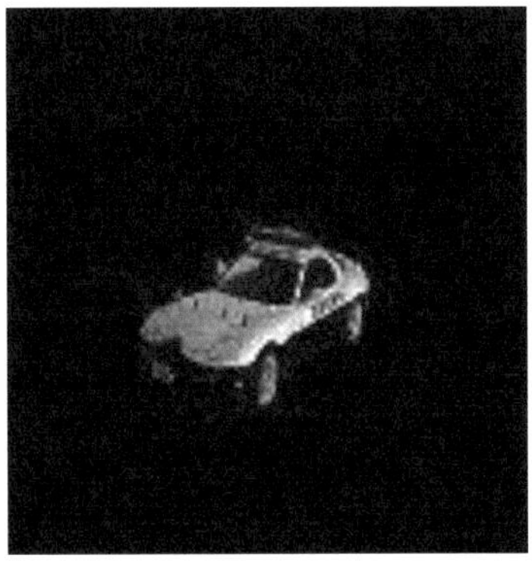

Fig. 5. RX-7 Mazda Efini Police patrol car used in the training and test sets

Fig. 6. Car park scene used in the training and test sets

It was proven experimentally that by choosing different values of the classification levels for the true-class Cl_T and false-class Cl_F objects, one can control the M-HONN system's behaviour to suit different application requirements, similarly with all the HONN-type systems. Thus we define:

$$\Delta Cl = \left| Cl_T - Cl_F \right| \tag{34}$$

where ΔCl is the absolute distance of the classification levels between the true-class objects and the false-class objects. When we increase ΔCl, then the resulting M-HONN system behaves more like a high-pass biased filter, which generally gives sharp correlation peaks and good clutter suppression but is more sensitive to intra-class distortions. Now, when we decrease ΔCl, then the resulting M-HONN system behaves more like a minimum variance synthetic discriminant function (MVSDF) (Kumar, 1986) filter with relatively good intra-class distortion invariance but producing broad correlation peaks. In effect, when ΔCl increases, the M-HONN system possesses better discriminatory properties but when ΔCl decreases the M-HONN system has better generalising properties. By plotting the isometric correlation planes of M-HONN system for different ΔCl values, one could observe that by increasing ΔCl value it leads to an increased emphasis of the high spatial frequency content of the composite images comprising M-HONN system, which in turn leads to a more localised response, sharper peaks, and reduction in the plane's sidelobes. By decreasing ΔCl value it leads to an increased emphasis on peripheral lower spatial frequency content of the composite images comprising M-HONN system, which in turn leads to a broader peaks in the correlation plane.

Next, we summarise the tests series for assessing M-HONN system's peak sharpness and detectability, distortion range, and discrimination ability, which we have all described them in full details in our previous work (Kypraios et al., 2008). We focus afterwards in analysing the performance of the M-HONN object recognition system within cluttered scenes.

5.1 Peak sharpness and detectability

Here we assessed (Jamal-Aldin et al., 1997; Jamal-Aldin et al., 1998; Kumar & Hassebrook, 1990) M-HONN system's ability to detect non-training in-class images that are oriented at the intermediate angle of view between the training images (Refregier, 1990; Refregier, 1991). The training set consisted of still images out-of-plane rotated between $[20\ 70]$ degrees at increments of 20°. We tested the M-HONN system with the true-class object's intermediate car poses over the same range at 10° increments. Two randomly chosen intermediate car poses, at 130° and at 140°, were added in the training set of the M-HONN system to create a false-class. We set the target of the false-class object to be $T_{\text{false}}=-40$ and of the true-class object to be $T_{\text{true}}=+40$. The M-HONN system had no information on the non-training, intermediate car images in the construction of its composite image. We explicitly constrained the correlation peak in the constraint matrix. Thus, we constrained the correlation peaks in the constraint matrix to be $+1$ for the images of the true-class object and 0 for the images of the false-class object. The randomly chosen mask Γ_c applied on both the training set and the test set was built from the training set image at 60°, i.e. $c=60^{\circ}$:

$$\Gamma_{60^{\circ}} = W^{x_{60^o}} \times L^{x_{60^o}} = \begin{bmatrix} w_{11}^{x_{60^o}} & w_{12}^{x_{60^o}} & L & w_{1n-1}^{x_{60^o}} & w_{1n}^{x_{60^o}} \\ w_{21}^{x_{60^o}} & w_{22}^{x_{60^o}} & L & w_{2n-1}^{x_{60^o}} & w_{2n}^{x_{60^o}} \\ & & & & \\ w_{m1}^{x_{60^o}} & w_{m2}^{x_{60^o}} & L & w_{mn-1}^{x_{60^o}} & w_{mn}^{x_{60^o}} \end{bmatrix} \times \begin{bmatrix} l_{11}^{x_{60^o}} & L & l_{1q}^{x_{60^o}} \\ l_{21}^{x_{60^o}} & L & l_{2q}^{x_{60^o}} \\ & & \\ l_{n1}^{x_{60^o}} & L & l_{nq}^{x_{60^o}} \end{bmatrix} \tag{35}$$

where $W^{x_{60^o}}$ and $L^{x_{60^o}}$ are the matrices of the input and layer weights. $w_{mn}^{x_{60^o}}$ are the input weights from the input neuron of the input vector element at row m and column n to the associated hidden layer for the training image $x_{60^o}(m,n)$ at 60° angle of view. $l_{mn}^{x_{60^o}}$ are the layer weights from the hidden neuron of the layer vector element at row m and column n to the associated output neuron. We set q = 1 since the output layer had only one neuron for a single class of objects. In M-HONN system, instead of multiplying each training image with the corresponding weight connections as done for the constrained- HONN (C-HONN) system, we keep constant the weight connection values which are set to be equal to a (randomly) chosen image included in the training set, here to be $x_{60^{\circ}}(m,n)$.

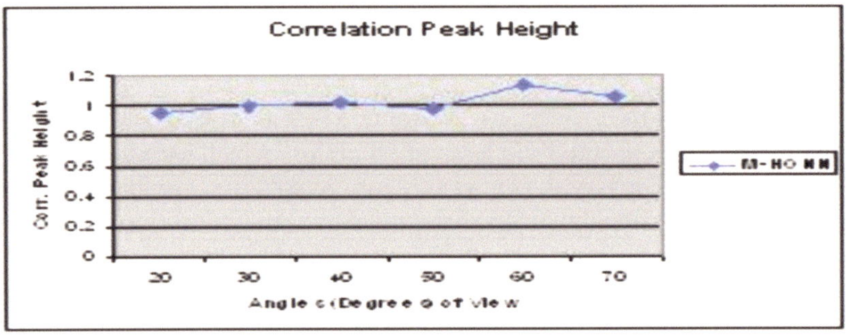

(a)

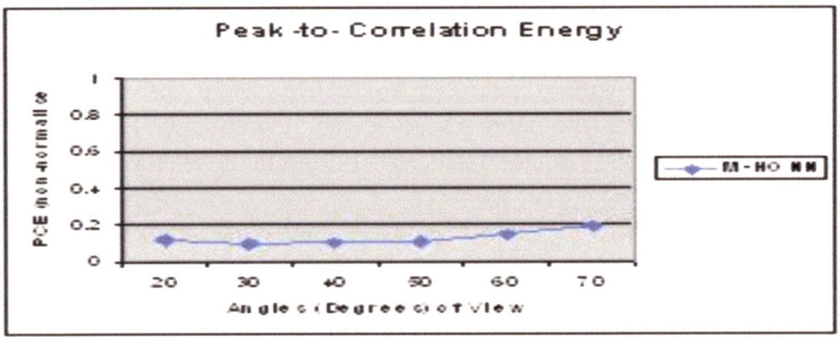

(b)

Fig. 7. (Adapted by Kypraios et al., 2008) shows (a) correlation peak-height versus the out-of-plane rotation angles of the object over the range of 20° to 70°. We tested the M-HONN system with the true-class object's intermediate car poses over the same range out-of-plane rotated at 10° increments; (b) the non-normalised PCE values of the test images at 10° increments versus the angles of view over the range of 20° to 70°.

Fig. 7 (a) shows the plot of the correlation-peak height for each input image for the M-HONN system. From the plot it is shown that the M-HONN system is invariant to the out-of-plane rotation, since it has produced consistent correlation peaks for both the in-class training and non-training images around the fixed-correlation peak-height value of unity. The consistency of the correlation peak values that the M-HONN system has exhibited demonstrate the system's ability to interpolate well between the intermediate car poses at 10° increments. Earlier (Kypraios et al., 2008; Kypraios, 2009; Kypraios, 2010), we have shown the NNET includes information for reference and non-reference images of the true-class object. Hence, the NNET interpolates non-linearly between the reference and non-reference images to follow the activation function graph. Moreover, the NNET is able to generalize between all the reference and non-reference images.

Fig. 7 (b) shows the non-normalised peak-to-correlation energy (PCE) (Kumar & Hassebrook, 1990) values for the M-HONN system. From the graph, it can be observed that the M-HONN system produced PCE values for the intermediate non-training images close to those produced by the training car images. In effect, the system maintains correlation peak sharpness for the in-class training and non-training images.

5.2 Distortion range

The second tests series (Jamal-Aldin et al., 1997; Jamal-Aldin et al., 1998; Kumar & Hassebrook, 1990) was carried out to assess the distortion range (Refregier, 1990; Refregier, 1991, Kypraios et al., 2008) of the M-HONN system. The training set consisted of images for a distortion range over 0° to 90°. We used several smaller test sets, which consisted of two in-class training images at a widely separated angle within the range $\left[10^\circ\,20^\circ\,30^\circ\,40^\circ\,50^\circ\,60^\circ\,70^\circ\,80^\circ\right]$ and a third non-training in-class image lying on the bisector angle of the two in-class training images (see Fig. 8 (a)). The intermediate non-training car pose image was $\hat{\Theta}_3 \in \left[5^\circ, 40^\circ\right]$ i.e. $\Theta_3 = \left[5^\circ\,10^\circ\,15^\circ\,20^\circ\,25^\circ\,30^\circ\,35^\circ\,40^\circ\right]$. Three randomly chosen training images, out-of-plane rotated at $110^\circ, 130^\circ$ and 140°, were added in the training set of the M-HONN system which fell inside the false-class. The targets of the true-class objects and of the false-class objects were found to be best set for the tests series as $T_{true} = +40$ and $T_{false} = -40$. The M-HONN system has no information built into it on the test images of the intermediate car poses. We constrained the correlation peaks in the constraint matrix to be $+1$ for the images of the true-class object and 0 for the images of the false-class object.

Fig. 8 (b) shows the correlation-peak height for each input image for the M-HONN system. It is found the system has good performance in recognising all the intermediate car poses of the test set. The correlation-peak height of the in-class input images, intermediate between two training images, lie within a band of greater than 76% of the pre-specified peak-height constant in the constraint matrix C for the M-HONN system. From the graph it can be observed that the system tolerated orientation over a range of $\hat{\Theta}_3 \in \left[5^\circ, 40^\circ\right]$.

5.3 Discrimination ability

The third tests series (Jamal-Aldin et al., 1997; Jamal-Aldin et al., 1998; Kumar & Hassebrook, 1990) was carried out to assess the discrimination ability (Refregier, 1990; Refregier, 1991, Kypraios et al., 2008) of the M-HONN system. In the tests, M-HONN system tried to discriminate between objects of different classes while retaining invariance to in-class distortions. The training set consisted of images of the Jaguar S-type for adistortion range over 20° to 70° at 10° increments. The test set consisted of one training image out-of-plane rotated at 40° of the Jaguar S-type and a second image of the out-of-class RX-7 Police patrol car at the same angle of out-of-plane rotation. Two different training set configuration of still images were experimented with. Firstly, we added two images of the Jaguar S-type at 130° and 140° for the false-class of the system's training set. We constrained the false-class images of the objects to zero correlation peak-height in the synthesis of the M-HONN system's composite image. Secondly, we conducted experiments with no inclusion in the system's composite image of any false-class images. For both cases, we aimed in observing if there was any change in the class separation ability of the M-HONN system. We constrained the true-class objects to unity correlation peak-height and we used the same as before Targets for the false- and true- class images of the NNET block. The target of the false-class object is $T_{false} = -40$, and the Target of the true-class object is $T_{true} = +40$ in the training set of the NNET block for the M-HONN system. It had no built-in information on the test images.

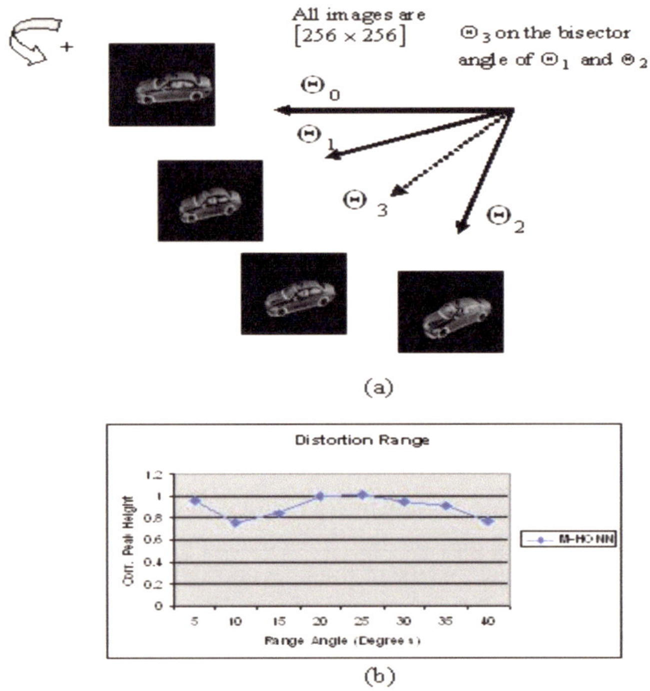

Fig. 8. (Adapted by Kypraios et al., 2008) shows (a) the reference angle, Θ0, and the two in-class training images at the angles Θ1 and Θ2. The test image is on the bisector at angle Θ3; (b) the correlation peak-heights for each input image over a range of Θ3 = [5° 40°] for the M-HONN system.

From the conducted experiments we drew Table 1. The forth column of Table 1 records the values taken for the in-class training image and the fifth column contains all the values taken for the out-of-class training image. It is shown from the third column of Table 1 that M-HONN system gave sufficient discrimination ability between the two objects, the Jaguar S-type car and the RX-7 Police patrol car. It produced 12% class separation (with the false-class images included in the synthesis of the composite image with zero correlation peak-height constraint). By not including any false-class images in the system's composite image, but by setting to unity correlation peak-height constraint the true-class images and keeping constant the target of the false-class object to $T_{false} = -40$ and the target of the true-class object to $T_{true} = +40$, the M-HONN system increased the class separation to 27%. Thus, the two different training set still images configurations that we had experimented with (in first, false-class images zero peak constrained and, in second, false-class images not included in the system's composite image) helped us make a useful observation about the M-HONN system's ability to distinguish between two different classes. More specifically, the false-class images included in the composite image, and zero peak constrained, were taken from the true-class object in different poses not included in the training set. In effect, when we tested the RX-7 police patrol car images, the system separated the input images from the trained images (unity peak constrained) of the true-class object and the false-class images (of the same true-class but zero peak constrained) as a third class. Apparently, that caused the drop of the M-HONN system discrimination ability by almost half. We have found to be a solution to the problem by including false-class images not belonging in the same the true-class object but from a different one which it could increase further the discrimination ability of M-HONN system.

			Correlation Peak Height	
Object Recognition System	False Class BG	Discrimination Ability %	Jaguar S-type	RX-7 Mazda Efini
M-HONN	zero – peak constrained	11.9967	1.0878	0.9573
M-HONN	NOT included	26.9758	1.1299	0.8251

Table 1. (adapted by Kypraios et al., 2008) Discrimination Ability of M-HONN system

5.4 Clutter tolerance

5.4.1 Training sets

We have conducted several tests (Kypraios et al., 2009) for evaluating the performance of the M-HONN system in recognising multiple objects of the same class or of different classes. Several training sets were created for testing the system's performance with still images and with video sequences. The first training set consisted of still images of the Jaguar S-type car for a distortion range over 0° to 360° out-of-plane rotated at 10° increments. The second training set consisted of still images of the RX-7 Police patrol car for a distortion range approximately over 0° to 360° out-of-plane rotated at 10° increments. The third training set consisted of video frames of a Ferrari Testarossa car within a background clutter scene. The fourth training set consisted of still images of different car park scenes. A fifth training set consisted of video frames we have taken showing a sequence of a Jaguar S-type car and a Ferrari Testarossa car within a background clutter scene. All the training and test sets of the still images and of the video sequence frames were used in grey-scale bitmap format, and they were sized to 256x256. All the test and train input still images and video frames were concatenated row-by-row into a vector form prior being processed by the NNET block of the M-HONN system.

5.4.2 Biologically-inspired knowledge representation and learning

As S. Haykin in his work on artificial neural network architectures (S. Haykin, 1999) observes, pattern recognition systems need to be re-designed in novel architectures, if they are to be solving more complex problems. He argues that such novel architectures should be designed with separate blocks of a recognition unit and a knowledge learning unit, and that the implementation of such designs can be only possible with the combination of artificial neural networks architectures with other tools as a hybrid. Some of the elements (S. Haykin, 1999) that such biologically-inspired hybrid systems need to exploit are, the non-linearity of the input information, learning and adaptation to the input information, and provide an attentional mechanism for the hybrid system to be able to select certain information to be included in its learning against other input. Therefore, knowledge representation and learning becomes a central issue in the design and implementation of such hybrid biologically-inspired pattern recognition systems (Lee & Portier, 2007).

Aler et al. in their work discuss the knowledge representation and its role in knowledge learning (Aler et al., 2000). Aler et al. argue the effects that altering the knowledge representation can have on the problem knowledge learned and problem solving. They consider any problem solving system to consist of a domain theory which specifies the task to be solved, the initial problem states and the aimed problem goals, and a control knowledge which guides the decision-making process. They were able to demonstrate the effects of knowledge representation to the efficiency of the problem solving process.

Recent work we have conducted (Kypraios, 2010) has demonstrated the problem solving ability of the HONN-type systems, such as the M-HONN system for multiple objects recognition. We have shown the system is able to solve, in particular, different visual tasks. Fig. 9 shows the first problem we have tested M-HONN system for recognising different angles of view of the input object. The training set consisted of still images of the Jaguar S-type car out-of-plane rotated over a range 0° to 170° to belong in the true-class, and still images of the Jaguar S-type car out-of-plane rotated over a range 180° to 360° to belong in the false-class. The true-class images were constrained to unit correlation peak-height in the synthesis of the M-HONN system's composite image, and the false-class images were constrained to zero correlation peak-height in the synthesis of the M-HONN system's composite image (see Fig. 10). We have set the true-class target classification levels (here we assume there is only one *class=1*, so there is no need to set any target connections for a second output neuron) to be $T_{true}^{class\,1} = +40$, and for false-class the target classification levels were set to be $T_{false}^{class\,1} = -40$. The test set consisted of multiple Jaguar S-type car objects inserted in plain background at different non-training out-of-plane rotation angles over a range 0° to 360°. As shown on Fig. 9, M-HONN system was able to correctly recognise the Jaguar S-type car poses over the range 0° to 170° to belong in the true-class, and the Jaguar S-type car poses over the range 180° to 360° to belong in the false-class. We have indicated with the solid line the recognised true-class objects and with the dashed line the recognised false-class objects.

Fig. 11 shows the second test we conducted to demonstrate the system's ability of problem solving where we want the system to recognise only the true-class objects of the Jaguar S-type car over a range 0° to 360°, and reject the false-class objects of the RX-7 Mazda Efini

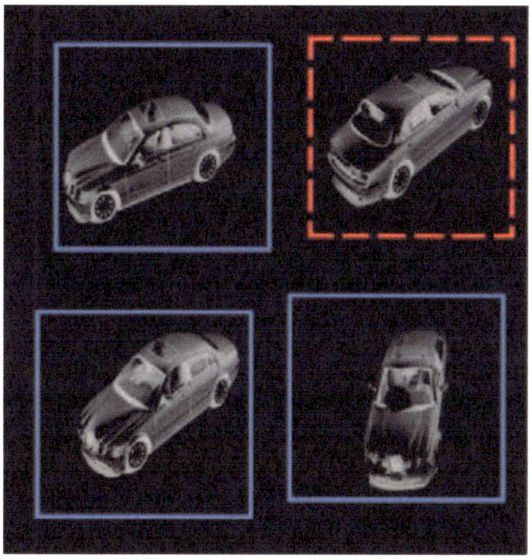

Fig. 9. It shows the first visual problem for testing the M-HONN object recognition system's ability of problem solving. M-HONN system tries to recognise certain angles of view of the input object while rejecting others. The training set consisted of still images of the Jaguar S-type car out-of-plane rotated over a range 0° to 170° to belong in the true-class, and still images of the Jaguar S-type car out-of-plane rotated over a range 180° to 360° to belong in the false-class. We have indicated with the solid line the recognised true-class objects and with the dashed line the recognised false-class objects.

Police patrol car over approximately the same range. The training set consisted of still images of the Jaguar S-type car out-of-plane rotated over a range 0° to 360° to belong in the true-class, and still images of the RX-7 Mazda Efini Police patrol car out-of-plane rotated over approximately a range 0° to 360° to belong in the false-class. The true-class images were constrained to unit correlation peak-height in the synthesis of the M-HONN system's composite image, and the false-class images were constrained to zero correlation peak-height in the synthesis of the M-HONN system's composite image. We have set the true-class target classification levels (here we assume there is only one *class=1*, so there is no need to set any target connections for a second output neuron) to be $T_{true}^{class\,1} = +240$, and for false-class the target classification levels were set to be $T_{false}^{class\,1} = -240$. Here, we have set higher target classification level values for increasing the inter-class discrimination abilities of the M-HONN system. It worth mentioning that we could have set *class=2* and, then, set a target classification level for $T_{true}^{class\,2}$ with no need to include false-class objects, but adjust the constraint matrix of the system's composite image to class 1 and class 2 different fixed correlation peak-height values. The test set consisted of non-training input still images of Jaguar S-type car objects inserted in plain background at different out-of-plane rotation angles over a range 0° to 360°, and input still images of RX-7 Mazda Efini Police patrol cars inserted in plain background at different out-of-plane rotation angles over a range 0° to 360°. As shown on Fig. 11, M-HONN system was able to successfully recognise the Jaguar S-type car poses over the range 0° to 360° to belong in the true-class, and the RX-7 Mazda Efini car poses over approximately the same range 0° to 360° to belong in the false-class. Again, we have indicated with the solid line the recognised true-class objects and with the dashed line the recognised false-class objects.

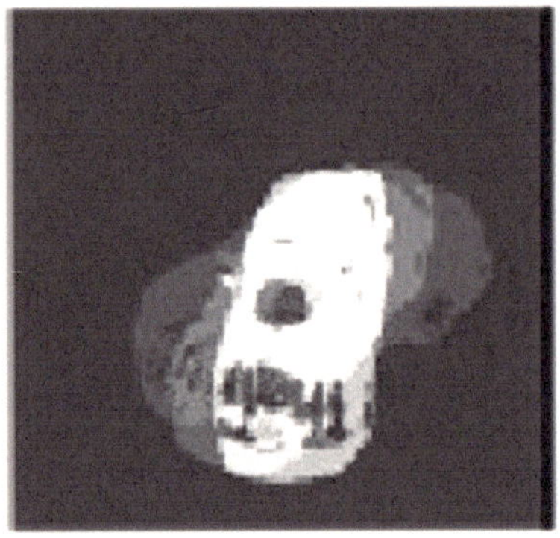

Fig. 10. It shows the composite image the M-HONN system synthesised for a training set consisting of still images of the Jaguar S-type car out-of-plane rotated over a range 0° to 360°.

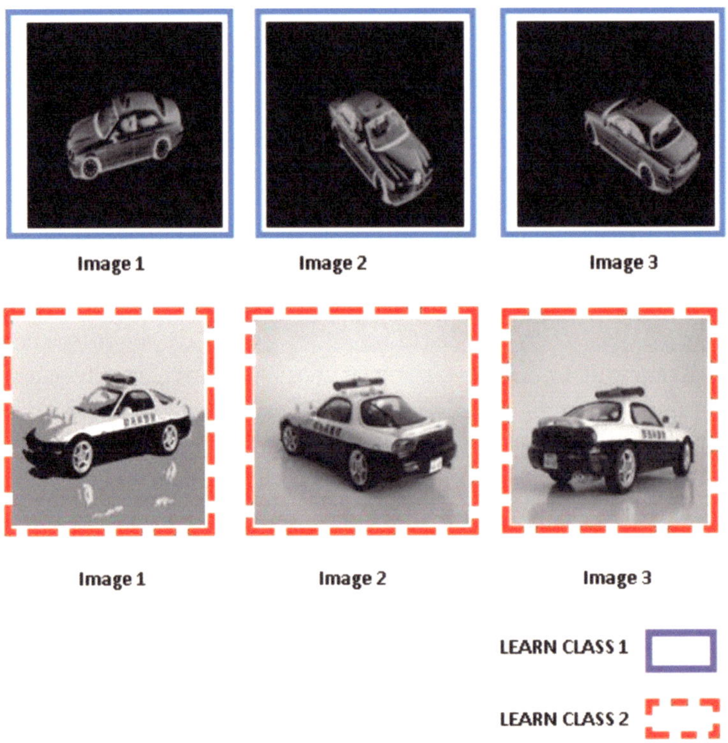

Fig. 11. It shows the second visual problem for testing the M-HONN object recognition system's ability of problem solving. M-HONN system tries to recognise only the true-class objects of the Jaguar S-type car and reject all the false-class objects. The training set consisted of still images of the Jaguar S-type car out-of-plane rotated over a range 0° to 360° to belong in the true-class, and still images of the RX-7 Mazda Efini Police patrol car out-of-plane rotated over approximately a range 0° to 360° to belong in the false-class. We have indicated with the solid line the recognised true-class objects and with the dashed line the recognised false-class objects.

Additional tests we conducted have demonstrated the effect that has the input mask Γ_c in the synthesis of the composite image of the M-HONN system. Thus, in one of the tests we created a training set consisting of Jaguar S-type car objects out-of-plane rotated over a range 20° to 70° at 10° increments to belong in true-class 1, RX-7 Mazda Efini Police patrol car objects out-of-plane rotated over approximately a range 20° to 70°at 10° increments to belong in true-class 2, and a random car park scene to belong in false-class. The true-class 1 images were constrained to unit correlation peak-height, the true-class 2 images were constrained to half-a-unit correlation peak-height, and the false-class images were constrained to zero correlation peak-height in the synthesis of the M-HONN system's composite image. We have set the true-class 1 and true-class 2 target classification levels to be $T_{true}^{class\,1} = +180$ and $T_{true}^{class\,2} = +90$, and for false-class 1 and false-class 2 the target classification levels were set to be $T_{false}^{class\,1} = -10$ and $T_{false}^{class\,2} = -10$. The test set (see Fig. 12) consisted of input still images of a Jaguar S-type car object and a RX-7 Mazda Efini Police patrol car object both inserted in a car park background scene (not the one we included in the training set), positioned off-the-centre and out-of-plane rotated over a range 20° to 70°. During the process of inserting the objects in to the car park scene some Gaussian noise is added, too. The M-HONN system was able to correctly discriminate between class 1 and class 2. However, in this test the emphasis was to study the effect that knowledge representation in the form of the composite image synthesis has on the problem solving. In effect, as shown in Fig. 13, when we have chosen to build the input mask Γ_c, which we applied it on both the training set and the test set, from the training set image of true-class 1 object of the Jaguar S-type car, then the system synthesised its composite image by non-linearly revealing more features for the true-class 1 object of the Jaguar S-type car, allowing less features for the true-class 2 object of the RX-7 Mazda Efini Police patrol car and completely suppressing any features of the background car park scene. When we have chosen to build the input mask Γ_c from the training set image of true-class 2 object of the RX-7 Mazda Efini Police patrol car, then the system synthesise its composite image (see Fig. 14) by non-linearly revealing more features for the true-class 2 object of the RX-7 Mazda Efini Police patrol car, allowing less features for the true-class 1 object of the Jaguar S-type car and completely suppressing any features of the background car park scene.

Fig. 12. It shows one of the test set input images used for assessing the M-HONN system's performance within clutter

From the above observations and conducted experiments, the M-HONN system, as all the HONN-type systems, combine in their design a knowledge representation unit being the optical correlator block with a knowledge learning unit being the NNET block. Moreover, HONN-type systems, such as M-HONN, have been proven in previous work we have done (Kypraios et al., 2002) to non-linearly combine the weighted, extracted by the NNET block, input training set. In effect, in HONN-type systems the attentional mechanism is provided by the extracted weights of the NNET block to be able to select certain features to be included in its composite image against other ones. Additionally, the M-HONN system, as shown above, can learn and adapt to the input information depending on the created training set itself. Here, the created training set comprises the domain theory of the task to be solved, the initial problem states and the problem goals are given by the true-class and false-class classification levels, and the synthesised composite image provides the control knowledge which guides the decision-making process.

Fig. 13. It shows the synthesised composite image of the M-HONN system. The training set set consisted of Jaguar S-type car objects out-of-plane rotated over a range 20° to 70° at 10° increments to belong in true-class 1, RX-7 Mazda Efini Police patrol car objects out-of-plane rotated over approximately a range 20° to 70°at 10° increments to belong in true-class 2, and a random car park scene to belong in false-class. When we have built the input mask from the training set image of true-class 1 object of the Jaguar S-type car, then the system synthesised its composite image by non-linearly revealing more features for the true-class 1 object of the Jaguar S-type car, allowing less features for the true-class 2 object of the RX-7 Mazda Efini Police patrol car and completely suppressing any features of the background car park scene.

5.4.3 Multiple objects recognition

Here, we summarise several tests we previously conducted for explicitly testing the M-HONN system's ability to recognise multiple objects of different classes (Kypraios et al., 2008). In the first series of conducted tests, the training set consisted of three Jaguar S-type car images out-of-plane rotated at 40° 60° and 80° to belong in class 1, and three Ferrari Testarossa extracted video frames from a recorded video sequence to belong in class 2. For our application purposes it was found to be adequate to set $T_{true}^{class1} = +40$ and $T_{true}^{class2} = +40$ for the true-class target classification levels and $T_{false}^{class1} = -40$ and $T_{false}^{class2} = -40$ for the false-class classification levels. We constrained true-class 1 of the Jaguar S-type object images to unit correlation peak-height constraint, and true-class 2 of the Ferrari Testarossa car to half-a-unit correlation peak-height constraint in the synthesis of the M-HONN system's composite image. Fig. 15 (a) and Fig. 15 (b) show the output correlation planes response of the M-HONN system for class 1, which are normalised to the overall maximum correlation plane peak-height value for all the input images. Fig. 15 (c) and Fig. 15 (d) show the output correlation plane response of the M-HONN system for class 2, which are normalised to the overall maximum correlation plane peak-height value for all the input images. From the recorded results we have shown that the M-HONN system has accommodated the recognition of class 1 and class 2 objects by output neuron 1 and output neuron 2, respectively.

Fig. 14. It shows the synthesised composite image of the M-HONN system. The training set set consisted of Jaguar S-type car objects out-of-plane rotated over a range 20° to 70° at 10° increments to belong in true-class 1, RX-7 Mazda Efini Police patrol car objects out-of-plane rotated over approximately a range 20° to 70°at 10° increments to belong in true-class 2, and a random car park scene to belong in false-class. Now we have built the input mask from the training set image of true-class 2 object of the RX-7 Mazda Efini Police patrol car, then the system synthesised its composite image by non-linearly revealing more features for the true-class 2 object of the RX-7 Mazda Efini Police patrol car, allowing less features for the true-class 1 object of the Jaguar S-type car and completely suppressing any features of the background car park scene.

In the second series of conducted tests, we aimed to assess the ability of the M-HONN system to recognise multiple objects of different classes within a cluttered video sequence. Fig. 16 shows indicatively four of the video frames from the recorded video sequence. The frame rate of the video sequence was 25 frames per second (fps). The training consisted of images of the Jaguar S-type car out-of-plane rotated over 20° to 80° degrees at 20° increments. We added two images of the Jaguar S-type car out-of-plane rotated at 130° and 140° to fall inside the false-class object for increasing the peak sharpness and class discrimination abilities of the M-HONN system. For our conducted tests we found the best values for the true-class 1 and true-class 2 classification values to be $T_{\text{true}}^{\text{class 1}} = +240$ and $T_{\text{true}}^{\text{class 2}} = +240$, respectively, and the best values for the false-class 1 and false-class 2 classification values to be $T_{false}^{class\,1} = -240$ and $T_{false}^{class\,2} = -240$. We constrained true-class 1 of the Jaguar S-type object images to unit correlation peak-height constraint, true-class 2 of the Ferrari Testarossa car to half-a-unit correlation peak-height constraint, and false-class 1 and false-class 2 to zero correlation peak-height constraints in the synthesis of the M-HONN system's composite image. Fig. 16 shows the locked window unit of chosen size 70x70 on top of the maximum correlation peak-height values. With the dashed line we have shown the secondary correlation peaks of the output plane and with the solid line we have shown the maximum correlation peak-height value of the output plane. M-HONN system successfully suppressed the unknown background clutter throughout the length of the video sequence and recognised correctly class 1 and class 2 objects. It is emphasised that we have not included any background information in the training set of the system.

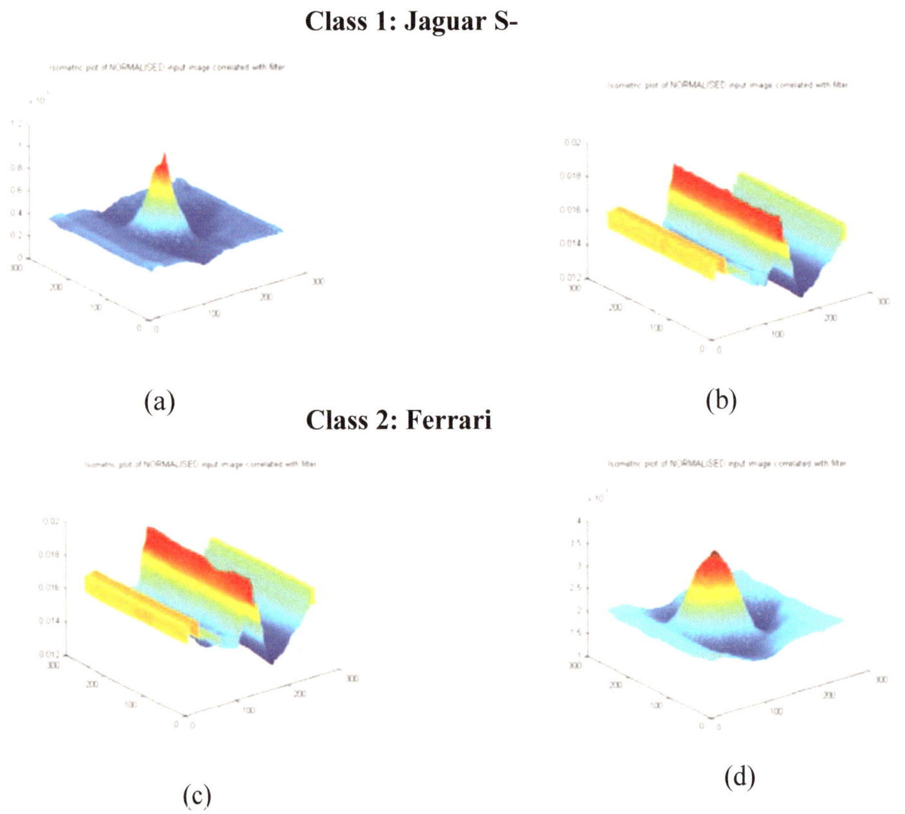

Fig. 15. (Adapted by Kypraios et al., 2009) It shows (a) for the first output layer neuron, and (b) for the second output layer neuron the isometric output correlation plane response of the M-HONN system for Class 1 (normalised to the maximum correlation plane peak-height value), and (c) and (d) the isometric output correlation plane response of the M-HONN system for Class 2 (normalised to the maximum correlation plane peak-height value).

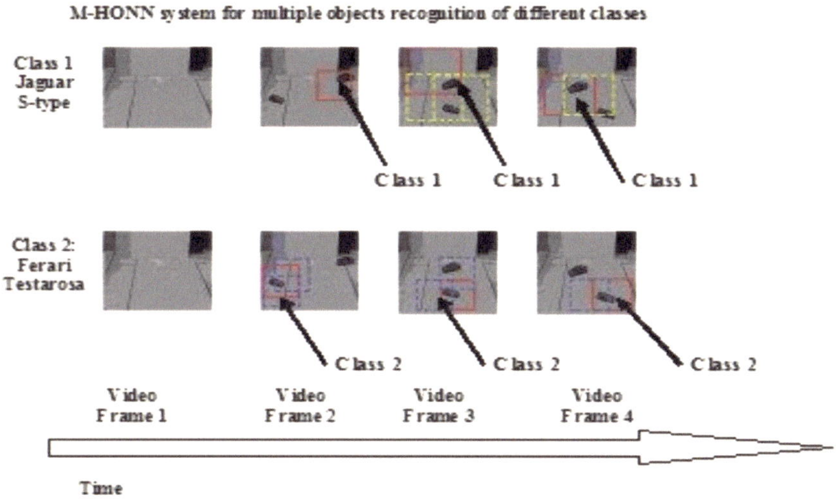

Fig. 16. It shows indicatively four of the video frames from the recorded video sequence. The locked window unit is on top of the maximum correlation peak-height values. With the dashed line we have shown the secondary correlation peaks of the output plane and with the solid line we have shown the maximum correlation peak-height value of the output plane.

6. Conclusion and future work

We have described the design and implementation of the M-HONN system. In particular, we focused in the design and implementation of the M-HONN system for multiple objects recognition of the same and of different classes. The inherited shift invariance properties by the optical correlator block of the system can accommodate for the recognition of multiple objects of the same class. The cross-correlation of each masked test set image with the transformed reference kernel returns an output correlation plane peak value for each cross-correlation step. Thus, the maximum peak height values of the output correlation plane correspond to the recognised true-class objects. By augmenting the output layer of the NNET block of the M-HONN system we can accommodate for the recognition of multiple objects of different classes. In effect, we increase the number of the output layer neurons proportionally with the number of the different object classes. We assign one output neuron to each different class. It was proven experimentally that by choosing different values of the classification levels for the true-class Cl_T and false-class Cl_F objects we can control the M-HONN system's behaviour and it can be varied from more like a high-pass biased filter, which generally gives sharp correlation peaks and good clutter suppression but is more sensitive to intra-class distortions, to more like a MVSDF filter behaviour, which generally gives broader correlation peaks but is more robust to intra-class distortions of the input objects.

We have assessed the performance of the M-HONN system by conducting several series of tests. We assessed the system's ability to detect non-training in-class images that are oriented at the intermediate angle of view between the training images. From the recorded results, we were able to show the system's ability to interpolate well between the intermediate car poses. The system maintained correlation peak sharpness for the in-class training and non-training images. More specifically, the M-HONN system is able to interpolate non-linearly between the reference and non-reference images to follow the activation function graph. The NNET block is able to generalize between all the reference and non-reference images. Next, we have tested the M-HONN system's distortion range. From the recorded results, we have shown that the system has exhibited a high distortion range recognising all the intermediate car poses of the test set over the range $\hat{\Theta}_3 \in \left[5^{\circ}, 40^{\circ} \right]$ (bisector angle). The third series of tests we conducted were for assessing the discrimination ability of the M-HONN system. From the recorded results, we have shown that the system successfully discriminate between objects of different classes while retaining invariance to in-class distortions.

We have analysed the M-HONN system's biologically-inspired hybrid design and we have found to combine a knowledge representation unit being the optical correlator block with a knowledge learning unit being the NNET block, as for the G-HONN type systems. We conducted several experiments for testing the system's problem solving abilities. The M-HONN system was able to solve the visual task of recognising certain Jaguar S-type car poses to belong in the true-class from other Jaguar S-type car poses. Also, the M-HONN system was able to solve the visual task of recognising only the true-class objects of the Jaguar S-type car.

The last series of tests aimed to assess the M-HONN system's performance of recognising multiple objects of different classes within clutter. We have tested the system with a recorded video sequence. The system successfully suppressed the unknown background clutter during the whole length of the video sequence and recognised correctly class 1 and class 2 objects. In overall, the M-HONN system was able to correctly recognise true-class objects out-of-plane rotated, translated off-the-centre and inserted into background scenes. It is emphasised that the system was able to recognise the true-class objects within an unknown background clutter scene since we have not included any background information in its training set. Additionally, all the invariance properties were simultaneously exhibited by the M-HONN system with a single pass over the input data sets. In effect, as we could see from its transfer function, M-HONN system is not either a multiple stages-type of filter or any pre-processing of the input data is required for maintaining its invariance properties. There is no need for a separate background segmentation pre-processing stage prior the system's object tracking as in the case of other motion based segmentation and object tracking techniques. Instead, the M-HONN system is able to successfully suppress the background clutter and track throughout the video sequence the recognised true-class object.

In future, we would like to assess the performance of each output neuron of the M-HONN system's NNET block individually and record separately their performance metrics values for the detectability, distortion range, and discrimination ability. Also, we believe that the M-HONN system's design can be extended to accommodate three-dimensional (3D) object recognition. Similarly to stereo vision systems (Lowe, 1987; Xu & Zhang, 1996; Sumi et al., 2002), the M-HONN system's design can be extended with a second input mask for processing different angles of the captured data, and incorporating the corresponding transformed images into its composite image synthesis.

7. References

Aler, R., Borrajo, D. & Isasi, P. (2000). Knowledge representation issues in control knowledge learning, *Proceedings of 25th International Conference on Machine Learning*, Morgan Kaufmann, pp. 1-8, ISBN 1558607072

Bahri, Z. & Kumar, B. V. K. (1988). Generalized Synthetic Discriminant Functions, *Journal of Optical Society of America*, Vol.5, No.4, pp. 562-571

Beale, R. & Jackson, T. (1990). *Neural Computing : An Introduction*, Institute of Physics Publishing, Hilger, ISBN 0852742622, 9780852742624, Bristol, Philadelphia

Bottou, L., Fogelman- Soulié, F., Blanchet, P. & Lienard, J. S. (1990). Speaker Independent Isolated Digit Recognition : Multilayer Perceptrons vs Dynamic Time Warping, *Neural Networks*, Vol.3, pp. 453-465

Casasent, D. (1984). Unified synthetic discriminant function computational formulation, *Applied Optics*, Vol.23, No.10, 1620-1627

Casasent, D., Neiberg, L. M. & Sipe, M. A. (1998). Feature Space Trajectory Distorted Object Representation for Classification and Pose Estimation, *Optical Engineering*, Vol.37, No.3, pp. 914-923

Caulfield, H. J. & Maloney, W. T. (1969). Improved discrimination in optical character recognition, *Applied Optics*, Vol.08, No.11, 2354-2356

Caulfield, H. J. (1980). Linear combinations of filters for character recognition: a unified treatment, *Applied Optics*, Vol.19, No.23, 3877-3878

Delopoulos, A., Tirakis, A. & Kollias, S. (1994). Invariant Image Classification Using Triple-Correlation-Based Neural Networks, *IEEE Transactions on Neural Networks*, Vol.5, No.3, pp. 392-408

Dobnikar, A., Ficzko J., Podbregar, D. & Rezar, U. (1991/92). Invariant pattern classification neural network versus FT approach, *Microprocessing and Microprogramming*, Vol. 33, pp. 161-168

Giles, C. L. & Maxwell, T. (1987). Learning, Invariance and Generalisation in Higher-Order Neural Networks, *Applied Optics*, Vol.26, pp. 4972-4978

Hagan, M. T., Demuth, H. B. & Beale, M. H. (1996). *Neural Network Design*, PWS Publishing, ISBN 0-9717321-0-8, Boston, MA

Haykin, S. (1999). *Neural Networks-A Comprehensive Foundations*, 2nd Edition, Prentice Hall International, Inc.

Jamal-Aldin, L. S., Young, R. C. D. & Chatwin, C. R. (1997). Application of non-linearity to wavelet-transformed images to improve correlation filter performance, *Applied Optics*, Vol. 36, No. 35, pp. 9212-9224

Jamal-Aldin, L. S., Young, R. C. D. & Chatwin, C. R. (1998). Synthetic discriminant function filter employing nonlinear space-domain preprocessing on bandpass-filtered images, *Applied Optics*, Vol. 37, No. 11, pp. 2051-2062

Kanaoka, T., Chellapa, R., Yoshitaka, M. & Tomita, S. (1992). A Higher-Order Neural Network for Distortion Invariant Pattern Recognition, *Pattern Recognition Letters*, Vol.13, pp. 837-841

Khotanzad, A. & Hong, H. (1990). Invariant Image Recognition by Zernike Moments, *IEEE Transactions on Pattern Analysis and Machine Intelligence,* Vol. 12, pp. 489-497

Kumar, B. V. K. & Hassebrook, L. (1990) Performance measures for correlation filters, *Applied Optics,* Vol. 29, No. 20, pp. 2997-3006

Kumar, B. V. K. (1986). Minimum Variance Synthetic Discriminant Functions, *Journal Optics Society America A,* Vol.3, pp. 1579-1584

Kumar, B. V. K. (1992). Tutorial Survey of Composite Filter Designs for Optical Correlators, *Applied Optics,* Vol.31, No.23, 4773-4801

Kypraios, I. (2009). A Comparative Analysis of the Hybrid Optical Neural Network-type Filters Performance within Cluttered Scenes, *51st International Symposium ELMAR, IEEE Region 8/IEEE Croatia/EURASIP,* Vol.1, pp. 71-77

Kypraios, I. (2010). *Hybrid optical neural network-type filters for multiple objects recognition within cluttered scenes,* Object Recognition, InTech, ISBN 978-953-307-222-7

Kypraios, I. (February 2010). A Digital/Optical Neuronal Model for the Cognitive Interaction Between Retina Sensor and the Human Brain Visual Cortex, *Poster Presentation, INCF UK Node Congress Analysing and Modelling the Neural Systems in Health and Disease, Informatics Forum,* Edinburgh

Kypraios, I., Lei, P. W., Birch, P. M., Young, R. C. D. & Chatwin C. R. (2008). Performance Assessment of the Modified-Hybrid Optical Neural Network Filter, *Applied Optics,* Vol.47, No.18, pp. 3378-3389

Kypraios, I., Young, R. C. D. & Chatwin, C. R. (2004b). Performance assessment of Unconstrained Hybrid Optical Neural Network filter for Object Recognition Tasks in Clutter, *Optical Pattern Recognition XV, Proceedings of SPIE,* Vol.5437, pp. 51-62

Kypraios, I., Young, R. C. D. & Chatwin, C. R. (2009). Modified-Hybrid Optical Neural Network Filter for Multiple Objects Recognition within Cluttered Scenes, *Optics and Photonics for Information Processing III, Proceedings SPIE,* Vol.7442, pp. 74420P-74420P-12

Kypraios, I., Young, R. C. D., Birch, P. M. & Chatwin, C. R. (2004a). Object Recognition Within Cluttered Scenes Employing a Hybrid Optical Neural Network Filter, *Optical Engineering Special Issue on Trends in Pattern Recognition,* Vol.43, pp. 1839-1850

Kypraios, I., Young, R. C. D., Birch, P. M. & Chatwin, C. R. (2003). A non-linear training set superposition filter derived by neural network training methods for implementation in a shift invariant optical correlator, *Proceedings SPIE Defense & Security, Optical Pattern Recognition XIV,* Vol. 5106, pp. 84-95, Orlando, Florida, USA

Kypraios, I., Young, R. C. D., Chatwin C. R. (2002). An Investigation of the Non-Linear Properties of Correlation Filter Synthesis and Neural Network Design, *Asian Journal of Physics,* Vol.11, No.3, pp. 313-344

LeCun, Y. (1989). Generalisation and Network Design Strategies, *Connectionism in Perspective,* Pfeirer, R., Schreter, Z., Fogelman-Soulié, F. & Steels, L., Elsevier Science, Amsterdam

LeCun, Y., Boser, B., Denker, J. S., Henderson, D., Howard, R. E., Hubbard, W., Jackel, L. D. (1990). Handwritten Digit Recognition with a Backpropagation Network, *Advances in Neural Information Processing Systems,* Touretzky, D., Morgan Kaufmann, Vol.2, pp. 396-404

Lee, I. & Portier, B. (11-13 July 2007). An empirical study of knowledge representation and learning within conceptual spaces for intelligent agents, *6th IEEE/ACIS International Conference Computer and Information Science*, pp. 463-468, Melbourne, Australia

Looney, C. G. (1997). *Pattern Recognition Using Neural Networks-Theory and Algorithms for Engineers and Scientists,* Oxford University Press, New York-Oxford

Lowe, D. G. (1987). Three-dimensional object recognition from single two dimensional images, *Artificial Intelligence, Elsevier,* Vol. 31, No. 3, pp. 355-395

Lynn, P. A. & Fuerst, W. (1998). *Introductory Digital Signal Processing- with Computer Applications,* John Wiley & Sons Ltd.

Mahalanobis, A., Kumar, B. V. K., Song, S., Sims, S. R. F. & Epperson, J. F. (1994). Unconstrained Correlation Filters, *Applied Optics,* Vol.33, No.17, pp. 3751-3759

Nguyen, D. & Widrow, B. (1989). The Truck Backer-Upper: An Example of Self-Learning in Neural Networks, *Proceedings of the IEEE International Joint Conference on Neural Networks,* Vol.2, pp. 357-363

Nguyen, D. & Widrow, B. (1990). Improving the Learning Speed of 2-Layer Neural Networks by Choosing Initial Values of the Adaptive Weights, *Proceedings of the IEEE International Joint Conference on Neural Networks,* Vol.3, pp. 21-26

Perantonis, S. & Lisboa, P. (1992). Translation, Rotation and Scale Invariant Pattern Recognition by High-Order Neural Networks and Moment Classifiers, *IEEE Transactions on Neural Networks,* Vol.3, No.2, pp. 241-251

Proakis, J. G. & Manolakis, D. G. (1988). *Introduction to Digital Signal Processing,* Prentice Hall International Paperback Editions

Refregier, Ph. (1990). Filter design for optical pattern recognition: multicriteria optimisation approach, *Optics Letters*, Vol. 15, No. 15, pp. 854- 856

Refregier, Ph. (1991). Optimal trade-off filters for noise robustness, sharpness of the correlation peak and Horner efficiency, *Optics Letters,* Vol. 16, No. 11, pp. 829-831

Shvedov, A., Schmidt, A. & Yakubovich, V. (1979). Invariant Systems of Features in Pattern Recognition, *Automation Remote Control,* Vol. 40, pp. 131-142

Simard, P. & LeCun, Y. (1992). Reverse TDNN : An Architecture for Trajectory Generation, *Advances in Neural Information Processing Systems,* Moody, J., Hanson, S. & Lipmann, R., Morgan Kauffmann, Vol.4, pp. 579-588

Spirkovska, L. & Reid, M. (1992). Robust Position, Scale and Rotation Invariant Object Recognition Using Higher-Order Neural Networks, *Pattern Recognition,* Vol.25, pp. 975-985

Stamos, E. (2001). *Algorithms for Designing Filters for Optical Pattern Recognition,* D.Phil. Thesis, Department of Electronic and Electrical Engineering, University College London

Sumi, Y., Kawai, Y., Yoshimi, T. & Tomita, F. (2002). 3D Object recognition in cluttered environments by segment-based stereo vision, *International Journal of Computer Vision, Springer,* Vol. 46, No. 1, pp. 5-23

Talukder, A. & Casasent, D. (1999). Non-Linear Features for Product Inspection, *Optical Pattern Recognition X, Proceedings of SPIE,* Vol.3715, pp. 32-43

The Mathworks (August 2008). Neural Network Processing Toolbox 13: User's Guide for version Matlab 6.5, Available from http://www.mathworks.com

Vander Lugt, A. (1964). Signal Detection By Complex Spatial Filtering, *IEEE Transactions on Information Theory,* Vol.10, pp. 139-145

Waibel, A., Hanazawa, T., Hinton, G , Shikano, K. & Lang, K. (1989). Phoneme Recognition Using Time-Delay Neural Networks, *IEEE Transactions on Acoustics, Speech Signal Processing,* Vol.37, No.3, pp. 328-339

Wood, J. (1996). Invariant Pattern Recognition: A Review. *Pattern Recognition,* Vol.29, No.1, pp. 1-17

Xu, G. & Zhang, Z. (1996). *Epipolar Geometry in Stereo, Motion, and Object Recognition: A Unified Approach,* Springer, Kluwer Academic Publishers, ISBN 0-7923-4199-6, The Netherlands

Yuceer, C. & Oflazer, K. (1993). A Rotation, Scaling and Translation Invariant Pattern Classification System, *Pattern Recognition,* Vol.26, No.5, pp. 687-710

Section 2

Colour Processing

4

The Contribution of Color to Object Recognition

Inês Bramão, Luís Faísca, Karl Magnus Petersson and Alexandra Reis
Cognitive Neuroscience Research Group, Departamento de Psicologia, Faculdade de Ciências Humanas e Sociais, & Institute of Biotechnology & Bioengineering/CBME, Universidade do Algarve, Faro, Portugal

1. Introduction

The cognitive processes involved in object recognition remain a mystery to the cognitive sciences. We know that the visual system recognizes objects via multiple features, including shape, color, texture, and motion characteristics. However, the way these features are combined to recognize objects is still an open question. The purpose of this contribution is to review the research about the specific role of color information in object recognition. Given that the human brain incorporates specialized mechanisms to handle color perception in the visual environment, it is a fair question to ask what functional role color might play in everyday vision. Humans possess trichromatic color vision that most likely developed for specialized uses. For instance, color vision could be used to detect ripe fruit against a background of foliage (Gegenfurtner, 2003; Surridge, Osorio, & Mundy, 2003). Traditionally, theories of object recognition suggest that objects are recognized based on shape information, largely ignoring the role of color information (Biederman, 1987; Marr & Nishihara, 1978). However, more recently, a large body of behavioral, functional neuroimaging, and neurophysiological evidence suggests that color information make an important contribution to object recognition (for a review, see Tanaka, Weiskopf, & Williams, 2001). In the first part of this chapter we discuss the relevance of research on color effects in object recognition, while reviewing the neural mechanisms that support color perception. In the second part of the chapter we present a review of the literature exploring the color effects on object recognition and we discuss some apparently contradictory results described in the scientific literature. We also present the main results of a meta-analysis in which the behavioral literature on the effect of color in object recognition has been explored and integrated (Bramão, Reis, Petersson, & Faísca, 2011). In the third section, we review some of our own behavioral and electrophysiological data that might explain some of the conflicting results found in the literature, and we discuss the level at which color information might contributes to object recognition. We argue that the color effects in object recognition depend on the color diagnosticity status of the specific objects.

2. Color processing in the human brain

All mammals possess dichromatic or monochromatic color vision, but only primates have trichromatic color vision. What is the ecological advantage of having trichromatic color vision? Primates evolved trichromatic vision from their dichromatic ancestors approximately 40 million years ago following the duplication of a gene coding for the L-cone (Jacobs, 1993; Jacobs & Rowe, 2004; Yokoyama, 2000). It is likely that color serve as a cue for object recognition; for example, animals may use color to assess the health of other members of their species; and color can aid image segmentation (Allen, 1879). But the dominant view is that trichromatic color vision emerged as a specific adaptation for finding fruits and young leaves against a background of mature leaves (e.g., Osorio & Vorobyev, 1996; Regan et al., 2001). This notion is particularly attractive, as many fruits gradually turn yellow, red or orange, and finally brown during ripening. These colors are strikingly visible to trichromats, but dichromats have difficulty distinguishing them from a dappled background of green leaves (**Figure 1**).

Fig. 1. The left image (A) shows in full color a picture of ripe fruit against a leafy background. To remove any advantage in seeing fruit conferred by trichromacy, (B) on the right side have had all the hue and saturation information removed, but are otherwise identical to image (A). The fruit in (B) is much less salient than in (A).

As the human brain evolved, it preserved the mechanism to handle color vision. Several physiological and anatomical studies have established the human color center in the V4 area located in the posterior part of the fusiform gyrus. However, this color center is a part of a more broadly distributed cortical network responsible for color processing, which includes V1, V2, V4, and regions beyond the inferior temporal cortex (e.g., Bartels & Zeki, 2000; Lueck et al., 1989; McKeefry & Zeki, 1997; Zeki & Bartels, 1999; Zeki et al., 1991). Nevertheless, it is unclear what role these brain regions play within the color processing system. Evidence suggests that the first stage of color processing, located in the V1 and V2, primarily registers the presence and intensity of different wavelengths. A second stage, located in the V4, is involved in automatic color constancy operations (Zeki & Marini, 1998). Color constancy is a property of the visual system that ensures that the perceived surface color remains relatively constant under varying illumination conditions. A very interesting case study reported by Zeki and colleagues (Zeki, Aglioti, McKeefry, & Berlucchi, 1999) shows the specific roles of V1, V2 and V4 within the color processing system. After an electric shock that led to vascular insufficiency, the patient PB became virtually blind, although he retained the capacity to perceive colors consciously. The psychophysical results suggested that color constancy were severely deficient in the patient and that his color vision was merely based on wavelength discrimination. Functional neuroimaging studies showed that, when he viewed and recognized colors, significant increases in activity were restricted to V1 and V2, and no significant activation of V4 was observed. Finally, a third and final stage in color processing involves object colors. This is supported by the inferior temporal and probably also by the prefrontal cortex (Zeki & Marini, 1998). Little is known, however, about the neural mechanisms underlying higher-level aspects of color processing (cortical brain regions believed to be important for color perception are shown in **Figure 2**).

Given that the brain has developed specialized mechanisms to handle color perception information in the visual environment, it is a fair question to ask what functional role color might play in everyday vision, in particular in object recognition.

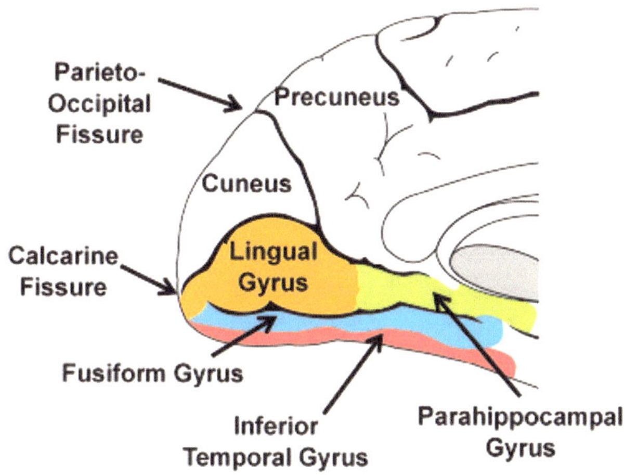

Fig. 2. Schematic view of the human brain. The regions that are important for various aspects of color perception are shown. These regions include the lingual gyrus and the posterior portion of fusiform gyrus, located below the calcarine fissure.

3. Does color information improve object recognition?

Traditionally, theories of object recognition suggest that objects are recognized based only on shape information, largely ignoring the potential role of color information (Biederman, 1987; Marr & Nishihara, 1978). For instance, in the recognition-by-components (RBC) model, proposed by Biederman (1987), objects are described as spatial arrangements of a restricted set of roughly 30 basic component shapes, such has wedges and cylinders, called geons. This idea suggests an analogy with words, which are constructed from a restricted set of phonemes. Biederman (1987) suggested that the first stage of object recognition involves the segmentation of the contour in regions of sharp concavity. This segmentation divides the contour into a number of parts that then are matched against the set of geons. Biederman (1987) used view-invariant representations. According with the RBC model, geons are defined by properties that are invariant over different views. Object representations are simply assemblies of geons constructed by inferring the qualitative spatial relations between them. Because geons and the relationships between them are viewpoint-invariant, the recognition process is likewise viewpoint-invariant. One strong point of this theory is the fact that geons are not only view-invariant, but also to other surface properties, such as size, color or texture.

However, more recently, a large body of behavioral, neuroimaging and neurophysiological studies suggest that color might contribute to object recognition. Tanaka and colleagues (Tanaka, Weiskopf, & Williams, 2001) proposed the "Shape + Surface" model of object recognition that takes into consideration the recent evidence for the role of color information in object recognition (**Figure 3**). The model recognizes that object recognition is primarily a shape-driven system (e.g., blue strawberries are still recognized as strawberries); however, color and possibly other surface properties, such as texture, are perceptual inputs for the object representation system. The Shape + Surface model draws a distinction between surface color at the input level and stored color knowledge and considers object recognition to be jointly determined by the bottom-up influence of surface color and the top-down influence of color knowledge. According to this model, visual color knowledge can be triggered either by the perceptual object during object recognition or by its lexical label during mental imagery. Finally, the model maintains a separation between linguistic and visual representations of object color. For example, it is possible to know that strawberries are red without having to consult a visual representation.

By examining whether there is an advantage to recognizing the typical colored version of an object (e.g., a red strawberry) over its black and white or atypical color version (e.g., a purple strawberry), it is possible to verify whether color information contributes to object recognition. However, this relatively straightforward test has yielded mixed results. Some studies have shown that recognition times are essentially unaffected by color information (Biederman & Ju, 1988; Davidoff & Ostergaard, 1988; Ostergaard & Davidoff, 1985). However, other studies have found that objects presented in their typical color version are recognized faster than when individuals are presented with their black and white or atypical color versions (e.g., Humphreys, Goodale, Jakobson, & Servos, 1994; Price & Humphreys, 1989; Therriault, Yaxley, & Zwaan, 2009; Wurm, Legge, Isenberg, & Luebker, 1993).

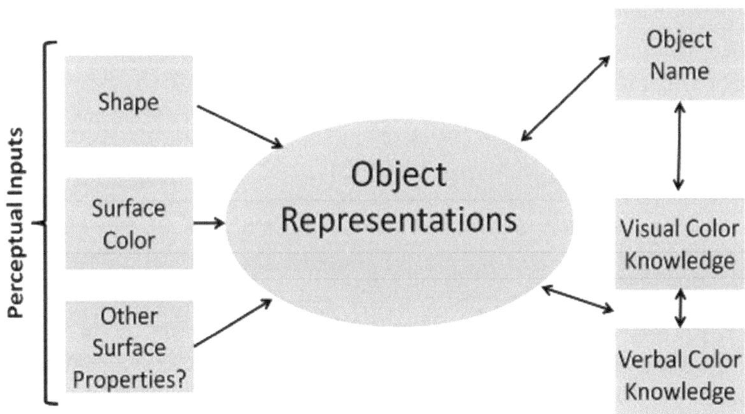

Fig. 3. The Shape + Surface model of object recognition. Adapted from Tanaka, Weiskopf and Williams (2001).

Different explanations have been proposed for these apparently contradictory results. For instance, color information may facilitate the recognition of objects within structurally similar categories (e.g., animals, fruits) but not structurally dissimilar categories (e.g., body parts, musical instruments, tools). Objects belonging to structurally similar categories activate a larger set of structural representations, leading to a higher competition within the visual system, and thus color can help resolve this competition (Price & Humphreys, 1989). Other studies have proposed that color can provide useful information when objects are high color diagnostic objects, that is, when objects are strongly associated with a color (Nagai & Yokosawa, 2003; Tanaka & Presnell, 1999). For example, a color diagnostic object, such as a strawberry, is strongly associated with the color red. A comb, however, which is a non-color diagnostic object, is not strongly associated with any particular color.

In a recent meta-analysis we systematically review the scientific literature on the effect of color information on object recognition (Bramão, Reis, Petersson, & Faísca, 2011). Thirty-five independent experiments, comprising 1535 participants, were included in this meta-analysis. Overall, we found a moderate significant effect of color on object recognition (d = 0.28, $p < 0.001$), establishing in that way that color information plays a role in object recognition and should be considered in the visual object recognition models (**Figure 4**).

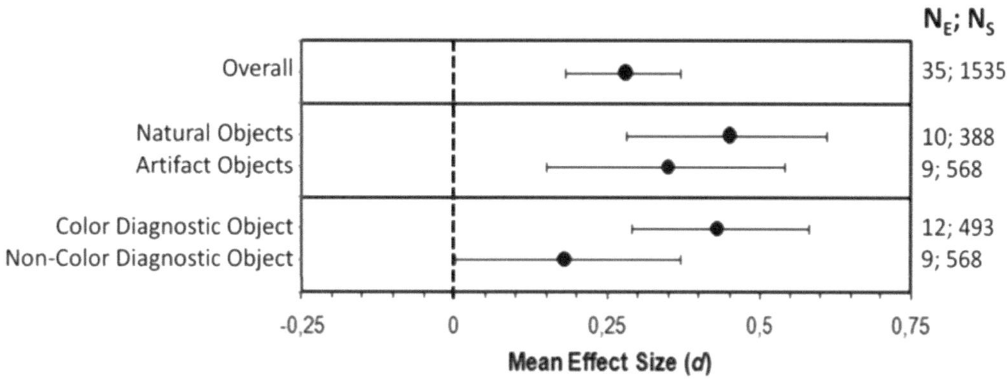

Fig. 4. Mean effect size (d) and 95% confidence intervals. The moderator variables tested in specific meta-analytic comparison are labeled on the left side. Labels to the right side of the figure indicate the number of independent effect sizes (experiments) which contributed to each meta-analysis (N_E), and the number of subjects these effect sizes were based upon (N_s). Adapted from Bramão, Reis, Petersson and Faísca (2011).

Additionally, we tested the specific moderator effect of a series of potential moderator variables on the role of the color information during object recognition (e.g., *stimuli type, object recognition task, etc…*). Here, we just present the results concerning the *object's semantic category* and *color diagnosticity* (for the complete analysis, see Bramão, Reis, Petersson, & Faísca, 2011). The impact of color in the recognition of objects from different semantic categories was first addressed by Price and Humphreys (1989). The authors found that object naming was facilitated by color when objects were from natural categories. Because objects from natural categories tend to be more structurally similar than artifacts, the competition within the object recognition system is greater for natural objects, and color information appears to be an important cue in resolving this competition. Wurm and colleagues (Wurm, Legge, Isenberg, & Luebker, 1993) showed that prototypical images exhibit a smaller color advantage compared to non-prototypical images. These observations led to the idea that color plays an important role in object recognition when shape is not diagnostic or typical. Moreover, the observed color advantage for natural objects might be related to the fact that they are typically strongly associated with a specific color and therefore, their color tends to be more diagnostic compared to artifacts. This interaction between category and color diagnosticity was addressed by Nagai and Yokosawa (2003), who reported a color advantage for high color diagnostic objects regardless of their category. Corroborating this idea, other studies have reported a similar color advantage for natural objects and artifacts (Bramão, Faísca, Forkstam, Reis, & Petersson, 2010; Rossion & Pourtois, 2004; Uttl, Graf, & Santacruz, 2006). Our meta-analysis also supports the idea that color is important for the recognition of objects from both categories: we observed that color facilitates the ability to recognize both natural (d = 0.45, $p < 0.001$) and artifact objects (d = 0.36, $p < 0.001$) (**Figure 4**; Bramão, Reis, Petersson, & Faísca, 2011).

Color diagnosticity, however, showed a great moderator effect on the influence of color on object recognition: studies using color diagnostic objects showed a significant color effect (d = 0.43, $p < 0.001$), whereas a marginal color effect was found in studies that used non-color diagnostic objects (d = 0.18, p = 0.06) (**Figure 4**; Bramão, Reis, Petersson, & Faísca, 2011). Color diagnosticity is probably the most investigated property in studies exploring the role of color information in object recognition. According to the color diagnosticity hypothesis, color diagnostic objects are the most likely candidates to show an advantage due to color information in object recognition tasks (Nagai & Yokosawa, 2003; Tanaka & Presnell, 1999). For example, Tanaka and Presnell (1999) showed that the presence of color information has a significant impact on the recognition of high color diagnostic objects and no effect on the recognition of objects with low color diagnosticity. In a control condition, when high and low color diagnostic objects were matched for structural complexity, reliable color effects were still found, suggesting that color made a unique contribution to recognition in a manner that is independent of shape. Similar results were found in the recognition of everyday scenes (Oliva & Schyns, 2000). Scenes that are rich in color diagnostic content (e.g., coast, forest) are best recognized in their typical color versions when compared to black and white or atypical color versions. On the other hand, non-color diagnostic scenes (e.g., city, shopping area) showed no difference in recognition performance across the typical, black-and-white and atypical color versions (Oliva & Schyns, 2000). Thus, the concept of color diagnosticity generalizes to the recognition of both objects and scenes.

However, recent studies have failed to replicate this finding and have documented that color information, independent of the color diagnosticity status of the object, improves its recognition (Rossion & Pourtois, 2004; Uttl, Graf, & Santacruz, 2006). For example, Rossion and Pourtois (2004) colored the 260 line-drawings from the Snodgrass and Vanderwart (1980) set with texture and shadow details. Norms for the color diagnosticity level of the objects were collected and correlated with the advantage provided by color alone in the naming responses. The authors did not report a significant correlation between these two measures (r = 0.05), showing that color information improves object recognition independently of its color diagnosticity level.

The interactions between color diagnosticity and the observed advantage due to color information are not well understood, and the reasons for the apparently contradictory results reported in the literature are not obvious. One possibility is that color information helps the recognition of color and non-color diagnostic objects at different levels of visual processing. To recognize an object, different processing stages must be resolved (Humphreys, Price, & Riddoch, 1999). First, the perceptual input must be encoded and matched against a template form stored in the long-term memory. Next, the semantic object representations are accessed, and, finally, the object name is activated. Color information might be useful for recognition of both color and non-color diagnostic objects in the early stages of the visual processing. Specifically, this information could be used to match the perceptual input with a known shape representation or, at an even earlier visual processing stage, segregate and organize the visual input. However, in the later stages of the recognition process, color information might play different roles depending upon the color diagnosticity status of the specific objects. Although color information might be important for semantic representation of a color diagnostic object, color information is probably not as important for semantic representation of a non-color diagnostic object. When we think about the properties of a strawberry, the property red is one of the first that comes to mind; however, if we think about the features of a comb, its color is not one of the first properties one might think of. Thus, we proposed that color information might participate in the recognition of color and non-color diagnostic objects at different levels of visual processing. More specifically, we hypothesize that color information participates in the recognition of both types of objects in the early visual perceptual stages, helping both segmentation and organization of the perceptual input. Studies have indicated that color information is an important cue in the early visual processing stages (Gegenfurtner & Rieger, 2000; Wurm, Legge, Isenberg, & Luebker, 1993); however, these studies did not control for or manipulate the color diagnosticity level of the presented objects. Color information is expected to play an additional role during the recognition of color diagnostic objects at the semantic levels of visual processing. Color is an intrinsic property of these objects. For example, Naor-Raz and Tarr (2003), using a variation of the Stroop paradigm, asked participants to name the displayed color of objects and words. They found that color is an intrinsic property of color diagnostic objects at multiple levels. Thus, the presence of color information in an image of a color diagnostic object might be important for the activation of semantic object representation and recognition of the object.

4. The influence of color information on the recognition of color diagnostic and non-color diagnostic objects

In this section we present the results from two studies that aimed to clarify the conflicting results found in the literature and to test the hypothesis that the color effects in object recognition depend on the color diagnosticity status of the specific objects. More specifically, we hypothesize that color information influences the recognition of both color and non-color diagnostic objects at the low-level of vision (e.g., improving the segmentation and the organization of perceptual input). However, color is expected to play an additional role in the recognition of color diagnostic objects at higher levels of the visual processing.

In a first study, participants performed three object recognition tasks with different cognitive demands at the perceptual, semantic and phonological levels: an object verification task, a category verification task, and a name verification task. Humphreys and colleagues argued that performance of these tasks poses different challenges for the cognitive system (Humphreys, Price, & Riddoch, 1999; Humphreys & Riddoch, 2006; Humphreys, Riddoch, & Quinlan, 1988; Riddoch & Humphreys, 1987). In the name verification task, participants were instructed to verify the name of visually presented objects. A number of processing stages must be completed before accessing the name representation. First, the early visual processes must encode the object shape and other perceptually available information. The encoded information must then be matched with the structural descriptions stored in long-term memory. The stored semantic and conceptual information about the object must be activated, and subsequently, the name representation is accessed. During this process, different forms of stored memory must be accessed, including knowledge about the object's shape (structural description), its functional and other meaning-related properties (semantic representation), and its name (lexical representation). In the category verification task, participants were instructed to verify the object's semantic category (natural or artifact). In contrast to name verification, category verification only depends on access to the stored structural description and the semantic representation. In the object verification task, participants were instructed to verify whether the presented object was a known object, and this only requires access to the structural description (Humphreys, Price, & Riddoch, 1999; Humphreys & Riddoch, 2006). By comparing the performance on these tasks, using both colored and black-and-white images, we attempted to determine the processing level at which color information facilitates the recognition of color and non-color diagnostic objects (**Figure 5**). If color information improves the recognition of color diagnostic objects both at the early visual and the semantic levels, then we expect to find an effect of the perceptual color for these objects when the task requires access to the structural description (i.e., in object verification). Furthermore, a larger effect of color information is to be expected for color diagnostic objects when the task requires access to both structural descriptions and semantic representations (i.e., in category verification). In the name verification task, we predicted color effects similar to those in the category verification task, given that no specific role of color is expected for accessing the lexical representation (i.e., the name) of an object *per se*. However, if color only modulates non-color diagnostic object recognition at the early visual processing stages, then we expect to find a perceptual color effect when the task requires access to the structural descriptions (i.e., in object verification). Moreover, we predicted that the perceptual color effect would remain constant for these objects on the remaining tasks, suggesting that only the early visual processing stages are affected by color information for these objects (Bramão, Inácio, Faísca, Reis, & Petersson, 2011).

In another study, we used ERPs to investigate this question. In contrast to behavioral measures, the ERPs permit the analysis of cognitive processes with a temporal resolution of milliseconds and represent an optimal approach to study the level at which visual processing of color information modulates object recognition. In a recognition task, subjects were presented with color and black-and-white versions of color and non-color diagnostic objects (**Figure 5**). Color effects were investigated in two early visual ERP components, the P1 and N1, and in two visual ERP components modulated by higher visual processes, the N350 and N400 (Bramão et al., Submitted). The P1 is an early scalp-recordable response to presented visual stimuli, which peaks at approximately 100 ms following stimulus onset and is best represented over the occipital sensors. This component has been associated with low-level visual processing but is also sensitive to attention (Mangun & Hillyard, 1991). The P1 is followed by a negative deflection peaking approximately 150 ms after stimulus onset termed N1, which has been observed primarily over the occipito-temporal region, and is an electrophysiological index of perceptual processing, where increased visual processing demands are reflected in more negative values (Johnson & Olshausen, 2003; Kiefer, 2001; Rossion et al., 2000; Tanaka, Luu, Weisbrod, & Kiefer, 1999; Wang & Kameda, 2005; Wang & Suemitsu, 2007). Based on our previous research, we predicted that the ERP associated with black-and-white stimuli would elicit a more positive P1 response and a more negative N1 response in occipital sites compared to color stimuli for both color and non-color diagnostic objects recognition.

The late visual N300 and N400 components are ERPs related to semantic processing. N300 is a negative ongoing component that peaks at approximately 300 ms after stimulus presentation and has an anterior topographic distribution (Barrett & Rugg, 1990; McPherson & Holcomb, 1999; Pratarelli, 1994). The N300 appears specific for visual stimuli and reflects a neural system that supports object model selection and generic memory. The N300 is the earliest marker of successful object categorization, with increased negative magnitude over frontal regions for unidentified objects compared to correctly-categorized stimuli (Hamm, Johnson, & Kirk, 2002; McPherson & Holcomb, 1999; Schendan & Kutas, 2002, 2007). The N300 is followed by the N400 component, which is a negative deflection over central-parietal regions peaking at approximately 400 ms after stimulus onset. The N400 is widely used as an index of semantic processing, with an increase in negative magnitude for semantically unrelated compared to semantically related material (Kutas & Hillyard, 1980a, 1980b). Both the N300 and N400 ERP components are related to late visual processing, with the N300 reflecting early object categorization (e.g., activation of object structural features that lead to a categorical representation), and the N400 being sensitive to information extracted after initial categorization (Hamm, Johnson, & Kirk, 2002). According to our expectations, we predicted that color effects in these two components would be restricted to color diagnostic objects.

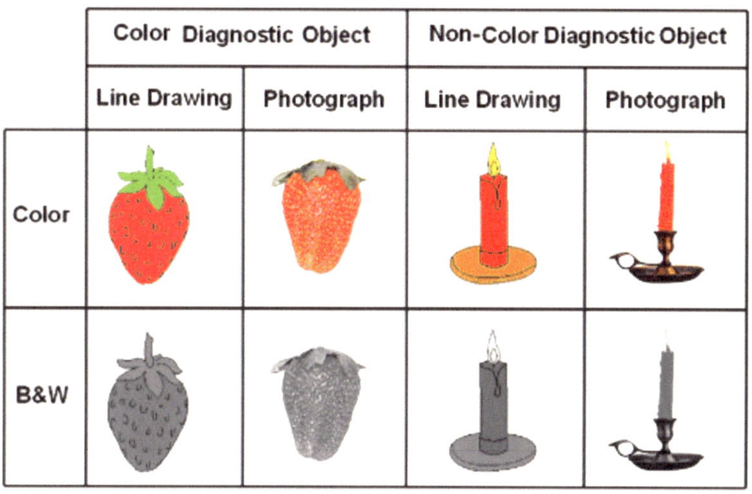

Fig. 5. Example of the stimuli used in our experiments.

Our behavioral results showed that, during non-color diagnostic object recognition,,the role of color was restricted to tasks that required high visual perceptual demanding. During color diagnostic object recognition, however, color was found to play a role in tasks that required high semantic processing (**Figure 6**; Bramão, Inácio, Faísca, Reis, & Petersson, 2011).

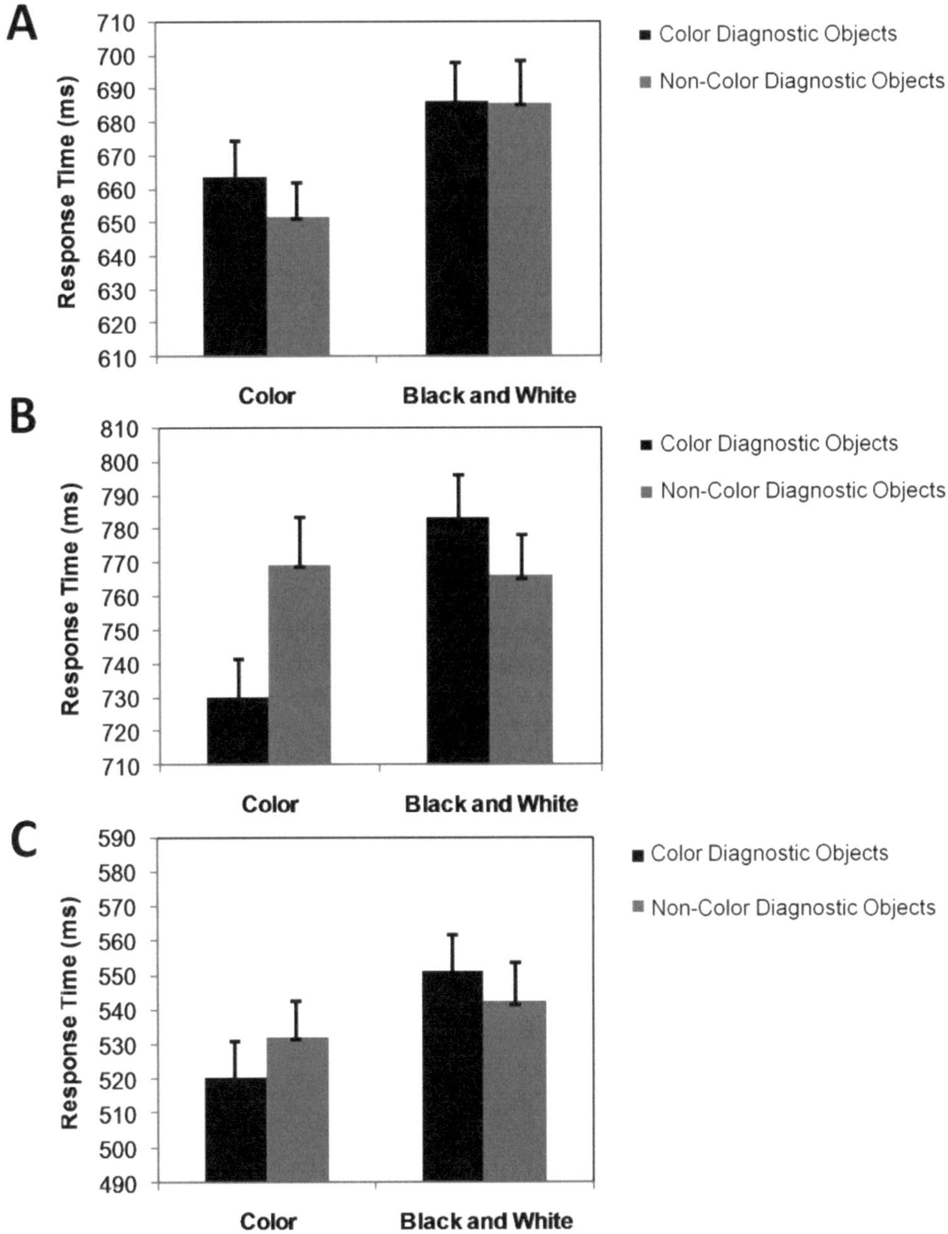

Fig. 6. Three-way interaction between the factors task, diagnosticity color object and presentation mode on verification times. A - Object verification task, B - Category verification task, C - Naming verification task. Bars represent standard error (Bramão, Inácio, Faísca, Reis, & Petersson, 2011).

The electrophysiological results corroborate our behavioral results. Independent of the color diagnosticity status, an early color effect was found (~100 ms after stimulus onset), suggesting that color aids image segmentation, thus lowering the visual demand of early visual processing stages. For color diagnostic objects, color effects occurred later (~350 ms after stimulus onset). These later color effects indicate that color is involved in the later stages of the recognition process for color diagnostic objects (**Figure 7**; Bramão et al., Submitted).

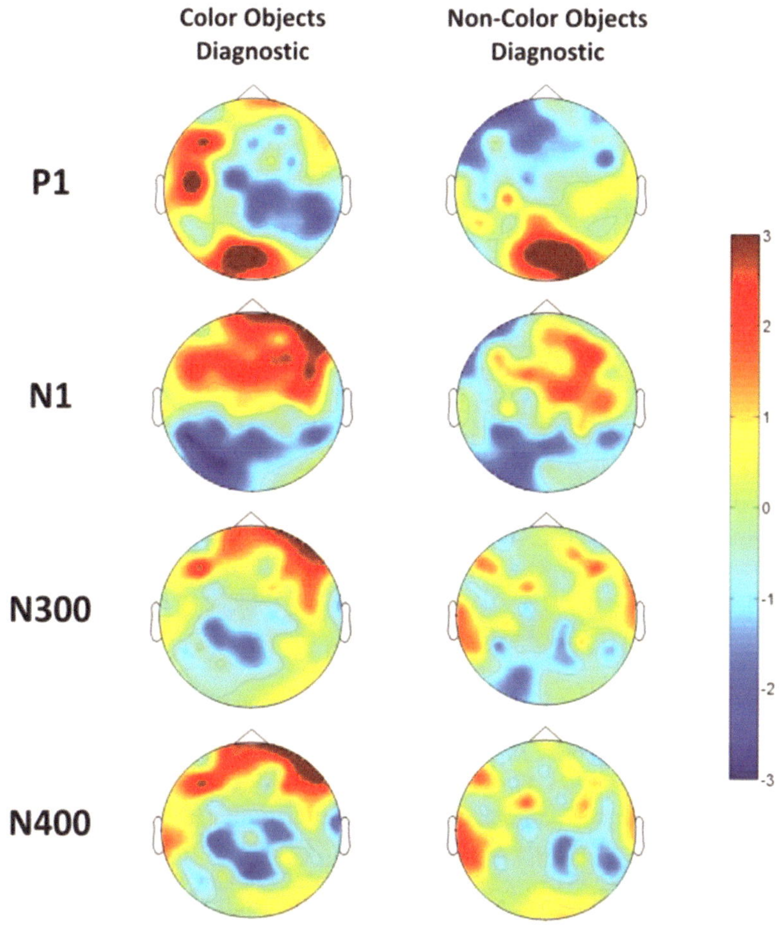

Fig. 7. Topographic distribution of the black-and-white *vs.* color objects in the time windows of interest for the color diagnostic and non-color diagnostic objects (Bramão et al., Submitted).

All together, these results suggest that color information contributes to the recognition of both color and non-color diagnostic objects but at different stages of visual processing. Color information has proven to be an important cue for solving the early perceptual demands at the initial stages of visual processing for both types of objects. Moreover, for color diagnostic object recognition, color information also contributes in the later stages of the visual processing.

The major outcome of these studies is that the influence of color on object recognition depends on object diagnosticity status. Tanaka and Presnell (1999) proposed that color information contributes to object recognition only when objects are color diagnostic (see also, Nagai & Yokosawa, 2003; Oliva & Schyns, 2000). However, recent studies have reported results that suggest that color contributes to the recognition of both color and non-color diagnostic objects (Rossion & Pourtois, 2004; Uttl, Graf, & Santacruz, 2006). We have provided data that may clarify these apparently contradictory results. Our studies suggest that color information affects different levels of visual processing during the recognition of color and non-color diagnostic objects. For the recognition of non-color diagnostic objects, color information is an important cue for the initial image segmentation and visual input organization, making the selection of a structural description, stored in the long-term visual memory, easier and faster, thus resulting in faster object verification. Moreover, our results also show an absence of color effects for non-color diagnostic objects in the later stages of the visual process. However, for color diagnostic objects, we observed an additional role for color information. Beyond the facilitation that color information confers on the initial visual stages, our results showed a strong color effect in the later stages of object recognition. It appears that color affects the later stages of recognition of color diagnostic objects in two different ways. First, color information triggers the selection of the structural object description from long-term visual memory. When we see an object, color and shape are likely processed in a parallel fashion. Some studies suggest that the same neural circuits, in early visual cortical regions, process information about color, shape and luminance (Gegenfurtner, 2003). At some point, this information must be combined to achieve a unitary representation of the visual world. One possibility is that this information is combined during the selection of structural description, where color might act as a cue that limits the range of candidate structural descriptions. The results also suggest that the templates corresponding to color diagnostic objects are stored in our visual memory system in a typical color format. Second, color information contributes to the activation and retrieval of the semantic network associated with these objects.

5. Conclusions

Previous research has established a role for color information in the early and late visual processes of object recognition. However, many of these studies did not control for the color diagnosticity status of the objects or investigated only high-color diagnostic objects (Davidoff, 1991; Davidoff, Walsh, & Wagemans, 1997; Gegenfurtner & Rieger, 2000; Goffaux et al., 2005; Lu et al., 2010; Wurm, Legge, Isenberg, & Luebker, 1993). For example, Davidoff (1991) proposed a model of object recognition where color contributes to object recognition in the later stages of the visual processing. In this model, the author proposed the existence of two separate representations, one for object structure and another for object function, termed *has-a* and *is-a* representations, respectively. Object color, according to this model, is part of the *has-a* properties, so that recognition of an object's color takes place after the initial visual representation has accessed the *has-a* color knowledge. The absence of color at the stored object structure was first questioned by Price and Humphreys (1989). Price and Humphreys (1989) argued that there are separated representations for color and shape, but that these representations are richly interconnected and that appropriated color objects activate color representations that in turn activate associated shape representations (Humphreys et al., 1994; Price and Humphreys, 1989). Actually, the data presented in this work shows that the role of color in object recognition dependents on the correlation between color and shape. When the correlation between color and shape is high, as it is in the case of the color diagnostic objects, color information is especially important at the semantic representation level, whereas when the correlation between color and shape is low, as it is in the case of the non-color diagnostic objects, color information improves object recognition only at the early stages of the visual processing. These results suggest that color improves object recognition in the early stages of the visual processing for all objects. However, because non-color diagnostic objects are not strongly associated with a color, no further color advantage is expected at the higher processing levels.

The results reviewed in this contribution advance our current understanding of the role of color information during object recognition and its relationship with the object's color diagnosticity status. Together our results showed that color modulates the recognition of color and non-color diagnostic objects at different levels of visual processing: for color diagnostic objects, color plays an important role at the semantic level; for non-color diagnostic objects, color plays a role at the pre-semantic recognition level.

6. Acknowledgements

This work was supported by Fundação para a Ciência e Tecnologia (REEQ/879/PSI/2005; PTDC/PSI-PCO/110734/2009; IBB/CBME, LA, FEDER/POCI 2010), Max Planck Institute for Psycholinguistics, Donders Institute for Brain, Cognition and Behaviour, Radboud University Nijmegen, Vetenskapsrådet (8276), Hedlunds Stiftelse and Stockholm County Council (ALF, FoUU). Inês Bramão was supported by a PhD fellowship (FCT/SFRH/BD/27381/2006).

7. References

Allen, G. (1879). *The Colour-sense: Its Origin and Development*. London: Trubner & Co.

Barrett, S., & Rugg, M. (1990). Event-Related potentials and the semantic matching of pictures. *Brain and Cognition, 14*, 201-212.

Bartels, A., & Zeki, S. (2000). The architecture of the colour centre in the human visual brain: new results and a review. *European Journal of Neuroscience, 12*, 172-193.

Biederman, I. (1987). Recognition-by-components: A theory of human image understanding. *Psychological Review, 94*, 115-147.

Biederman, I., & Ju, G. (1988). Surface versus edge-based determinants of visual recognition. *Cognitive Psychology, 20*, 38-64.

Bramão, I., Faísca, L., Forkstam, C., Reis, A., & Petersson, K. M. (2010). Cortical brain regions associated with color processing: An FMRI study. *The Open Neuroimaging Journal, 4*, 164-173.

Bramão, I., Francisco, A., Inácio, F., Faísca, L., Reis, A., & Petersson, K. M. (Submitted). Electrophysiological evidence for color effects on the recognition of color diagnostic and non-color diagnostic objects.

Bramão, I., Inácio, F., Faísca, L., Reis, A., & Petersson, K. M. (2011). The influence of color information on the recognition of color diagnostic and non color diagnostic objects. *The Journal of General Psychology, 138*, 1-17.

Bramão, I., Reis, A., Petersson, K. M., & Faísca, L. (2011). The role of color information on object recognition: A review and meta-analysis. *Acta Psychologica, 138*, 244–253.

Davidoff, J. (1991). *Cognition Through Color*. Cambridge: MIT Press.

Davidoff, J., & Ostergaard, A. (1988). The role of colour in categorial judgement. *Quarterly Journal of Experimental Psychology, 40*, 533-544.

Davidoff, J., Walsh, V., & Wagemans, J. (1997). Higher-level cortical processing of color. *Acta Psychologica, 97*, 1-6.

Gegenfurtner, K. (2003). Cortical mechanisms of colour vision. *Nature Reviews Neuroscience, 4*, 563-572.

Gegenfurtner, K., & Rieger, J. (2000). Sensory and cognitive contributions of color to the recognition of natural scenes. *Current Biology, 10*, 805–808.

Goffaux, V., Jacques, C., Mouraux, A., Oliva, A., Schyns, P., & Rossion, B. (2005). Diagnostic colours contribute to the early stages of scene categorization: Behavioural and neurophysiological evidence. *Visual Cognition, 12*, 878-892.

Hamm, J., Johnson, B., & Kirk, I. (2002). Comparison of the N300 and N400 ERPs to picture stimuli in congruent and incongruent contexts. *Clinical Neurophysiology, 113*, 1339-1350.

Humphreys, G. W., Goodale, M. A., Jakobson, L. S., & Servos, P. (1994). The role of surface information in object recognition: Studies of a visual form agnosic and normal subjects. *Perception, 23*, 1457-1481.

Humphreys, G. W., Price, C., & Riddoch, M. J. (1999). From objects to names: A cognitive neuroscience approach. *Psychological Research, 62*, 118-130.

Humphreys, G. W., & Riddoch, M. J. (2006). Features, objects, action: The cognitive neuropsychology of visual object processing, 1984–2004. *Cognitive Neuropsychology, 23*, 156-183.

Humphreys, G. W., Riddoch, M. J., & Quinlan, P. (1988). Cascade processing in picture identification. *Cognitive Neuropsychology, 5*, 67-103.

Jacobs, G. H. (1993). The distribution and nature of color vision among mammals. *Biological Reviews, 68*, 413-471.

Jacobs, G. H., & Rowe, P. W. (2004). Evolution of vertebrate color vision. *Clinical and Experimental Optometry, 87*, 206-216.

Johnson, J., & Olshausen, B. (2003). Timecourse of neural signatures of object recognition. *Journal of Vision, 3*, 499-512.

Kiefer, M. (2001). Perceptual and semantic sources of category-specifc effects: Event-related potentials during picture and word categorization. *Memory and Cognition, 29*, 100-116.

Kutas, M., & Hillyard, S. (1980a). Event-related potentials to semantically inappropriate and surprisingly large words. *Biological Psychology, 11*, 99-116.

Kutas, M., & Hillyard, S. (1980b). Reading senseless sentences: brain potentials reflect semantic incongruity. *Science, 207*, 203-205.

Lu, A., Xu, G., Jin, H., Mo, L., Zhang, J., & Zhang, J. X. (2010). Electrophysiological evidence for effects of color knowledge in object recognition. *Neuroscience Letters, 469*, 405–410.

Lueck, C. J., Zeki, S., Friston, K., Deiber, M., Kennerd, C., & Frackowiak, R. (1989). The color centre in the cerebral cortex of man. *Nature, 340*, 386-389.

Mangun, G. R., & Hillyard, S. A. (1991). Modulations of sensory-evoked brain potentials indicate changes in perceptual processing during visual-spatial priming. *Journal of Experimental Psychology: Human Perception and Performance, 17*, 1057-1074.

Marr, D., & Nishihara, H. (1978). Representation and recognition of the spatial organization of three-dimensional shapes. *Proceedings of the Royal Society of London, Series B, 200*, 269-294.

McKeefry, D., & Zeki, S. (1997). The position and topography of the human colour centre as revealed by functional magnetic resonance imaging. *Brain, 120*, 2229-2242.

McPherson, W., & Holcomb, P. (1999). An electrophysiological investigation of semantic priming with pictures of real objects. *Psychophysiology, 36*, 53-65.

Nagai, J., & Yokosawa, K. (2003). What regulates the surface color effect in object recognition: Color diagnosticity or category? *Technical Report on Attention and Cognition, 28*, 1-4.

Naor-Raz, G., & Tarr, M. J. (2003). Is color an intrinsic property of object representation? *Perception, 32*, 667-680.

Oliva, A., & Schyns, P. G. (2000). Diagnostic colors mediate scene recognition. *Cognitive Psychology, 41*, 176-210.

Osorio, D., & Vorobyev, M. (1996). Colour vision as an adaptation to frugivory in primates. *Proceedings of the National Academy of Sciences, 263*, 593-599.

Ostergaard, A., & Davidoff, J. (1985). Some effects of color on naming and recognition of objects. *Journal of Experimental Psychology: Learning, Memory and Cognition, 11*, 579-587.

Pratarelli, M. (1994). Semantic processing of pictures and spoken words: Evidence from Event-Related brain potentials. *Brain and Cognition, 24*, 137-157.

Price, C., & Humphreys, G. W. (1989). The effects of surface detail on object categorization and naming. *The Quarterly Journal of Experimental Psychology, 41*, 797-827.

Regan, B. C., Julliot, C., Simmen, B., Viénot, F., Charles-Dominique, P., & Mollon, J. D. (2001). Fruits, foliage and the evolution of primate colour vision. *Philosophical Transactions of the Royal Society, 356*, 229–283.

Riddoch, M. J., & Humphreys, G. W. (1987). Visual Object Processing: A Cognitive Neuropsychological Approach. In G. W. Humphreys & M. J. Riddoch (Eds.), *Picture Naming*. London: Erlbaum UK.

Rossion, B., Gauthier, I., Tarr, M. J., Despland, P., Bruyer, R., Linotte, S., et al. (2000). The N170 occipito-temporal component is delayed and enhanced to inverted faces but not to inverted objects: an electrophysiological account of face-specific processes in the human brain. *Neuroreport, 11*, 69-74.

Rossion, B., & Pourtois, G. (2004). Revisiting Snodgrass and Vanderwart's object pictorial set: The role of surface detail in basic-level object recognition. *Perception, 33*, 217-236.

Schendan, H., & Kutas, M. (2002). Neurophysiological evidence for two processing times for visual object identification. *Neuropsychologia, 40*, 931–945.

Schendan, H., & Kutas, M. (2007). Neurophysiological evidence for the time course of activation of global shape, part, and local contour representations during visual object categorization and memory. *Journal of Cognitive Neuroscience, 19*, 734-749.

Snodgrass, J. G., & Vanderwart, M. (1980). A standardized set of 260 pictures: norms for name agreement, image agreement, familiarity, and visual complexity. *Journal of Experimental Psychology: Learning, Memory and Cognition, 6*, 174-215.

Surridge, A., Osorio, D., & Mundy, N. (2003). Evolution and selection of trichromatic vision in primates. *Trends in Ecology and Evolution, 18*, 198-205.

Tanaka, J., Luu, P., Weisbrod, M., & Kiefer, M. (1999). Tracking the time course of object categorization using event-related potentials. *Neuroreport, 10*, 829-835.

Tanaka, J., & Presnell, L. (1999). Color diagnosticity in object recognition. *Perception & Psychophysics, 61*, 1140-1153.

Tanaka, J., Weiskopf, D., & Williams, P. (2001). The role of color in high-level vision. *Trends in Cognitive Sciences, 5*, 211-215.

Therriault, D. J., Yaxley, R. H., & Zwaan, R. A. (2009). The role of color diagnosticity in object recognition and representation. *Cognitive Processing, 10*, 335-342.

Uttl, B., Graf, P., & Santacruz, P. (2006). Object color effects identification and repetition priming. *Scandinavian Journal of Psychology, 47*, 313-325.

Wang, G., & Kameda, S. (2005). Event-related potential component associated with the recognition of three-dimensional objects. *Neuroreport, 16*, 767-771.

Wang, G., & Suemitsu, K. (2007). Object recognition learning differentiates the representations of objects at the ERP component N1. *Clinical Neurophysiology, 118*, 372-380.

Wurm, L. H., Legge, G. E., Isenberg, L. M., & Luebker, A. (1993). Color improves object recognition in normal and low vision. *Journal of Experimental Psychology: Human Perception and Performance, 19*, 899-911.

Yokoyama, S. (2000). Molecular evolution of vertebrate visual pigments. *Progress in Retinal and Eye Research, 19*, 385-419.

Zeki, S., Aglioti, S., McKeefry, D., & Berlucchi, G. (1999). The neurological basis of conscious color perception in a blind patient. *Proceedings of the National Academy of Sciences, 96*, 14124-14129.

Zeki, S., & Bartels, A. (1999). The clinical and functional measurement of cortical (in)activity subdivisions (V4 and V4a) of the human colour centre in the visual brain, with special reference to the two subdivisions (V4 and V4a) of the human colour centre. *Philosophical Transactions of the Royal Society, 354*, 1371-1382.

Zeki, S., & Marini, L. (1998). Three cortical stages of colour processing in the human brain. *Brain, 121*, 1669-1685.

Zeki, S., Watson, J., Lueck, C. J., Friston, K., Kennard, C., & Frackowiak, R. (1991). A direct demonstration of functional specialization in human visual cortex. *Journal of Neuroscience, 11*, 641-649.

Section 3

Optical Correlators, and Artificial Neural Networks

5

Advances in Adaptive Composite Filters for Object Recognition

Victor H. Diaz-Ramirez[1], Leonardo Trujillo[2] and Sergio Pinto-Fernandez[1]
[1]*Instituto Politecnico Nacional - CITEDI*
[2]*Instituto Tecnologico de Tijuana*
México

1. Introduction

The problem of object recognition is one of the most common problems that is addressed by researchers and engineers that want to develop artificial vision or image analysis systems. In order to recognize an object within an image or video sequence we must basically solve two different but related tasks. Firstly, it is essential to detect the target object within the scene image, and secondly its exact location within the image must be estimated. While the general concept of object recognition is straightforward, even a brief review of modern literature reveals a wide range of proposals and systems (Goudail & Refregier, 2004; Szeliski, 2010). However, one of the most common and successful approaches are local feature-based systems that normally employ two basic steps (Lowe, 2004; Tuytelaars & Mikolajczyk, 2008). First, object features are extracted from the scene image, and afterwards a classification step is used to determine if the observed features belong to the target object; a process known as feature matching. Feature-based systems have achieved very good results and are widely used in many application domains. Nevertheless, feature based systems suffer from two noteworthy drawbacks. First, they can be computationally expensive[1], and second their overall performance depends upon some ad-hoc decisions that might require optimization (Brown et al., 2011; Olague & Trujillo, 2011; Pérez & Olague, 2008; Theodoridis & Koutroumbas, 2008; Trujillo & Olague, 2008).

An attractive alternative to feature-based systems is given by correlation filtering algorithms, an approach that has been intensively investigated over the last decades (Vijaya-Kumar et al., 2005). A correlation filter is basically a linear system whose output is the maximum-likelihood estimator of the targets coordinates in the observed scene (Goudail & Refregier, 2004; Refregier, 1999). In other words, detection is carried out by searching for correlation peaks in the system output, and the coordinates of these peaks provide the position estimates that localize the objects within the scene. An advantage of correlation filtering is that it possesses a strong mathematical foundation. Moreover, the design process of correlation filters usually considers the optimization of various performance criteria (Vijaya-Kumar & Hassebrook,

[1] While some implementations can achieve very high frame rates, they nevertheless are far behind the almost instantaneous results that optical-electronic systems can achieve with correlation filters such as those described in this chapter.

1990). As result, correlation filters have been used to develop reliable object recognition systems that exhibit robust performance even when used in highly noisy conditions (Javidi & Hormer, 1994; Javidi & Wang, 1997; Javidi et al., 1996). Correlation filters are commonly implemented using hybrid opto-digital correlators, thus exploiting the inherent parallelism of optics and achieving a very high rate of operation. Optical correlators follow two basic types of architectures: the 4F correlator (4FC) (Vanderlugt, 1964; 1992) and the joint transform correlator (JTC) (Javidi & Horner, 1989; Weaver & Goodman, 1966). Both architectures allow fast object recognition, however they are very sensitive to ambient disturbances and to misalignments in the optical setup (Nicolás et al., 2001). On the other hand, it is also possible to effectively implement correlation filters using a digital computer and efficient algorithms for the fast Fourier transform. In fact, currently there are several very large scale integration (VLSI) devices that can be used to digitally implement correlation filtering algorithms that operate in real-time, such as field programmable gate arrays (FPGA) (Rakvic et al., 2010) and graphics processing units (GPU) (Sanders & Kandrot, 2010).

In general, correlation filters can be broadly classified into two main classes, analytical filters and composite filters. Analytical filters are typically given by a closed form mathematical expression that is directly derived from the respective signal and noise models while optimizing specific quality metrics (Javidi & Wang, 1997; Kerekes & Vijaya-Kumar, 2006; Vijaya-Kumar et al., 2000; Yaroslavsky, 1993). On the other hand, composite filters are constructed by combining a set of training images, which are explicit representations of the target object and their expected distortions (Bahri & Kumar, 1988; Kerekes & Vijaya-Kumar, 2008; Vijaya-Kumar, 1992). It is assumed that when the training images are properly chosen, we can synthesize composite filters that achieve very good and robust performance in recognizing the target object. The rest of this chapter deals with composite correlation filters, while the interested reader is referred to (Javidi & Hormer, 1994; Vijaya-Kumar et al., 2005) for more information regarding analytical filters. Composite filters can be further classified as constrained or unconstrained filters. Constrained filters are designed in such a manner that the filter's output at the origin of the training images must be equal to a prespecified value (Kerekes & Vijaya-Kumar, 2008; Vijaya-Kumar, 1992). These restrictions are known as the equal output correlation-peak (EOC) constraints. Synthetic discriminant functions (SDF) (Hester & Casasent, 1980) and minimum average correlation energy (MACE) (Mahalanobis et al., 1987), are two popular constrained filters. Unconstrained filters avoid the EOC constraints in order to expand the solutions space for filter synthesis, thus achieving a higher robustness to scene distortions when compared to constrained filters. Maximum average correlation height (MACH) filters (Mahalanobis et al., 1994) and optimal trade-off SDF (OTSDF) filters (Goudail & Refregier, 2004; Vijaya-Kumar et al., 1994) are examples of widely used unconstrained filters. The MACH filters maximize the average response at the origin of the training images and also minimize an average dissimilarity measure over the training set. Thus, MACH filters are robust to distorted versions of the target which are not included in the training set (called intraclass distortions). Several versions of MACH filters exist, among these the generalized MACH (GMACH) filter achieves the lowest variations in correlation peaks among the set of training images (Alkanhal et al., 2000; Nevel & Mahalanobis, 2003). This means that the GMACH filter yields an optimized response to intraclass distortions. The OTSDF filters, on the other hand, provide a compromise between multiple performance criteria by optimizing their weighted sum (Vijaya-Kumar et al., 1994).

As result, OTSDF filters can yield a balanced performance in recognizing a target corrupted by several types of concurrent noise processes. Recently, a composite filter which performs a compromise between a constrained and unconstrained filter using two mutually exclusive training sets was proposed (Diaz-Ramirez, 2010). This constrained filter improves tolerance to intraclass distortions without lowering the signal to noise ratio.

A main drawback of both constrained and unconstrained composite filters is that their performance strongly depends upon the proper selection of the training set of images. In fact, the training images are commonly chosen based on the experience of the designer in an ad-hoc manner. Therefore, it is not possible to guarantee optimal performance in the general case, given that it is not possible to a priori determine the optimal set of training patterns.

To overcome these shortcomings, recent works propose an adaptive approach towards filter synthesis (Aguilar-Gonzalez et al., 2008; Diaz-Ramirez & Kober, 2007; Diaz-Ramirez et al., 2006; Gonzalez-Fraga et al., 2006; Martinez-Diaz et al., 2008; Ramos-Michel & Kober, 2008). In such an approach, the goal is to construct a composite filter with optimal performance characteristics for a fixed set of patterns, rather than a filter that achieves average performance over an ensemble of images. One possible way to implement an adaptive approach for filter synthesis is to use an incremental search algorithm. Such an algorithm can use all available information about the objects to be recognized, as well as examples of false objects or background samples that should be rejected. The adaptive process for filter synthesis can also account for additive sensor noise by training with images corrupted by a particular noise model. Therefore, adaptive filters can exhibit a high amount of robustness to noise during the imaging process.

This chapter presents recent advances in the design of adaptive composite correlation filters for robust object recognition. We describe two different design approaches, based on the basic models of constrained and unconstrained filters. We show that the resultant adaptive constrained filters can achieve a high recognition rate with a low computational complexity, by simply using EOC constraints with complex values. Furthermore, unconstrained adaptive filters can be constructed to produce robust recognition in highly noisy conditions. The remainder of the chapter is organized follows. Section 2 presents a brief review of the most successful composite filters for object recognition. Then, Section 3 describes two proposed algorithms to synthesize adaptive composite filters. Computer simulation results obtained with the proposed adaptive filters are presented in Section 4. These results are discussed and compared in terms of performance metrics with those obtained with existing composite filters in noisy scenes. Finally, Section 5 summarizes our conclusions.

2. Composite correlation filters

In this Section, the main strategies for composite correlation filter designs are recalled. We consider constrained SDF and MACE filters, as well as unconstrained MACH and OTSDF filters. Basically, composite filters can be used for intraclass distortion-tolerant pattern recognition; i.e., detection of distorted patterns belonging to the same class of objects. Let $\{S\} = \{T_i(\mu,\nu)|i = 1,...,N\}$ be a set consisting of N different training images expressed in the frequency domain, where each one represents a distorted versions of the target object $t(x,y)$, where $T(\mu,\nu)$ is the Fourier transform of $t(x,y)$. Composite filters must be able to recognize the target and all the distorted versions in $\{S\}$ using a single correlation operation.

2.1 Constrained composite filters

Synthetic Discriminant Functions (SDF) filter

An SDF filter can be expressed as a linear combination of the Fourier transformed training images $T_i(\mu,\nu)$, as follows,

$$H(\mu,\nu) = \sum_{i=1}^{N} a_i T_i(\mu,\nu) \tag{1}$$

where $\{a_i | i = 1,\ldots,N\}$ are unknown coefficients that must be chosen to satisfy the inner-product conditions (Vijaya-Kumar, 1992)

$$c_i = \langle T_i(\mu,\nu), H(\mu,\nu)\rangle \tag{2}$$

The quantities $\{c_i\}$ represent the EOC constraints, that is, prespecified values in the correlation output at the origin of each training image. Let $\mathbf{T}$ be a matrix with N columns and d rows (the number of pixels in each training image) where its ith column is given by $\mathbf{t}_i$, a $d \times 1$ vector constructed by placing the elements of $T_i(\mu,\nu)$ in lexicographical order. Let $\mathbf{a}$ and $\mathbf{c}$ respectively represent column vectors of $\{a_i\}$ and $\{c_i\}$. In matrix-vector notation, filter $H(\mu,\nu)$ and constraints $\{c_i\}$ can be rewritten as

$$\mathbf{h}_{\text{SDF}} = \mathbf{Ta} \tag{3}$$

and

$$\mathbf{c}^* = \mathbf{T}^+ \mathbf{h}_{\text{SDF}} \tag{4}$$

where superscripts "$*$" and "$+$" represent the complex conjugate and the conjugate transpose, respectively. Combining Eqs. (3) and (4) the solution of the system of equations is $\mathbf{a} = \left(\mathbf{T}^+\mathbf{T}\right)^{-1}\mathbf{c}$, and if matrix $\left(\mathbf{T}^+\mathbf{T}\right)$ is nonsingular the filter solution is

$$\mathbf{h}_{\text{SDF}} = \mathbf{T}\left(\mathbf{T}^+\mathbf{T}\right)^{-1}\mathbf{c}^* \tag{5}$$

Minimum Average Correlation Energy (MACE) filter

The MACE filter is able to produce sharp correlation peaks by suppressing lateral sidelobes (Mahalanobis et al., 1987). This can be done by minimizing the average correlation energy (ACE) in the filter output, subject to the prespecified EOC constraints. The effect of minimizing the ACE measure is that the resultant correlation function would yield values close to zero everywhere except at the central location for training images, where the EOC constraints occur (Mahalanobis et al., 1987). Let $\mathbf{D}$ be a $d \times d$ diagonal matrix where the entries along the main diagonal are obtained by computing $\mathrm{E}\left\{|\mathbf{t}_i|^2; i = 1,\ldots,N\right\}$, which are the average power spectra of the training images. In matrix-vector notation, filter $\mathbf{h}_{\text{MACE}}$ which minimizes

$$\text{ACE} = \mathbf{h}_{\text{MACE}}^+ \mathbf{D} \mathbf{h}_{\text{MACE}} \tag{6}$$

and is subject to meet the EOC constraints

$$\mathbf{c}^* = \mathbf{T}^+\mathbf{h}_{\text{MACE}} \tag{7}$$

is given by (Mahalanobis et al., 1987)

$$\mathbf{h}_{\text{MACE}} = \mathbf{D}^{-1}\mathbf{T}\left(\mathbf{T}^+\mathbf{D}^{-1}\mathbf{T}\right)^{-1}\mathbf{c}^* \tag{8}$$

Multiclass pattern recognition

Two-class problem

Assume that there are several distorted versions of a target object $\{t_i(x,y)\}$ and various objects to be discriminated $\{f_i(x,y)\}$; in other words, a two-class pattern recognition problem. Then, the goal is to design a constrained composite filter to recognize images from the training set of true-class objects (target class), given by

$$\{T\} = \{T_1(\mu,\nu), T_2(\mu,\nu), \ldots, T_{N_T}(\mu,\nu)\} \tag{9}$$

and to reject training images from the false-class (unwanted class), given by

$$\{F\} = \{F_1(\mu,\nu), F_2(\mu,\nu), \ldots, F_{N_F}(\mu,\nu)\} \tag{10}$$

A two-class composite filter can be constructed by combining all of the given training images in a set $\{S\} = \{T\} \cup \{F\}$. Afterwards, to solve the two-class pattern recognition problem we can set the filter output as

$$\{c_i = 1; i = 1, 2, \ldots, N_T\} \tag{11}$$

for the true-class objects, and

$$\{c_i = 0; i = N_T + 1, N_T + 2, \ldots N_T + N_F\} \tag{12}$$

for the false-class objects. In this manner, the vector $\mathbf{c}$ of EOC constraints is given by

$$\mathbf{c} = [1, 1, \ldots 1, 0, 0, \ldots, 0]^T \tag{13}$$

It can be seen that both SDF and MACE filters with equal output correlation peaks can be used for intraclass distortion-tolerant pattern recognition or for interclass pattern recognition. For a two-class constrained composite filter, we can expect that the central correlation peak will be close to unity for the true-class objects and close to zero for objects of the false-class. Moreover, this approach can easily be extended to multi-class problems.

Multiclass problem

Suppose that the true-class subset $\{T\}$ is given by the union of K different subsets of training images, as follows

$$\{T\} = \bigcup_{k=1}^{K} \{T_k\} \tag{14}$$

where $\{T_k\}$ is a subset of training images that represents the kth true-class of objects to be recognized, which is given by

$$\{T_k\} = \left\{T_i^k(\mu,\nu)\,|i = 1,\ldots,N_T\right\} \tag{15}$$

Here, $T_i^k(\mu,\nu)$ is the ith Fourier transformed training image, which belongs to the kth true-class of objects. For simplicity, we assume that each subset $\{T_k\}$ contains N_T training images. The set $\{S\}$ of all training images can be constructed as follows

$$\{S\} = \left\{\bigcup_{k=1}^{K}\{T_k\}\right\} \cup \{F\} \tag{16}$$

According to the SDF approach a constrained filter can be constructed as a linear combination of all training images in $\{S\}$, subject to satisfy the prespecified EOC constraints $\{c_i\}$ (Vijaya-Kumar, 1992). In the basic two-class object recognition problem, we need to set the filter output to yield an intensity value equal to unity for any object that belongs to $\{T\}$, and to yield an intensity value of zero for any object that belongs to $\{F\}$; i.e.,

$$|c_{ki}|^2 = 1;\ \text{for}\ \left\{T_i^k(\mu,\nu)\right\} \in \{T\},\ k = 1,\ldots,K \tag{17}$$

and

$$\left|c_{(K+1)i}\right|^2 = 0;\ \text{for}\ \{T_i(\mu,\nu)\} \in \{F\} \tag{18}$$

Furthermore, to distinguish among objects from different true-classes $\{T_k\}$, the constraint vales $\{c_i\}$ must not only satisfy Eqs. (17) and (18), they must also provide information regarding the specific class of each training image. For this, we propose to use complex values $\{c_i\}$ with a magnitude value equal to unity for all, but each with a different prespecified phase value that indicates the class that correspond to each training image. The encoded phase values must be chosen to allow us to associate (in the complex correlation plane of the output) any unknown input patterns to one of the K different true-classes. This can be achieved by using the following EOC constraints,

$$\begin{aligned}
&\{c_i = \exp(i\phi_1),\ \text{for}\ i = 1,\ldots,N_T\};\forall\left\{T_i^1(\mu,\nu)\right\} \in \{T_1\}\\
&\{c_i = \exp(i\phi_2),\ \text{for}\ i = N_T+1,\ldots,2N_T\};\forall\left\{T_i^2(\mu,\nu)\right\} \in \{T_2\}\\
&\vdots \quad \vdots\\
&\{c_i = \exp(i\phi_K),\ \text{for}\ i = (K-1)N_T+1,\ldots,KN_T\};\forall\left\{T_i^K(\mu,\nu)\right\} \in \{T_K\}
\end{aligned} \tag{19}$$

Here, $\{\phi_k|k = 1,\ldots,K\}$ are prespecified phase values associated to the kth true-class of objects $\{T_k\}$. Observe that by using a constrained composite filter with complex EOC constraints, we satisfy the equal output intensity restrictions imposed by Eqs. (17) and (18), and at the same time we can classify any unknown input pattern from the input scene by comparing the obtained phase values $\hat{\phi}_k$ at coordinates of maximum intensities (correlation peaks), with the prespecified ϕ_k values previously defined in the filter constraints (Diaz-Ramirez et al., 2012).

2.2 Unconstrained composite filters

Maximum Average Correlation Height (MACH) filter

The MACH filter $\mathbf{h}_{\mathrm{MACH}}$ is designed to maximize the ratio between the intensity of the output average correlation height (ACH) and the average similarity measure (ASM) among training images (Mahalanobis et al., 1994). Hence, the MACH filter is designed to maximize the function $J = |\mathrm{ACH}|^2/\mathrm{ASM}$. Let $\mathbf{X}_i$ and $\mathbf{M}$, be both $d \times d$ diagonal matrices containing the elements of the training vectors $\mathbf{t}_i$, and the average training vector

$$\mathbf{m} = \frac{1}{N}\sum_{i=1}^{N}\mathbf{t}_i \tag{20}$$

Furthermore, the ACH measure can be described as the average of the output central correlation values produced by the training images, as

$$\mathrm{ACH} = \frac{1}{N}\sum_{i=1}^{N}\mathbf{t}_i^{+}\mathbf{h}_{\mathrm{MACH}} \tag{21}$$

Additionally, the ASM can be seen as the average error between the full correlation responses produced by the training images $\mathbf{v}_i = \mathbf{X}_i^{*}\mathbf{h}_{\mathrm{MACH}}$, and the correlation function produced by the average training image $\bar{\mathbf{v}} = \mathbf{M}^{*}\mathbf{h}_{\mathrm{MACH}}$, that is,

$$\mathrm{ASM} = \frac{1}{dN}\sum_{i=1}^{N}|\mathbf{v}_i - \bar{\mathbf{v}}|^2 \tag{22}$$

In a compact notation we can rewrite the ACH and ASM measures as follows,

$$\mathrm{ACH} = \mathbf{m}^{+}\mathbf{h}_{\mathrm{MACH}} \tag{23}$$

and

$$\mathrm{ASM} = \mathbf{h}_{\mathrm{MACH}}^{+}\mathbf{S}\mathbf{h}_{\mathrm{MACH}} \tag{24}$$

where

$$\mathbf{S} = \frac{1}{dN}\sum_{i=1}^{N}(\mathbf{X}_i - \mathbf{M})(\mathbf{X}_i - \mathbf{M})^{*} \tag{25}$$

Thus, filter $\mathbf{h}_{\mathrm{MACH}}$ is obtained by maximizing the following objective function (Mahalanobis et al., 1987):

$$J(\mathbf{h}_{\mathrm{MACH}}) = \frac{\mathbf{h}_{\mathrm{MACH}}^{+}\mathbf{m}\mathbf{m}^{+}\mathbf{h}_{\mathrm{MACH}}}{\mathbf{h}_{\mathrm{MACH}}^{+}\mathbf{D}\mathbf{h}_{\mathrm{MACH}}} \tag{26}$$

where the resultant MACH filter is given by

$$\mathbf{h}_{\mathrm{MACH}} = \mathbf{S}^{-1}\mathbf{m} \tag{27}$$

Generalized MACH (GMACH) filter

The GMACH filter $\mathbf{h}_{\mathrm{GMACH}}$ (Alkanhal et al., 2000), can be seen as a trade-off between a filter with EOC constraints and the MACH filter. Note, that the correlation output at the origin for

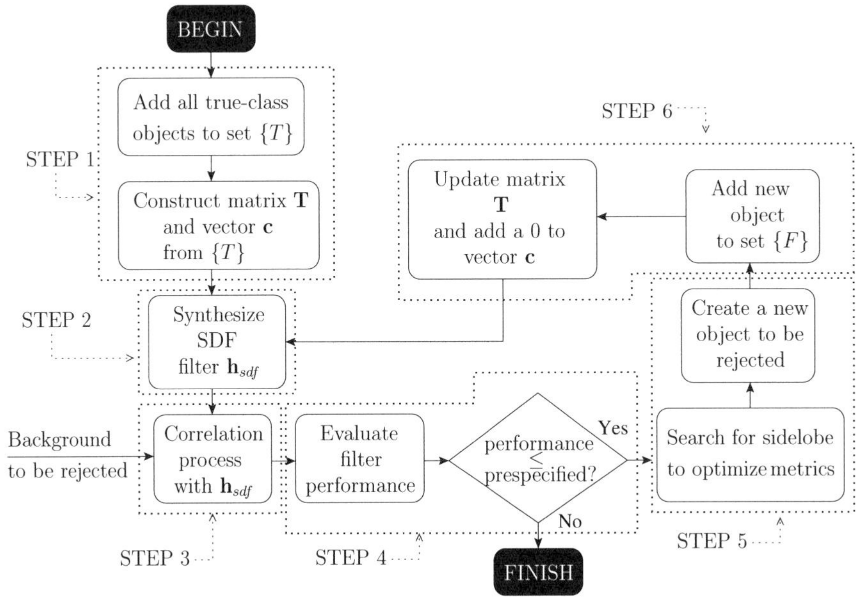

Fig. 1. Iterative training procedure to synthesize an adaptive constrained composite filter

the ith training image, is given by

$$c_i = \mathbf{h}^{+}_{\text{GMACH}}\mathbf{t}_i \tag{28}$$

Furthermore, the average correlation output at the origin is

$$\bar{c} = \mathbf{h}^{+}_{\text{GMACH}}\mathbf{m}_i \tag{29}$$

The output correlation variance can be written as (Alkanhal et al., 2000)

$$\sigma_c^2 = \frac{1}{N}\sum_{i=1}^{N}|c_i - \bar{c}|^2 = \mathbf{h}^{+}_{\text{GMACH}}\boldsymbol{\Omega}\mathbf{h}_{\text{GMACH}} \tag{30}$$

where

$$\boldsymbol{\Omega} = \frac{1}{N}\sum_{i=1}^{N}\mathbf{h}^{+}_{\text{GMACH}}\left(\mathbf{t}_i - \mathbf{m}\right)\left(\mathbf{t}_i - \mathbf{m}\right)^{+}\mathbf{h}_{\text{GMACH}} \tag{31}$$

is a covariance matrix estimate. The GMACH filter $\mathbf{h}_{\text{GMACH}}$ is designed to maximize the function (Alkanhal et al., 2000)

$$J(\mathbf{h}_{\text{GMACH}}) = \frac{|\bar{c}|^2}{\sigma_c^2} = \frac{\mathbf{h}^{+}_{\text{GMACH}}\mathbf{m}\mathbf{m}^{+}\mathbf{h}_{\text{GMACH}}}{\mathbf{h}^{+}_{\text{GMACH}}\boldsymbol{\Omega}\mathbf{h}_{\text{GMACH}}} \tag{32}$$

where the resultant filter is

$$\mathbf{h}_{\text{GMACH}} = \boldsymbol{\Omega}^{-1}\mathbf{m} \tag{33}$$

Optimal trade-off SDF (OTSDF) filter

In earlier sections, we have seen that most successful composite filters are designed to optimize certain performance criteria, namely ACE, ASM, and ACH. However, some of these metrics are in fact conflicting objectives, for instance ACE and ASM. For example, consider the MACE filter, which produces sharp correlation peaks by optimizing (minimizing) the output ACE. This means that the MACE filter has a great capacity to distinguish between target objects that should be recognized and false patterns that should be rejected. However, it is well known that MACE filter has a poor tolerance to intraclass distortions, which is characterized by the ASM metric. Therefore, OTSDF filters are designed to perform a compromise between several conflicting measures (Goudail & Refregier, 2004). For instance, an OTSDF filter can be obtained by minimizing the following function (Vijaya-Kumar et al., 1994):

$$\begin{aligned} J\left(\mathbf{h}_{\text{OTSDF}}\right) &= \omega_1 \text{ACE} + \omega_2 \text{ASM} - |\text{ACH}| \\ &= \omega_1 \mathbf{h}_{\text{OTSDF}}^{+} \mathbf{D} \mathbf{h}_{\text{OTSDF}} + \omega_2 \mathbf{h}_{\text{OTSDF}}^{+} \mathbf{S} \mathbf{h}_{\text{OTSDF}} - \left|\mathbf{h}_{\text{OTSDF}}^{+} \mathbf{m}\right| \end{aligned} \tag{34}$$

where ACE and ASM are functions to be minimized, ACH is a function to be maximized, and $\omega_1^2 + \omega_2^2 = 1$ are trade-off constants. The resultant OTSDF filter, is given by (Goudail & Refregier, 2004)

$$\mathbf{h}_{\text{OTSDF}} = \left(\omega_2 \mathbf{D} + \omega_2 \mathbf{S}\right)^{-1} \mathbf{m} \tag{35}$$

We can see that unconstrained filters cannot restrict their correlation responses at the origin of the training images in the same manner that a constrained filters does. Instead, these filters maximize the intensity value produced by the average training image and minimize the intensity response produced by unwanted patterns.

3. Adaptive composite filter designs

In Section 2 we described how a basic SDF filter is designed to satisfy the EOC constraints. This means that the filter is only able to control the output correlation points at the central location of the training images within the observed scene. This limited control yields the appearance of high correlation sidelobes over the entire image background. This undesirable property causes a drastic reduction in recognition performance for the SDF filter when it is used in highly cluttered scenes. However, this problem is solved by the MACE filter, which yields sharp correlation peaks at the central location of the training images and suppresses correlation sidelobes by minimizing the ACE metric. However, as we see in Section 2 the MACE filter has a poor tolerance to intraclass distortions. In contrast, the OTSDF filter removes the EOC constraints to gain more control over the output correlation plane. In this manner, the filter can suppress the correlation sidelobes more efficiently and can improve its tolerance to intraclass distortions. This is accomplished because the OTSDF filter optimizes the ACH, ASM, and ACE performance measures. However, note that these metrics are based on the calculation of spatial averages over the complete training set of images. This leads to the synthesis of composite filters which can only yield average performance over several similar applications and assumming stationary conditions.

In this chapter, we are interested in designing composite filters that are optimized in terms of performance metrics for a given set of patterns that are directly related to a particular

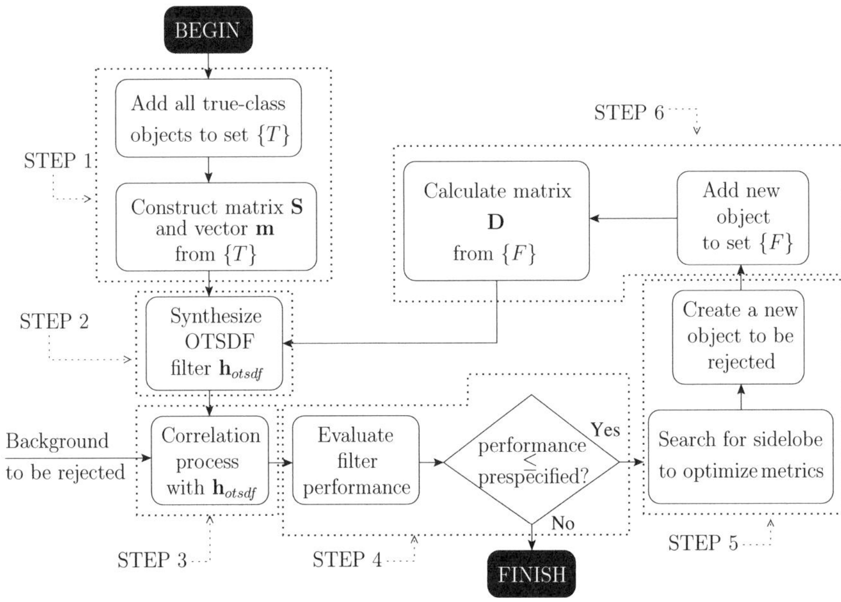

Fig. 2. Iterative training procedure to synthesize an adaptive unconstrained composite filter

application problem. First, we analyze the two-class pattern recognition problem, where the training set is given by $\{S\} = \{T\} \cup \{F\}$. We assume that the true-class training images $\{t_i(x,y)\} \in \{T\}$ are previously chosen by the filter designer and that the false-class images $\{f_i(x,y)\} \in \{F\}$ can be given by any known false objet to be rejected, or by unknown patterns that have similar structures to those of the target. If information of the background where detection will be carried out is available, the false-class images $f_i(x,y)$ can be given by small fragments taken from a synthetic image with similar statistical properties to those of the expected background in the image scene.

Let us define a set $\{U_F\}$ that contains all feasible image patterns that can be chosen as false-class images $f_i(x,y)$, an extremely vast set given the size and resolution of common digital images. The set $\{U_F\}$ can be seen as the universe of feasible training images from which we can obtain subset $\{F\}$. In this sense, we can see that an optimal subset $\{F_O\} \subset \{U_F\}$ of image patterns must exist, which is the set of false-class images that can be used to synthesize a composite filter that achieves optimal performance; i.e., when $\{F\} = \{F_O\}$. Note that the subset $\{F_O\}$ is a priori unknown, and its contents cannot be derived analytically from the problem definition. Therefore, a search and optimization strategy is required to find $\{F_O\}$[2].

In this chapter, the proposal is to use an adaptive iterative algorithm to search for $\{F_O\}$. The first step of the adaptation algorithm is to perform the correlation process between the background scene and a basic composite filter, initially trained with all available versions of the target and known false-class objects. The background function can be either described deterministically as an image or by a stochastic process. Next, we search for the coordinates of a point in the output correlation plane that allows us to improve the performance of the

[2] The theoretical goal is to find set $\{F_O\}$. However, in practice the goal is relaxed, instead searching for the best possible approximation to $\{F_O\}$.

filter. The goal is to incorporate a segment, or region, that is cropped from the synthetic background around a central point as a new false class image in $\{F\}$, call this new image taken from the background $f_n(x,y)$ that has a support region which is similar to that of the target image class. The new image $f_n(x,y)$ should provide the maximum performance increase, based on a chosen performance criteria, when compared to all other possible background segments that could have been chosen. After including $f_n(x,y)$ in $\{F\}$ a new composite filter is synthesized. This procedure is iteratively repeated until a prespecified performance level for the filter is reached. Note that the suggested training procedure can be used to synthesize adaptive composite filters based on constrained or unconstrained models. The general steps of the training procedure are summarized as follows:

- STEP 1: Include all available training images to a corresponding subset $\{T\}$ or $\{F\}$, and construct the training set $\{S\} = \{T\} \cup \{F\}$.
- STEP 2: Synthesize a composite filter trained for $\{S\}$ using a constrained or unconstrained filter model.
- STEP 3: Carry out the correlation between the actual composite filter and a synthetic image of the background.
- STEP 4: Calculate the performance metrics of the composite filter and set them the current performance level of the filter. If the performance level of the filter is greater than a prespecified value, the procedure is finished. Otherwise, go to next step.
- STEP 5: Find the maximum intensity value in the output correlation plane, and around this point extract a new training image to be rejected from the background. The region of support of this new training image is similar to that of the reference image of the target.
- STEP 6: Include the new false-image to set $\{F\}$ and update set $\{S\}$. Next, go to STEP 2.

Adaptive constrained filter design

An adaptive constrained filter can be constructed by training a simple SDF filter with the iterative procedure described above. First, all available views of the target are included in the true-class training set $\{T\}$. Next, we construct the matrix $\mathbf{T}$ and the vector of constraints $\mathbf{c}$, and a basic SDF filter $\mathbf{h}_{sdf}$ is synthesized using Eq. (5). At this point, the $\mathbf{h}_{sdf}$ filter is able to recognize all objects in subset $\{T\}$ with a single correlation operation. However, the filter may produce high correlation sidelobes when the target is embedded into a highly cluttered background. Nonetheless, we can train the filter $\mathbf{h}_{sdf}$ to optimize its ability to distinguish among the different views of the target and the background by optimizing the discrimination capability (DC) of the filter. The DC can be formally defined, as follows (Yaroslavsky, 1993):

$$\mathrm{DC} = 1 - \frac{\left|c^B_{max}\right|^2}{\left|c^T_{max}\right|^2} \tag{36}$$

where $\left|c^B_{max}\right|^2$ is the maximum intensity value in the output correlation plane over the background area, and $\left|c^T_{max}\right|^2$ is the maximum intensity value in the output correlation plane over the area occupied by the target. The background area and the target area are complementary. A filter with a DC value close to unity possesses a good capacity to

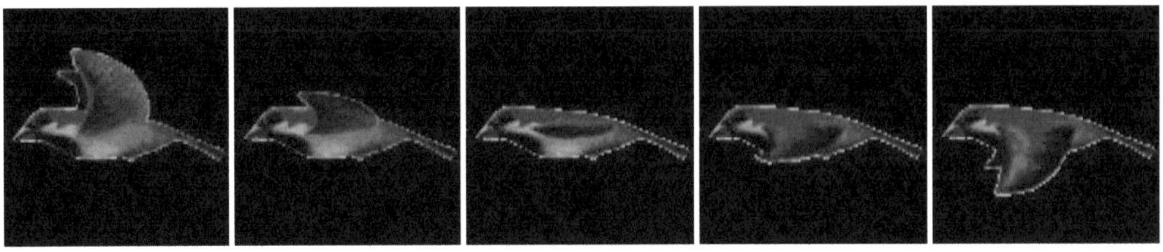

(a) (b) (c) (d) (e)

Fig. 3. Sample views of the target object

distinguish between targets and unwanted objects. Negative values of DC indicate that the filter is unable to recognize any target. Note that other discrimination metrics can be used in the training procedure; for instance, the peak to correlation energy (PCE) (Vijaya-Kumar & Hassebrook, 1990) and the peak to sidelobe (PSR) ratio (Kerekes & Vijaya-Kumar, 2008). To measure the DC of the filter we carry out the correlation process between $\mathbf{h}_{sdf}$ and a synthetic image of the background with similar statistical properties to those of the real background, then we calculate the DC using Eq. (36). If the DC of the $\mathbf{h}_{sdf}$ filter is greater than a prespecified value the training procedure is finished. Otherwise, we search for the coordinates of the highest sidelobe in the output correlation plane between $\mathbf{h}_{sdf}$ and the background image. These coordinates are set as the origin, and around the origin we construct a training image form the background. This new training image is included in the false-class subset $\{F\}$ and a new $\mathbf{h}_{sdf}$ filter is synthesized to recognize the object patterns in $\{T\}$ and reject the object patterns in $\{F\}$. This cycle can be continued until a desired DC value is reached. The training algorithm to synthesize an adaptive constrained composite filter is presented in Fig. 1.

Adaptive unconstrained filters

An unconstrained adaptive composite filter can be constructed by training a basic OTSDF filter and optimizing several performance criteria. It must be noted that since the OTSDF filter is not restricted to satisfy hard EOC constraints, the filter has more freedom to concurrently optimize multiple criteria. The flow diagram of the proposed iterative algorithm is presented in Fig. 2. The algorithm begins by constructing subset $\{T\}$ with all available views of the target objects. Next, we create the mean vector of training images $\mathbf{m}$ (see Eq. (20)) and matrix $\mathbf{S}$ using Eq. (25), then a basic OTSDF filter is synthesized following Eq. (35). The diagonal matrix $\mathbf{D}$ required in Eq. (35) can be constructed using all available known patterns that ought to be rejected; otherwise $\mathbf{D}$ is zero. The next step of the algorithm is to carry out the correlation process between the current $\mathbf{h}_{otsdf}$ filter and a synthetic image that is representative of the background. Afterwards, we evaluate the performance of the filter using the following objective function:

$$J(\mathbf{h}) = \frac{|\mathrm{ACH}|^2}{\mathrm{ACE}_{bg} + \mathrm{ASM}} = \frac{\mathbf{h}_{otsdf}^{+}\mathbf{m}\mathbf{m}^{+}\mathbf{h}_{otsdf}}{\mathbf{h}_{otsdf}^{+}\mathbf{D}_{bg}\mathbf{h}_{otsdf} + \mathbf{h}_{otsdf}^{+}\mathbf{S}\mathbf{h}_{otsdf}} \tag{37}$$

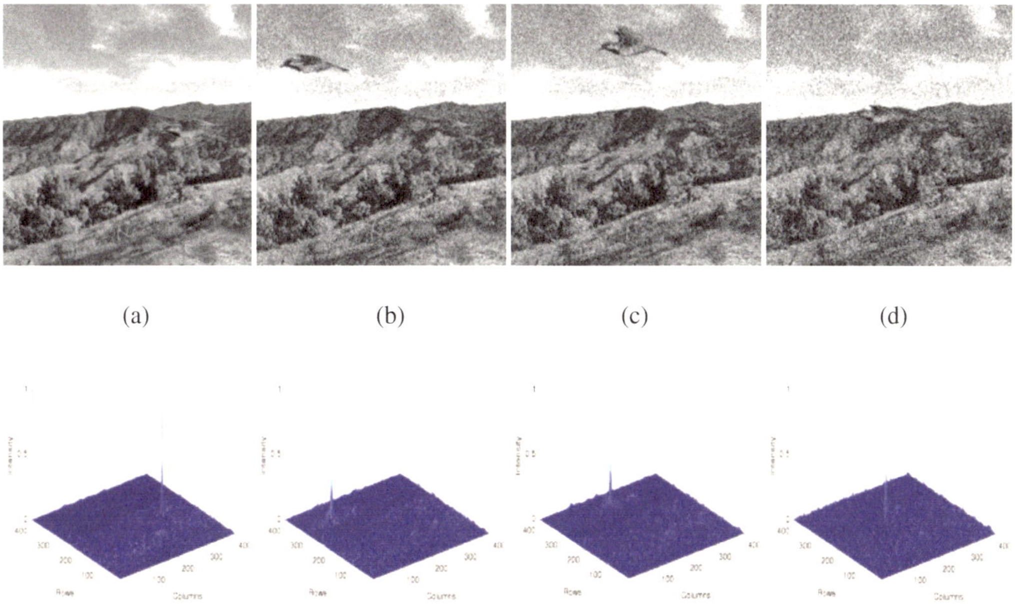

Fig. 4. Example of input test scene with noise variance of: (a) $\sigma_n^2 = 2/256$, (b) $\sigma_n^2 = 4/256$, (c) $\sigma_n^2 = 8/256$, (d) $\sigma_n^2 = 16/256$. Output correlation intensity plane obtained with ACF: (e) for scene shown in (a), (f) for scene shown in (b), (g) for scene shown in (c), (h) for scene shown in (d).

where $\mathbf{D}_{bg}$ is a diagonal matrix where the main diagonal is given by $|\mathbf{b}_g|^2$ which is the power spectrum vector of the representative image of the background. Note that the objective function increases when both of the ACE and ASM metrics are minimized and when the ACH metric is maximized. If the value of Eq. (37) is greater than a desired value then the training procedure is finished. Otherwise, we search for coordinates in the output correlation plane (between $\mathbf{h}_{otsdf}$ and the background image) that achieves the maximum improvement of the objective function. These coordinates are the center of the background region that is extracted and included as a new training image. This new training image is included in the false set $\{F\}$ and the matrix $\mathbf{D}$ is updated; finally a new filter $\mathbf{h}_{otsdf}$ is constructed. This cycle can be continued until a designed trade-off performance is obtained.

4. Experimental results

In this section, we analyze and discuss the simulation performance of the proposed adaptive filters for object recognition. These results are compared with those obtained with conventional MACE (Mahalanobis et al., 1987) and MACH (Mahalanobis et al., 1994) composite filters. The performance of the composite filters is evaluated in terms of recognition performance and location accuracy. Recognition performance is given by discrimination capability (see Eq. (36)), whereas location accuracy is characterized by the location errors

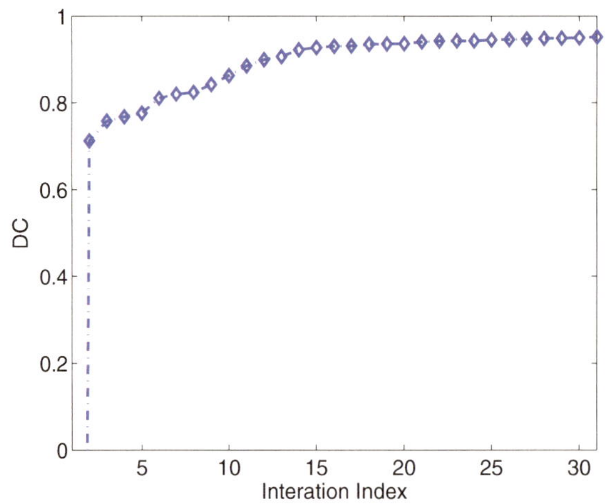

Fig. 5. DC performance of ACF vs iteration index during training procedure.

(LE) defined by (Kober & Campos, 1996):

$$\mathrm{LE} = \left[\left(\tau_x - \hat{\tau}_x \right)^2 + \left(\tau_y - \hat{\tau}_y \right)^2 \right]^{1/2} \tag{38}$$

where τ_x,τ_y and $\hat{\tau}_x,\hat{\tau}_y$ are the exact and estimated target coordinates, respectively. τ_x,τ_y are assumed to be known, whereas $\hat{\tau}_x,\hat{\tau}_y$ are estimated from correlation-peak location. The target is a flying bird whose sample views are shown in Fig. 3, which were extracted from a real video sequence. The input scene is defined with a non-overlapping signal model (Javidi & Wang, 1994; Kober et al., 2000) as follows,

$$f(x,y) = t_k\left(x - \tau_{x_k}, y - \tau_{y_k}\right) + \left[1 - w_k\left(x - \tau_{x_k}, y - \tau_{y_k}\right)\right] b(x,y) + n(x,y) \tag{39}$$

where $t_k(x,y)$ represents the kth view of the target, τ_{x_k},τ_{y_k} are random variables representing unknown coordinates of the target within the scene, $b(x,y)$ is the background, $n(x,y)$ is a zero-mean additive noise with variance σ_n^2, and $w_k(x,y)$ is the region of support of $t_k(x,y)$. The input scene can be interpreted as a view of the target embedded into a background

	$\sigma_n^2 = 2/256$	$\sigma_n^2 = 4/256$	$\sigma_n^2 = 8/256$	$\sigma_n^2 = 16/256$
ACF	DC=0.93±0.06	DC=0.91±0.07	DC=0.90±0.06	DC=0.87±0.06
	LE=0	LE=0	LE=0	LE=0
MACH	DC=0.92±0.01	DC=0.85±0.01	DC=0.68±0.04	DC=0.41±0.04
	LE=0.02±0.02	LE=0.02±0.02	LE=9.1±8.06	LE=25.2±9.2
MACE	DC=0.9±0.01	DC=0.81±0.03	DC=0.68±0.04	DC=0.51±0.04
	LE=0.02±0.02	LE=1.95±0.37	LE=14.57±11.06	LE=32.27±14.9

Table 1. DC and LE performance with 95% confidence of ACF, MACE and MACH filters while noise variance σ_n^2 is changed.

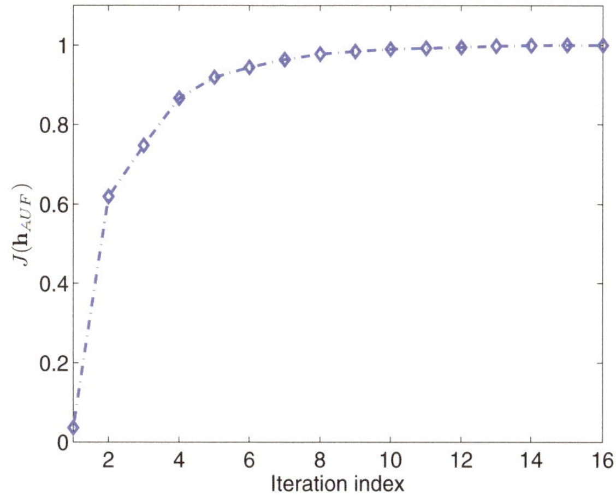

Fig. 6. Normalized performance of AUF in terms of objective function $J(\mathbf{h}_{AUF})$ vs iteration index during training procedure.

at unknown coordinates, and corrupted with additive noise. In our experiments, we use monochrome images of size 400×400 pixels. The signal range is $[0,1]$ with 256 quantization levels. The size of the target is of about 120×95 pixels, with the mean value and standard deviation of $\mu_t = 0.354$, $\sigma_t = 0.237$, respectively. The background image has a mean value $\mu_b = 0.73$ and standard deviation $\sigma_b = 0.21$. Fig. 4 (a)-(d) shows examples of the input test scene for different positions of the target and different amounts of noise. First, we design an adaptive constrained filter (ACF) trained to recognize the five views of the target shown in Fig. 3, using the iterative algorithm shown in Fig. 1. In the design process we use a different background image, which has similar statistical properties than the one used during the recognition experiments. Before the first iteration the DC value for the ACF is negative. However, after 31 iterations of the adaptation process the ACF reaches DC=0.95. This implies that a high level of control over the correlation plane for the input scene can be achieved. Fig. 5 shows the performance of the ACF in the design process in terms of the DC value versus the iteration index. To illustrate the performance of the proposed method, Fig. 4 (a)-(d) show four test scenes and Fig. 4 (e)-(h) presents the output intensity planes obtained

	$\sigma_n^2 = 2/256$	$\sigma_n^2 = 4/256$	$\sigma_n^2 = 8/256$	$\sigma_n^2 = 6/256$
AUF	DC=0.87±0.02	DC=0.82±0.06	DC=0.77±0.07	DC=0.68±0.11
	LE=0.8±0.21	LE=1.3±0.3	LE = 2.8±1.3	LE = 3.2±1.8
MACH	DC=0.71±0.04	DC=0.66±0.02	DC=0.49±0.04	DC=0.38±0.09
	LE=2.1±0.25	LE=2.95±0.67	LE=9.73±7.06	LE=13.37±9.9
MACE	DC=0.57±0.11	DC=0.41±0.18	DC=0.23±0.16	DC=0.18±0.25
	LE=6.03±0.88	LE=14.23±0.02	LE=23.1±11.66	LE=37.2±18.1

Table 2. DC and LE performance with 95% confidence of AUF, MACE and MACH filters while noise variance σ_n^2 is changed.

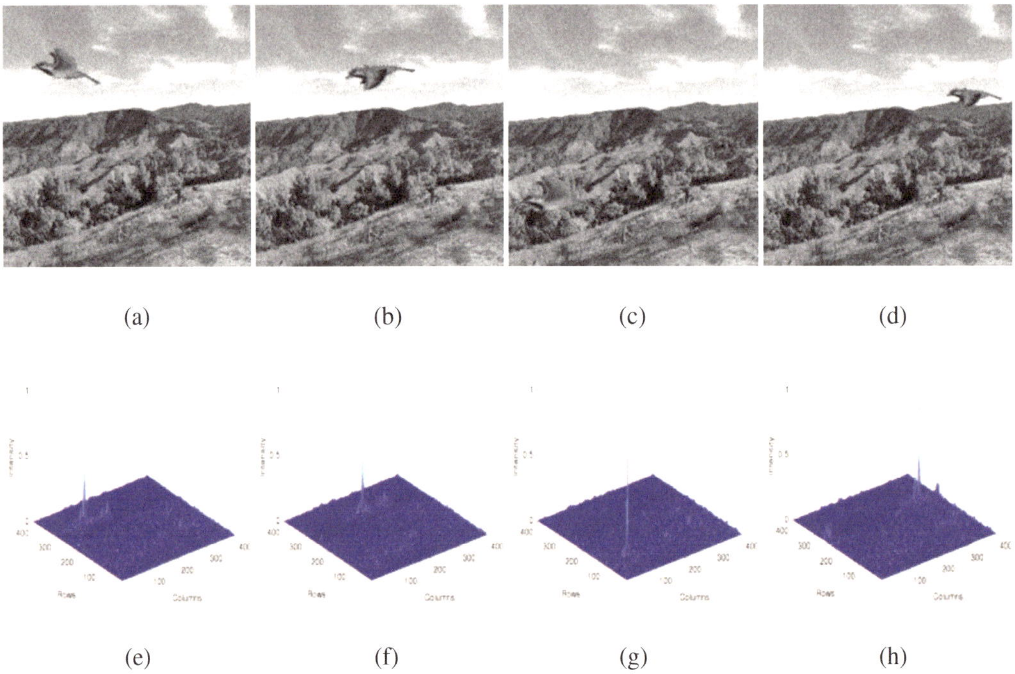

Fig. 7. Examples of input test scenes with a geometrically ditorted versions of the target and with additive noise variance $\sigma_n^2 = 2/256$. (a) Target rotated by -10 degrees, (b) Target rotated by 10 degrees, (c) Target with size enlarged by 20%, (d) Target with size reduced by 20%. Output correlation intensity plane obtained with AUF: (e) for scene shown in (a), (f) for scene shown in (b), (g) for scene shown in (c), (h) for scene shown in (d).

by the ACF on each scene. We can see one sharp correlation peak in each output intensity plane, indicating the presence of the target at the correct position. Moreover, observe that the output-correlation intensity values in the background area are very low in all the tests. Next, we compare the recognition performance of all considered composite filters when different views of the target are embedded into the background at unknown coordinates, and the variance of additive noise σ_n^2 is changed. To guarantee correct statistical results, 120 statistical trials of each experiment for different views of the target and realizations of random noise processes were carried out. With 95% confidence the performance results in terms of DC and LE are presented in Table 1. One can observe that the proposed ACF yields the best results in terms of DC and no location errors occurred. This means that the proposed ACF is robust to additive noise and to background disjoint noise.

Now, we design an adaptive unconstrained filter (AUF) trained to recognize the five views of the target including rotated versions from -10 to 10 degrees with increments of two degrees, and scaled versions with 0.8 and 1.2 scale factors. In this case, the true-class training set $\{T\}$ contains 70 training images. The AUF was synthesized using the iterative training algorithm shown in Fig. 2, reaching its maximum value in terms of the objective function "$J(\mathbf{h}_{AUF})$" (see Ec. (37)) after 16 iterations. The normalized performance of the AUF in the design process in terms of $J(\mathbf{h}_{AUF})$ versus the iteration index is shown in Fig. 6. To illustrate the performance of the AUF in recognizing geometrically distorted views of the target, Fig. 7

(a)-(d) exhibits several input test-scenes containing a distorted version of the target over the background at unknown coordinates. The output intensity planes obtained with the AUF for each of the input scenes are presented in Fig. 7 (e)-(h). It can be seen that the distorted target can be accurately located in each scene with the adaptive filter. Next, we test the recognition performance of AUF in recognizing geometrically distorted views of the target embedded within noisy scenes. To guarantee correct statistical results, 120 statistical trials of each experiment for different positions, rotations, and scale changes of the target (within the training intervals) and realizations of random noise processes were carried out. In each trial, we randomly choose a geometrically distorted view of the target which can be given by a rotated version of the target within the range of [-10,10] degrees or by a scaled version within the range of [0.8,1.2] scale factors. The distorted target is embedded into the background at unknown coordinates and the scene is corrupted with additive noise. Then, the constructed scene is correlated with the composite filters and the DC and LE metrics are calculated. The results are summarized in Table 2, it can be seen that the proposed AUF yields the best results in terms of DC and LE whereas the MACE filter yields the worst results.

Finally, the simulation results suggest that both ACF and AUF possess very good discrimination capability, outperforming conventional MACE and MACH filters in all our tests. Moreover, one can observe that the ACF is more robust than the AUF with respect to additive noise, and also yields a better location accuracy. In contrast, the AUF is more tolerant in recognizing geometrically distorted views which are embedded into a background.

5. Conclusions

In summary, the chapter presents an iterative approach to synthesize adaptive composite correlation filters for object recognition. The approach can be used to monotonically improve the quality of a simple composite filter in terms of quality metrics using all available information about the target object to be recognized, and false patterns to be rejected such as the background. Given a subset of true-class training images the proposed approach designs the impulse response of an optimized adaptive filter in terms of a particular performance criterion using an incremental search-based strategy. We designed an adaptive constrained filter with the suggested iterative algorithm optimizing the discrimination capability. According to the simulation results, the proposed adaptive constrained filter proved to be very robust in recognizing different views of a target within an input scene that is corrupted with additive noise. Moreover, the filter exhibits high levels of discrimination capability and location accuracy when compared with conventional MACE and MACH formulations. Furthermore, we synthesized an adaptive unconstrained composite filter optimized with respect to a proposed objective function based on the ACH, ACE, and ASM metrics. Here again, the experimental results suggest that the adaptive unconstrained filter provides a robust detection of geometrically distorted versions of the target when it is embedded within a highly cluttered background.

Finally, we can envision several lines of future research that can be derived from the algorithms and methods presented here. First, future experimental tests should consider real-world scenarios and applications to validate the usefulness of these filters in applied domains. Second, while the adaptive design process presented here has shown promising performance, it is evident that we cannot assume that an optimal strategy has been chosen. For instance, the proposed algorithm follows an iterative mechanism to build the final solution; i.e., it incrementally constructs the training set of images. However, from a search and optimization stand-point there is no reason to assume that this is in any way an optimal strategy for the filter design process. Therefore, it would be instructive to propose, design, and test other iterative search algorithms, such as population-based meta-heuristics, since the structure of the search space is not known a priori and is probably discontinuous and highly multi-modal. Finally, a comparative study of the developed composite filters with other object recognition approaches, particularly feature based methods, might provide a more comprehensive understanding regarding the domain of competence of each.

6. Acknowledgements

The research reported in this chapter was supported by Consejo Nacional de Ciencia y Tecnologia (CONACYT) and Secretaria de Investigacion y Posgrado del Instituto Politecnico Nacional (SIP-IPN), Mexico, through the projects CONACYT-0130504 and SIP20110110.

7. References

Aguilar-Gonzalez, P. M., Kober, V. & Ovseyevich, I. A. (2008). Pattern recognition in nonoverlapping background with noisy target image, *Pattern Recognition and Image Analysis* 20(2).

Alkanhal, M., Vijaya-Kumar, B. V. K. & Mahalanobis, A. (2000). Improving false alarm capabilities of the maximum average correlation height filter, *Opt. Eng.* 39: 1133–1141.

Bahri, Z. & Kumar, V. B. K. V. (1988). Generalized sinthetic discriminant functions, *J. Opt. Soc. Am. A* 5: 562–571.

Brown, M., Hua, G. & Winder, S. (2011). Discriminative learning of local image descriptors, *IEEE Trans. Pattern Anal. Mach. Intell.* 33(1): 43–57.

Diaz-Ramirez, V. H. (2010). Constrained composite filter for intraclass distortion invariant object recognition, *Optics and Lasers in Engineering* 48(12): 1153–1160.

Diaz-Ramirez, V. H. & Kober, V. (2007). Adaptive phase-input joint transform correlator, *Appl. Opt.* 46(26): 6543–6551.

Diaz-Ramirez, V. H., Kober, V. & Alvarez-Borrego, J. (2006). Pattern recognition with an adaptive joint transform correlator, *Appl. Opt.* 45(23): 5929–5941.

Diaz-Ramirez, V. H., Campos-Trujillo, O., Kober, V. & Aguilar-Gonzalez, P. M. (2012). Multiclass pattern recognition using adaptive correlation filters with complex constraints, *Opt. Eng.* 51(3):to appear.

Gonzalez-Fraga, J. A., Kober, V. & Alvarez-Borrego, J. (2006). Adaptive synthetic discriminant function filters for pattern recognition, *Opt. Eng* 45: 0570051–05700510.

Goudail, F. & Refregier, P. (2004). *Statistical Image Processing Techniques for Noisy Images, an application-oriented approach*, Kluwer Academic, Boston.

Hester, C. F. & Casasent, D. (1980). Multivariant technique for multiclass pattern recognition, *Appl. Opt.* 19: 1758–1761.

Javidi, B. & Hormer, J. L. (1994). *Real-Time Optical Information Processing*, Academic Press, San Diego.

Javidi, B. & Horner, J. L. (1989). Single spatial light modulator joint transform correlator, *Appl. Opt.* 25: 1027–1032.

Javidi, B. & Wang, J. (1994). Design of filters to detect a noisy target in nonoverlapping background noise, *J. Opt. Soc. Am. A* 11: 2604–2612.

Javidi, B. & Wang, J. (1997). Optimum filter for detecting a target in multiplicative noise and additive noise, *J. Opt. Soc. Am. A* 14(4): 836–844.

Javidi, B., Zhang, G. & Parchekani, F. (1996). Minimum square error filter for detecting a noisy target in background noise, *Appl. Opt.* 35(35).

Kerekes, R. A. & Vijaya-Kumar, B. V. K. (2006). Correlation filters with controlled scale response, *IEEE Trans. Imag. Proc.* 15(7): 1794–1802.

Kerekes, R. A. & Vijaya-Kumar, B. V. K. (2008). Selecting a composite correlation filter design: a survey and comparative study, *Opt. Eng.* 47(6): 067202.

Kober, V. & Campos, J. (1996). Accuracy of location measurement of a noisy target in a nonoverlapping background, *J. Opt. Soc. Am. A* 13(8): 1653–1666.

Kober, V., Seong, Y. & Choi, T. (2000). Trade-off filters for optical pattern recognition with nonoverlapping target and scene noise, *Patt. Rec. Image Anal.* 10(1): 149–151.

Lowe, D. G. (2004). Distinctive image features from scale-invariant keypoints, *Int. J. Comput. Vision* 60(2): 91–110.

Mahalanobis, A., Vijaya-Kumar, B. V. K. & Casasent, D. (1987). Minimum average correlation energy filters, *Appl. Opt.* 26: 3633–3640.

Mahalanobis, A., Vijaya-Kumar, B. V. K., Song, S., Sims, S. R. F. & Epperson, J. F. (1994). Unconstrained correlation filters, *Appl. Opt.* 33(17): 3751–3759.

Martinez-Diaz, S., Kober, V. & Ovseyevich, I. A. (2008). Adaptive nonlinear composite filters for pattern recognition, *Pattern Recognition and Image Analysis* 18(4): 84383.

Nevel, A. V. & Mahalanobis, A. (2003). Comparative study of maximum average correlation height filter variants using ladar imagery, *Opt. Eng.* 42(541).

Nicolás, J., Campos, J., Iemmi, C., Moreno, I. & Yzuel, M. J. (2001). Convergen optical correlator alignment based on frequency filtering, *Appl. Opt.* 41: 1505–1514.

Olague, G. & Trujillo, L. (2011). Evolutionary-computer-assisted design of image operators that detect interest points using genetic programming, *Image Vision Comput.* 29: 484–498.

Pérez, C. B. & Olague, G. (2008). Learning invariant region descriptor operators with genetic programming and the f-measure, *19th International Conference on Pattern Recognition (ICPR 2008), December 8-11, 2008, Tampa, Florida, USA*, IEEE, pp. 1–4.

Rakvic, R. N., Ngo, H., Broussard, R. P. & Ives, R. W. (2010). Comparing an FPGA to a cell for an image processing application, *EURASIP Journal on Advances in Signal Processing* 2010(764838).

Ramos-Michel, E. M. & Kober, V. (2008). Adaptive composite filters for pattern recognition in linearly degraded and noisy scenes, *Opt. Eng.* 47(4): 82203.

Refregier, P. (1999). Bayesian theory for target location in noise with unknown spectral density, *J. Opt. Soc. Am. A* 16: 276–283.

Sanders, J. & Kandrot, E. (2010). *CUDA by Example: An Introduction to General-Purpose GPU Programming, First Edition*, Addison-Wesley.

Szeliski, R. (2010). *Computer Vision : Algorithms and Applications*, Vol. 5 of *Texts in Computer Science*, Springer-Verlag.

Theodoridis, S. & Koutroumbas, K. (2008). *Pattern Recognition, Fourth Edition*, Academic Press.

Trujillo, L. & Olague, G. (2008). Automated design of image operators that detect interest points, *Evolutionary Computation* 16(4): 483–507.

Tuytelaars, T. & Mikolajczyk, K. (2008). Local invariant feature detectors: a survey, *Found. Trends Comput. Graph. Vis.* 3(3): 177–280.

Vanderlugt, A. (1964). Signal detection by complex filtering, *IEEE Trans. Info. Theory* IT-10: 139–145.

Vanderlugt, A. (1992). *Optical Signal Processing*, John Wiley, New York.

Vijaya-Kumar, B. V. K. (1992). Tutorial survey of composite filter designs for optical correlators, *Appl. Opt.* 31: 4773–4801.

Vijaya-Kumar, B. V. K., Carlson, D. W. & Mahalanobis, A. (1994). Optimal trade-off synthetic discriminant function filters for arbitrary devices, *Opt. Lett.* 19(19): 1556–1558.

Vijaya-Kumar, B. V. K. & Hassebrook, L. (1990). Performance measures for correlation filters, *Appl. Opt.* 29: 2997–3006.

Vijaya-Kumar, B. V. K., Mahalanobis, A. & Juday, R. D. (2005). *Correlation Pattern Recognition*, Cambridge University Press.

Vijaya-Kumar, B. V. K., Mahalanobis, A. & Takessian, A. (2000). Optimal tradeoff circular harmonic function correlation filter methods providing in-plane rotation response, *Appl. Opt.* 9(6): 1025–1034.

Weaver, C. S. & Goodman, J. L. (1966). Technique for optically convolving two functions, *Appl. Opt.* 5: 1248–1249.

Yaroslavsky, L. P. (1993). The theory of optical method for localization of objects in pictures, *in Progress in Optics, E. Wolf Ed. (Elsevier North-Holland)* XXXII: 145–201.

6

The Use of Contour, Shape and Form in an Integrated Neural Approach for Object Recognition

I. Lopez-Juarez
Centro de Investigacion y de Estudios Avanzados del IPN (CINVESTAV)
Mexico

1. Introduction

How objects are recognised by humans is still an open research field. But, in general there is an agreement that humans recognise objects as established by the similarity principle - among others- of the Gestalt theory of visual perception, which states that things which share visual characteristics such as contour, shape, form, size, colour, texture, value or orientation will be seen as belonging together (Ellis, 1950). This principle applies to human operators; for instance, when an operator is given the task to pick up a specific object from a set of similar objects; the first approaching action will probably be guided solely by visual information clues such as shape similarity. But, if further information is given (i.e. type of surface), then a finer clustering could be accomplished to identify the target object.

The task described above can also be accomplished by automated systems such as industrial robots that can be benefited from the integration of a robust invariant object recognition capability following the above assumptions and by using image features from the object's contour (boundary object information), its shape (i.e. type of curvature or topographical surface information) and form (depth information). These features can be concatenated in order to form an invariant vector descriptor which can be mapped into specific objects using Artificial Intelligence schemes such as Artificial Neural Network (ANN). In previous work, it was demonstrated the feasibility of the approach to learn and recognise multiple 3D working pieces using its contour from 2D images and using a vector descriptor called the Boundary Object Function (BOF) (Peña-Cabrera, et al., 2005). The BOF exhibited invariance with different geometrical pieces, but did not consider surface topographical information. In order to overcome this condition and to have a more robust descriptor, a methodology that includes a shape index using the Shape From Shading (SFS) method (Horn, 1970) is presented as well as the depth information coming from a stereo vision system. The main idea of the approach is to concatenate three vectors, (BOF+SFS+DI) so that not only the contour but also the object's curvature information (shape) and form are taken into account by the ANN.

In this article after presenting related work in Section 2 and original work in Section 3, the contour vector description (BOF), the SFS vector and the stereo disparity map (Depth) are explained in Sections 4, 5 and 6 respectively. A description of the learning algorithm using the FuzzyARTMAP ANN is given in Section 7 followed by Section 8 that describes the results of the proposed integrated approach. Finally, conclusions and future work is described in Section 9.

2. Related work

Some authors have contributed with techniques for invariant pattern classification using classical methods such as invariant moments (Hu, 1962); artificial intelligence techniques, as used by Cem Yüceer & Kemal Oflazer (Yüceer and Oflazer, 1993) which describes a hybrid pattern classification system based on pattern pre-processor and an ANN invariant to rotation, scaling and translation. Stavros J. & Paulo Lisboa developed a method to reduce and control the number of weights of a third order network using moment classifiers (Stavros and Lisboa, 1992) and Shingchern D. You & G. Ford proposed a network for invariant object recognition of objects in binary images using four sub-networks (Shingchern and Ford, 1994). Montenegro used the Hough transform to invariantly recognize rectangular objects (chocolates) including simple defects (Montenegro, 2006). This was achieved by using the polar properties of the Hough transform, which uses the Euclidian distance to classify the descriptive vector. This method showed to be robust with geometric figures, however for complex objects it would require more information coming from other techniques such as histogram information or information coming from images with different illumination sources and levels. Gonzalez et al. used a Fourier descriptor, which obtains image features through silhouettes from 3D objects (Gonzalez Garcia, et al., 2004). Their method is based on the extraction of silhouettes from 3D images obtained from laser scan, which increases recognition times. Another interesting method for 2D invariant object representation is the use of the compactness measure of a shape, sometimes called the shape factor, and which is a numerical quantity representing the degree to which a shape is compact. Relevant work in this area within the theory of shape numbers was proposed by Bribiesca and Guzman (Bribiesca and Guzman, 1980).

Worthington studied topographical information from image intensity data in grey scale using the Shape from Shading (SFS) algorithm (Worthington and Hancock, 2001). This information is used for object recognition. It is considered that the shape index information can be used for object recognition based on the surface curvature. Two attributes were used, one was based on low-level information using curvature histogram and the other was based on structural arrangement of the shape index maximal patches and its attributes in the associated region.

Lowe defines a descriptor vector named SIFT (Scale Invariant Feature Transform), which is an algorithm that detects distinctive image points and calculates its descriptor based on the histograms of the orientation of key points encountered (Lowe, 2004). The extracted points are invariants to scale, rotation as well as source and illumination level changes. These points are located within a maximum and minimum of a Gaussian difference applied to the space scale. This algorithm is very efficient, but the processing time is relatively high and furthermore the working pieces have to have a rich texture.

3. Original work

Classic algorithms such as moment invariants are popular descriptors for image regions and boundary segments; however, computation of moments of a 2D image involves a significant amount of multiplications and additions in a direct method. In many real-time industrial applications, the speed of computation is very important, the 2D moment computation is intensive and involves parallel processing, which can become the bottleneck of the system when moments are used as major features. In addition to this limitation, observing only the piece's contour is not enough to recognise an object since objects with the same contour can still be confused.

In order to cope with this limitation, in this paper a novel method that includes a parameter about the piece contour (BOF), the shape of the object's curvature (SFS) and the depth information from the stereo disparity map (Depth) is presented as main contribution.

The BOF algorithm determines the distance from the centroid to the object's perimeter and the SFS calculates the curvature of the way that light is reflected on parts, whereas the depth information is useful to differentiate similar objects with different height. These features (contour, form and depth) are concatenated in order to form a invariant vector descriptor which is the input to an Artificial Neural Network (ANN).

4. Object's contour

As mentioned earlier, the Boundary Object Function (BOF) method considers only the object's contour to recognise different objects. It is very important to obtain as accurately as possible, metric properties such as area, perimeter, centroid point, and distance from the centroid to the points of the contour of the object. In this section, a description of the BOF method is presented.

4.1 Metric properties

The metric properties for the algorithm are based on the Euclidean distance between two points in the image plane. The first step is to find the object in the image performing a pixel-level scan from top to bottom (first criterion) and left to right (second criterion). For instance, if an object in the image is higher than the others, this object will be considered first. In the event that all objects are from the same height, then the second criterion applies and the selected object will be the one located more to the left.

4.1.1 Perimeter

The definition of perimeter is the set of points that make up the shape of the object, in discrete form and is the sum of all pixels that lie on the contour, which can be expressed as:

$$P = \sum_i \sum_j \text{pixels}\,(i,j) \in \text{contour} \tag{1}$$

Equation (1) shows how to calculate the perimeter; the problem lies in finding which pixels in the image belong to the perimeter. For searching purposes, the system calculates the perimeter obtaining the number of points around a piece grouping X and Y points coordinates corresponding to the perimeter of the measured piece in clockwise direction. The perimeter calculation for every piece in the Region of Interest (ROI) is performed after the binarization. Search is always accomplished, as mentioned earlier, from top to bottom and left to right. Once a white pixel is found, all the perimeter is calculated with a search function as it is shown in figure 1.

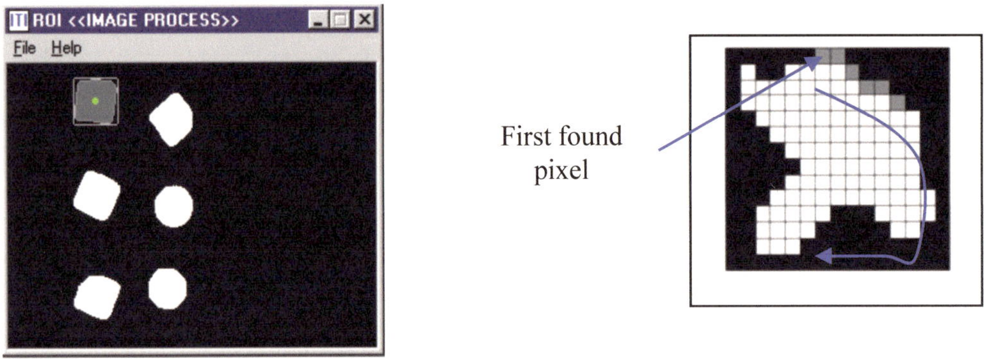

Fig. 1. Perimeter calculation of a workpiece.

The next definitions are useful to understand the algorithm:

- A nearer pixel to the boundary is any pixel surrounded mostly by black pixels in 8-connectivity.
- A farther pixel to the boundary is any pixel that is not surrounded by black pixels in 8-connectivity.
- The highest and lowest coordinates are the ones that create a rectangle (Boundary Box).

The search algorithm executes the following procedures once it has found a white pixel:

Searches for the nearer pixel to the boundary that has not been already located.

Assigns the label of actual pixel to the nearer pixel to the boundary recently found.

Paints the last pixel as a visited pixel.

If the new coordinates are higher than the last higher coordinates, the new values are assigned to the higher coordinates.

If the new coordinates are lower than the last lower coordinates, the new values are assigned to the lower coordinates.

Steps 1 to 5 are repeated until the procedure returns to the initial point, or no other nearer pixel to the boundary is found.

This technique will surround any irregular shape very fast, and will not process useless pixels of the image.

4.1.2 Area

The area of an object is defined as the space between a region, in other words, the sum of all pixels that form the object, which can be defined by equation (2):

$$A = \sum_i \sum_j \text{pixels}\,(i,j) \in \text{form} \tag{2}$$

4.1.3 Centroid

The centre of mass of an arbitrary shape is a pair of coordinates (Xc, Yc) in which all its mass is considered concentrated and on which all the resultant forces are acting on. In other words it is the point where a single support can balance the object. Mathematically, in the discrete domain, the centroid is defined as:

$$Xc = \frac{1}{A}\sum_{x,y} j \quad Yc = \frac{1}{A}\sum_{x,y} i \tag{3}$$

where A is obtained from eq. (2)

4.2 Generation of descriptive vector (BOF)

The generation of the descriptive vector called The Boundary Object Function (BOF) is based on the Euclidean distance between the object's centroid and the contour. If we assume that $P1(X_1, Y_1)$ are the centroid coordinates (X_C , Y_C) and $P2(X_2, Y_2)$ is a point on the perimeter, then this distance is determined by the following equation:

$$d(P_1, P_2) = \sqrt{(X_2 - X_1)^2 + (Y_2 - Y_1)^2} \tag{4}$$

The descriptive vector (BOF) in 2D contains the distance calculated in eq. (4) for the whole object's contour. The vector is composed by 180 elements where each element represents the distance data collected every two degrees. The vector is normalized by dividing all the vector elements by the element with maximum value. Figure 2 shows an example where the object is a triangle. In general, the starting point for the vector generation is crucial, so the following rules apply: the first step is to find the longest line passing through the centre of the piece, as shown in Figure 2(a), there are several lines. The longest line is taken and divided by two, taking the centre of the object as reference. Thus, the longest middle part of the line is taken as shown in Figure 2(b) and this is taken as starting point for the BOF vector descriptor generation as shown in Figure 2(c). The object's pattern representation is depicted in Figure 2(d).

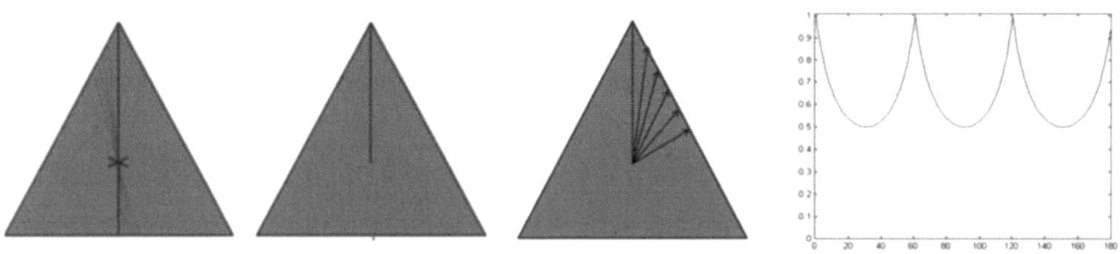

(a) (b) (c) (d)

Fig. 2. Example for the generation of the BOF vector.

5. Object's form

The use of shading is taught in art class as an important cue to convey 3D shape in a 2D image. Smooth objects, such as an apple, often present a highlight at points where a reception from the light source makes equal angles with reflection toward the viewer. At the same time, smooth object get increasingly darker as the surface normal becomes perpendicular to rays of illumination. Planar surfaces tend to have a homogeneous appearance in the image with intensity proportional to the angle between the normal to the plane and the rays of illumination. In other words, the Shape From Shading algorithm (SFS) is the process of obtaining three-dimensional surface shape from reflection of light from a greyscale image. It consists primarily of obtaining the orientation of the surface due to local variations in brightness that is reflected by the object, and the intensities of the greyscale image is taken as a topographic surface.

In the 70's, Horn formulated the problem of Shape From Shading finding the solution of the equation of brightness or reflectance trying to find a single solution (Horn, 1970). Today, the issue of Shape from Shading is known as an ill-posed problem, as mentioned by Brooks, causing ambiguity between what has a concave and convex surface, which is due to changes in lighting parameters (Brooks, 1983). To solve the problem, it is important to study how the image is formed, as mentioned by Zhang (Zang, et al., 1999). A simple model of the formation of an image is the Lambertian model, where the grey value in the pixels of the image depends on the direction of light and surface normal. So, if we assume a Lambertian reflection, we know that the direction of light and brightness can be described as a function of the object surface and the direction of light, and then the problem becomes a little simpler.

The algorithm consists in finding the gradient of the surface to determine the normals. The gradient is perpendicular to the normals and appears in the reflectance cone whose centre is given by the direction of light. A smoothing operation is performed so that the normal direction of the local regions is not very uneven. When this is performed, some normals still lie outside of the normal cone reflectance, so that it is necessary to rotate them to place these normals within the cone. This is an iterative process to finally obtain the kind of local surface curvature.

The procedure is as follows, first the light reflectance E in (i, j), is calculated using the expression:

$$E\,(i,j) = n_{i,j}^{k} \cdot s \tag{5}$$

where: S is the unit vector for the light direction, and the term $n_{i,j}^{k}$ is the normal estimation in the Kth iteration. The reflectance equation of the image is defined by a cone of possible normal directions to the surface as shown in Figure 3 where the reflectance cone has an angle of cos-1(E(i,j)).

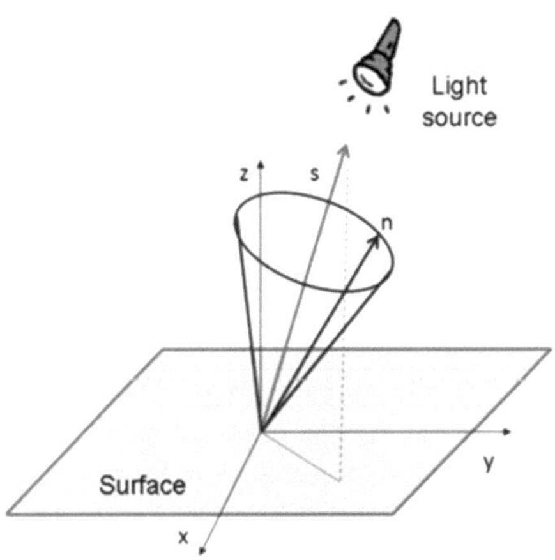

Fig. 3. Possible normal directions to the surface over the reflectance cone.

If the normals satisfy the recovered reflectance equation of the image, then these normals must fall on their respective reflectance cones.

5.1 Image's gradient

The first step is to calculate the surface normals which are calculated using the gradient of the image (I), as shown in equation (6).

$$\nabla I = [p\ q]^T = \begin{bmatrix} \frac{\partial I}{\partial x} & \frac{\partial I}{\partial y} \end{bmatrix}^T \tag{6}$$

Where [p q] are used to obtain the gradient and are known as Sobel operators.

5.2 Normals

Since the normals are perpendicular to the tangents, the tangents can be found by the cross product, which is parallel to (-p, -q, 1) T. Then we can write for the normal expression:

$$n = \frac{1}{\sqrt{p^2 + q^2 + 1}} (-p, -q)^T \tag{7}$$

Assuming that z component of the normal to the surface is positive.

5.3 Smoothness and rotation

Smoothing, in few words can be described as avoiding abrupt changes between normal and adjacent. The Sigmoidal Smoothness Constraint makes the restriction of smoothness or regularization, forcing the error of brightness to satisfy the matrix rotation θ, deterring sudden changes in direction of the normal through the surface.

With the normal smoothed, then the next step is to rotate these normals so that they lie in the reflectance cone as shown in Figure 4.

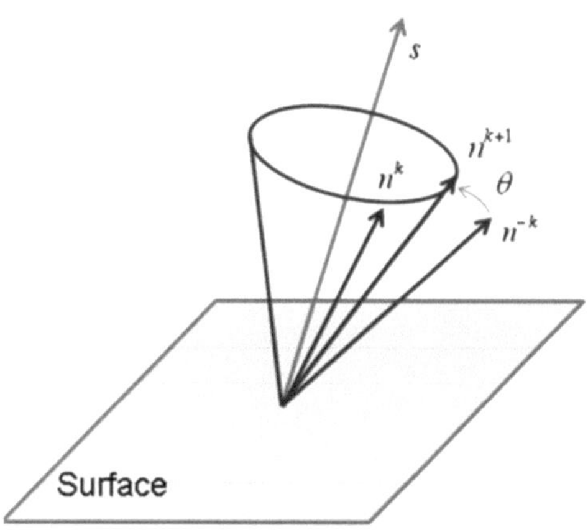

Fig. 4. Normals rotation within the reflectance cone.

Where $n_{i,j}^{k}$ are the smoothed normals, $n_{i,j}^{-k}$ are the normals after the smoothness and before the rotation, and $n_{i,j}^{k+1}$ are the normals after a rotation of θ degrees. The smoothness and rotation of the normals involve several iterations represented by the letter k.

5.4 Shape index

Koenderink separated the shape index in different regions depending on the type of curvature, which is obtained through the eigenvalues of the Hessian matrix, which is represented by K_1 and K_2 as given by the following equation (Koenderink &. Van Doorn, 1992).

$$\varphi = \frac{2}{\pi} \tan^{-1} \frac{k_2 + k_1}{k_2 + k_1} \quad ; \quad k_2 \geq k_1 \tag{8}$$

The result of the shape index φ has values between [-1, 1] which can be classified, according to Koenderink, depending on its local topography, as shown in table 1.

Cup	Rut	Saddle rut	Saddle Point	Plane	Saddle Ridge	Ridge	Dome
$\left[-1, -\frac{5}{8}\right)$	$\left[-\frac{5}{8}, -\frac{3}{8}\right)$	$\left[-\frac{3}{8}, -\frac{1}{8}\right)$	$\left[-\frac{1}{8}, -\frac{1}{8}\right)$	---	$\left[\frac{1}{8}, \frac{3}{8}\right)$	$\left[\frac{3}{8}, \frac{5}{8}\right)$	$\left[\frac{5}{8}, 1\right]$

Table 1. Classification of the Shape Index

Figure 5 shows the image from the surface local form depending on the value of the Shape Index, and Figure 6 shows an example of the SFS vector from a rectangular piece used during experiments.

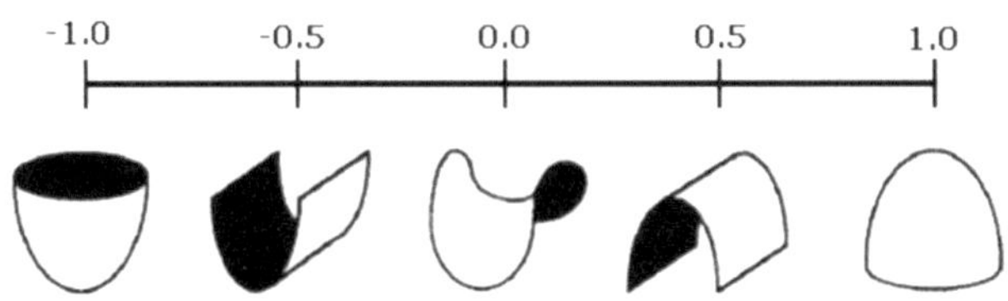

Fig. 5. Representation of local forms in the Shape Index classification.

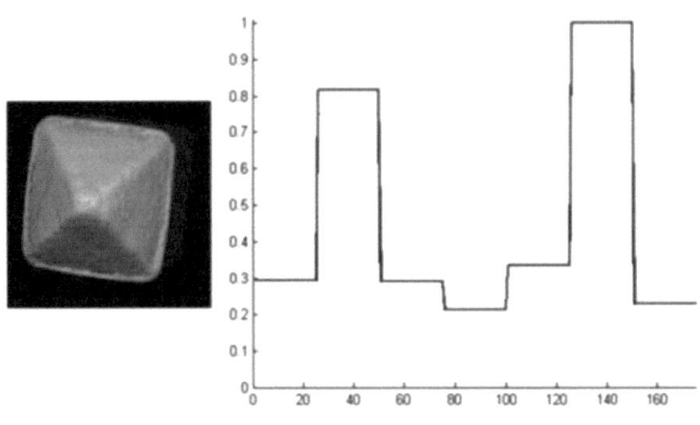

Fig. 6. SFS Vector Descriptor Example

6. Histogram of disparity map (depth)

With binocular vision, the vision system is able to interact in a three-dimensional world coping with volume and distance within the environment. Due to the separation between both cameras, two images are obtained with small differences between them; such differences are called disparity and form a so-called disparity map. The epipolar geometry describes the geometric relationships of images formed in two or more cameras focused on a point or pole.

The most important elements for this geometric system as illustrated in figure 7 are: the epipolar plane, consisting of the pole (P) and two optical centres (O and O′) from two chambers. The epipoles (e and e′) are the virtual image of the optical centres (O and O′). The baseline, that join the two optical centres and epipolar lines (l and l'), formed by the intersection of the epipolar plane with both images (ILEFT and IRIGHT) connects the epipoles with the image of the observed points (p, p′).

Epipolar line is crucial in stereoscopic vision, because one of the most difficult parts in stereoscopic analysis is to establish the correspondence between two images, mating stereo, deciding which point in the right image corresponds to which on the left.

The epipolar constraint allows you to narrow the search for stereoscopic, correspondence of two-dimensional (whole image) to a search in a dimension on the epipolar line.

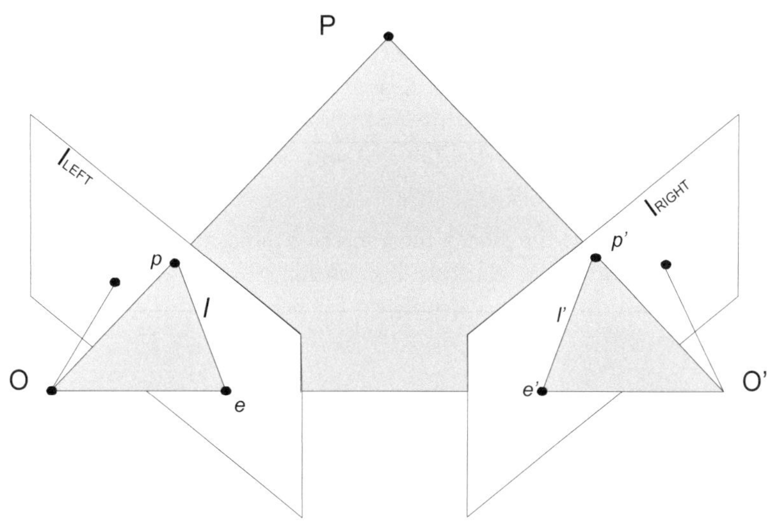

Fig. 7. Elements of epipolar geometry.

One way to further simplify the calculations associated with stereoscopic algorithms is the use of rectified images; that is, to replace the images by their equivalent projections on a common plane parallel to the baseline. It projects the image, choosing a suitable system of coordinates, the rectified epipolar lines are parallel to the baseline and they are converted to single-line exploration.

In the case of rectified images, given two points p and p′, located on the same line of exploration the left image and right image, with coordinates (u, v) and (u′, v′), the disparity is given as the difference d = u'- u. If B is the distance between the optical centres, also known as baseline, it can be shown that the depth of P is z = −B / d.

6.1 Stereoscopic matching algorithms

The stereoscopic matching algorithm reproduce the human stereopsis process so that a machine, for instance a robot, can perceive the depth of each point in the observed scene and thus is able to manipulate objects, avoid or recreate three-dimensional models. For a pair of stereoscopic images the main goal of these algorithms is to find for each pixel in an image its corresponding pixel in the other image (mating), in order to obtain a disparity map that contains the position difference for each pixel between two images which is proportional to the depth map. To determine the actual depth of the scene it is necessary to take into account the geometry of the stereoscopic system to obtain a metric map. As mating a single pixel is almost impossible, each pixel is represented by a small region that contains it, a so-called window correlation, thereby realizing the correlation between the windows of one image and the other, using the colour of pixels within. Once the disparity map is obtained, then the histogram of this map is the region of interest.

7. Learning and recognition

The selection of the ANN for this purpose was based on previous results where the convergence time for some ANN architectures was evaluated during recognition tasks of simple geometrical parts. The assessed networks were Backpropagation, Perceptron and Fuzzy ARTMAP using the BOF vector. Results showed that the FuzzyARTMAP network outperformed the other networks with lower training/testing times (0.838ms/0.0722ms) compared with Perceptron (5.78ms/0.159 ms) and Backpropagation (367.577ms/0.217 ms) (Lopez-Juarez, et al., 2010).

In the Fuzzy ARTMAP (FAM) network there are two modules ART_a and ART_b and an inter-ART module "Map-field" that controls the learning of an associative map from ART_a recognition categories to ART_b categories (Carpenter and Grossberg, 1992). This is illustrated in Figure 8.

The Map-field module also controls the match tracking of ART_a vigilance parameter. A mismatch between Map field and ART_a category activated by input Ia and ART_b category activated by input I_b increases ART_a vigilance by the minimum amount needed for the system to search for, and if necessary, learn a new ART_a category whose prediction matches the ART_b category. The search initiated by the inter-ART reset can shift attention to a novel cluster of features that can be incorporated through learning into a new ART_a recognition category, which can then be linked to a new ART prediction via associative learning at the Map field.

A vigilance parameter measures the difference allowed between the input data and stored patterns. Therefore, this parameter affects the selectivity or granularity of the network prediction. For learning, the FuzzyARTMAP has 4 important factors: Vigilance in the input module (ρ_a), vigilance in the output module (ρ_b), vigilance in the Map field (ρ_{ab}) and learning rate (β).

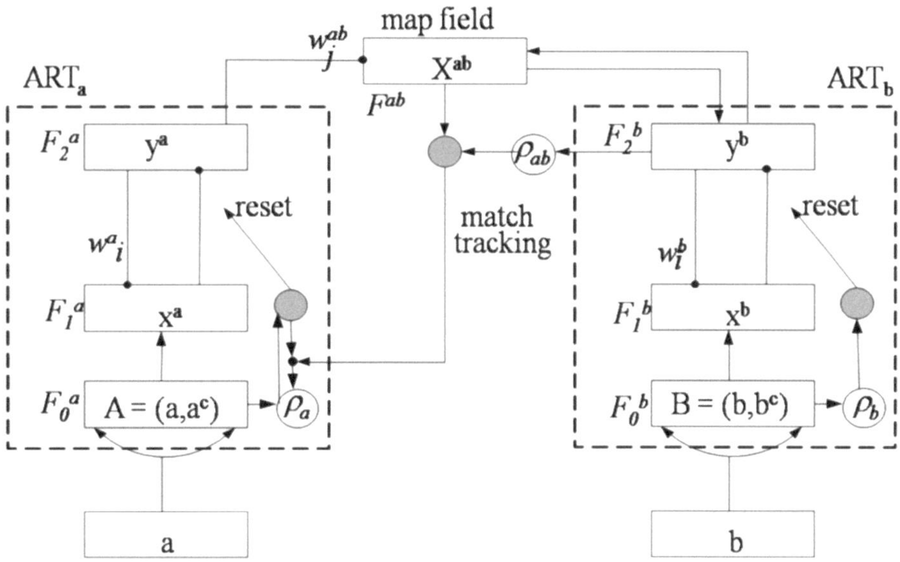

Fig. 8. FuzzyARTMAP Architecture

For the specific case of the work presented in this article, the input information is concatenated and presented as a sole input vector A, while the vector B receives the correspondence associated to the respective component, during the training process.

8. Experimental results

The experimental results were obtained using two sets of four 3D working pieces of different cross-section: square, triangle, cross and star. One set had its top surface rounded, so that these were referred to as being of rounded type. The other set had a flat top surface and referred to as pyramidal type. The working pieces are showed in figure 9.

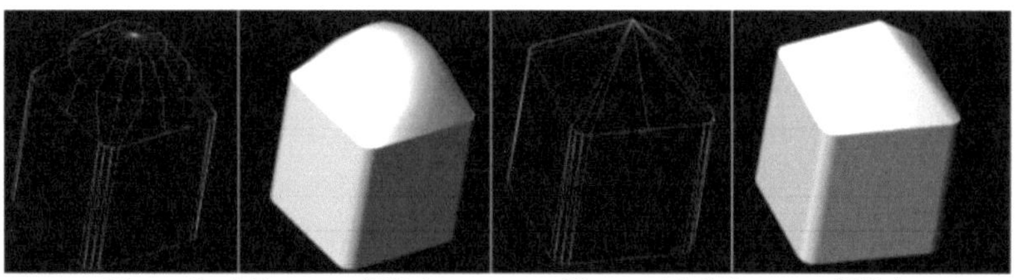

Rounded-Square (RSq) Pyramidal-Square (PSq)

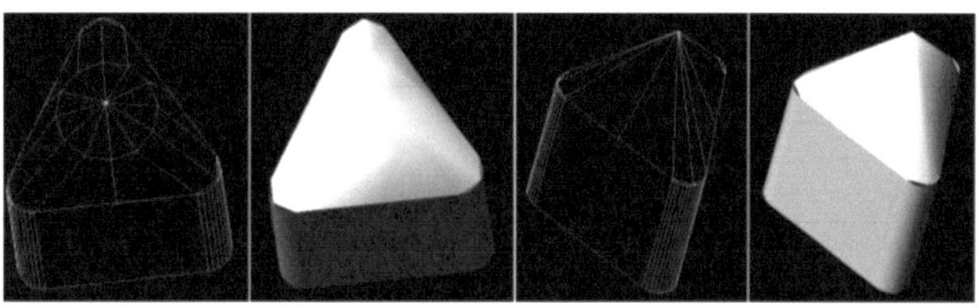

Rounded-Triangle (RT) Pyramidal-Triangle (PT)

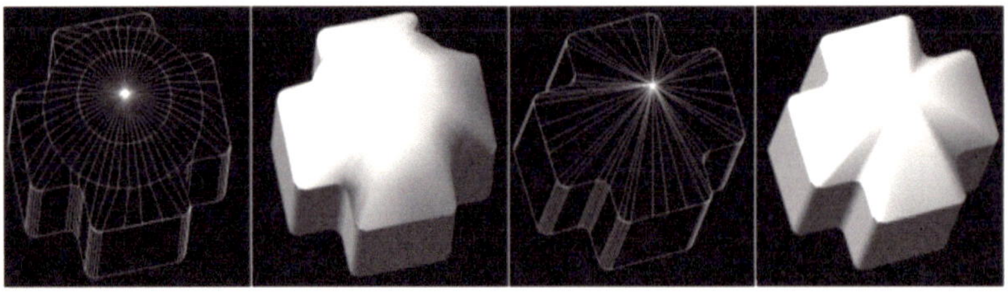

Rounded-Cross (RC) Pyramidal-Cross (PC)

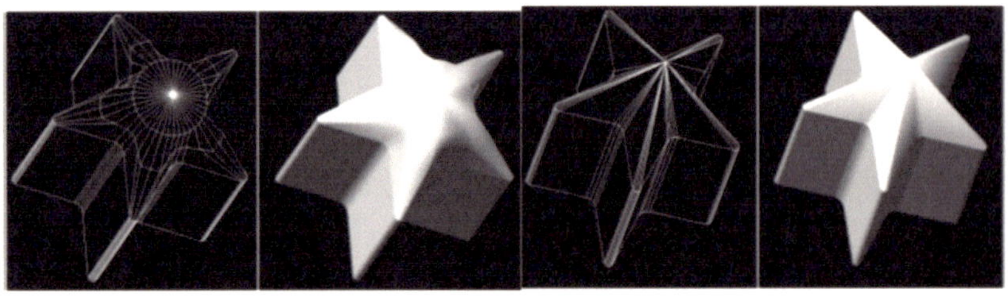

Rounded-Star (RSt) Pyramidal-Star (PSt)

Fig. 9. Working pieces.

The object recognition experiments by the FuzzyARTMAP (FAM) neural network were carried out using the above working pieces. The network parameters were set for fast learning ($\beta = 1$) and high vigilance parameter ($\rho_{ab} = 0.9$). There were carried out four types of experiments. The first experiment considered only the BOF taking data from the contour of the piece, the second experiment considered information from the SFS algorithm taking into account the reflectance of the light on the surface and the third experiment was performed using the depth information. The fourth experiment used the concatenated vector from the three object descriptors (BOF+SFS+Depth). An example of how an object was coded using the three descriptors is showed in figure 10. Two graphs are presented; the first graph corresponds to the descriptive vector from the Rounded-Square object and the other corresponding to the Pyramidal-square object. The BOF descriptive vector is formed by the 180 first elements (observe that both patterns are very similar since the object's cross-sectional shape is the same). Next, there are 175 elements corresponding to the SFS values (every shape corresponding to the 7 index values was repeated 25 times). The following 176 values corresponded to the Depth information obtained for the Disparity Histogram that contained 16 values that were repeated 11 times.

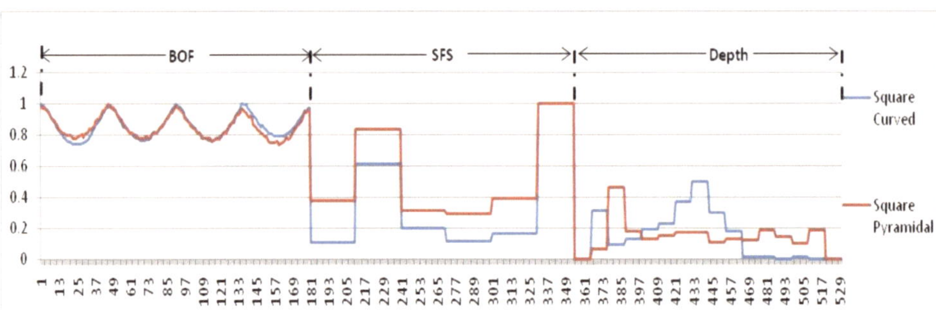

Fig. 10. Input vector example.

8.1 Recognition rates

Several experiments were defined to test the invariant object recognition capability of the system. For these experiments, the FuzzyARTMAP network was trained with 3 patterns, the objects were located in different orientation and location within a defined working space of 20cm x 27cm using different scales and also the slope of the plane was modified.

The overall results under the above conditions are illustrated in figure 11. The first row corresponded to the recognition rates obtained using only the BOF, SFS, and Depth vector.

It was observed a high recognition rate. For instance, using only the BOF, the system was able to recognize 99.8% from the whole set of objects.

In the second row it is shown the recognition rate using a combination of the BOF+SFS, and BOF+Depth vectors. It is important to notice that the recognition rate in both cases was lower than using the BOF vector alone (99.4% and 98.61%, respectively). In the last experiment, the complete concatenated vector BOF+SFS+Depth vector was used achieving 100% recognition rate varying the scale up to 20% and using a slope of 15^0.

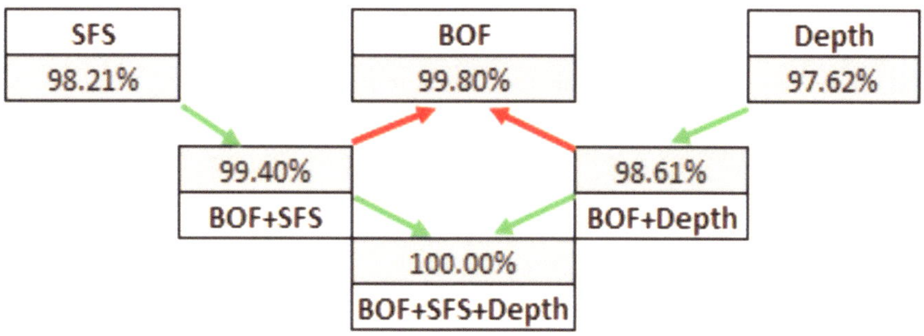

Fig. 11. Recognition rate results.

9. Conclusions

The research presented in this article provides an alternative methodology to integrate a robust invariant object recognition system using image features from the object's contour (boundary object information), its form (i.e. type of curvature or topographical surface information) and depth information from a stereo camera. The features can be concatenated in order to form an invariant vector descriptor which is the input to an Artificial Neural Network (ANN) for learning and recognition purposes.

Experimental results were obtained using two sets of four 3D working pieces of different cross-section: square, triangle, cross and star. One set had its surface curvature rounded and the other had a flat surface curvature so that these object were named of pyramidal type. Using the BOF information and training the neural network with this vector it was demonstrated that all pieces were recognised irrespective from its location an orientation within the viewable area. When information was concatenated (BOF + SFS and BOF + Depth), the robustness of the vision system lowered since the recognition rate in both cases was lower than using the BOF vector alone (99.4% and 98.61% respectively). But, using the complete concatenated vector BOF+SFS+Depth achieved 100% recognition rate invariant to scale up to 20% and also invariant to the inclination of the plane up to 15⁰. Further tests were conducted but the recognition was lower since for instance, increasing the slope angle it contributed to distort the contour as detected by the BOF hence making the recognition rate very sensitive.

10. References

Bribiesca E. and Guzman A. (1980). How to Describe Pure Form and How to Measure Differences in Shape Using Shape Numbers, *Pattern Recognition*, Vol. 12, No. 2, pp. 101-112.

Brooks, M. (1983). Two results concerning ambiguity in shape from shading. In *AAAI-83*, pp 36-39.

Carpenter, G., Grossberg. S. (1992). Fuzzy ARTMAP: A neural network architecture for incremental supervised learning of analog multidimensional maps. *IEEE Transactions on neural networks*, Vol. 3. No. 5.

Cem Yüceer and Kema Oflazer (1993). A rotation, scaling and translation invariant pattern classification system. *Pattern Recognition*, vol 26, No. 5. 1993. pp. 687-710.

Ellis W. D. (1950). A Sourcebook of Gestalt Psychology. New York: The Humanities Press.

Gonzalez Garcia, E.; Feliu Batlle, V.; Oliver, A.; Sanchez Rodriguez, L. (2004). Descriptores de Fourier para identificacion y posicionamiento de objetos en entornos 3D. *XXV Jornadas de Automatica.*

Horn, B.K.P. (1970). Shape from Shading: A Method for Obtaining the Shape of a Smooth Opaque Object from One View. *PhD thesis, MIT.*

Hu, M.K. (1962)Visual pattern recognition by moment invariants, *IRE Trans Inform Theory.* IT-8, pp. 179-187.

Koenderink, J &. Van Doorn, A (1992). Surface shape and curvature scale. *Image and Vision Computing*, Vol. 10, pp. 557-565.

Lopez-Juarez, I. Rios-Cabrera, R. Peña-Cabrera, M. and Osorio-Comparan, R. (2010). Learning and Fast Object Recognition in Robot Skill Acquisition: A New Method. In Advances in Pattern Recognition. *2nd Mexican Conference on Pattern Recognition*, MCPR 2010, Springer LNCS. Martínez-Trinidad, Carrasco-Ochoa, Kittler, (Eds.). ISBN: 978-3-642-15991-6. Vol. 6256. pp. 40-49.

Lowe, D. (2004). Distinctive Image Features from Scale-Invariant Keypoints. Computer Science Department. University of British Columbia. Vancouver, B.C., Canada.

Montenegro Javier. (2006). Hough-transform based algorithm for the automatic invariant recognition of rectangular chocolates. Detection of defective pieces. Universidad Nacional de San Marcos. *Industrial Data*, vol. 9, num 2.

Peña-Cabrera, M; Lopez-Juarez, I; Rios-Cabrera, R; Corona-Castuera, J (2005). Machine Vision Approach for Robotic Assembly. *Assembly Automation.* Vol. 25 No. 3, pp 204-216.

Stavros J. and Paulo Lisboa. (1992). Translation, Rotation , and Scale Invariant Pattern Recognition by High-Order Neural networks and Moment Classifiers. *IEEE Transactions on Neural Networks*, vol. 3, No. 2.

Shingchern D. You , Gary E. Ford. (1994). Network model for invariant object recognition. *Pattern Recognition Letters* 15. Pp 761-767.

Worthington, P.L. and Hancock, E.R. (2001). Object recognition using shape-from shading. *IEEE Transactions on Pattern Analysis and Machine Intelligence*, 23 (5). pp. 535-542.

Zhang, R; Tsai, P; Cryer, J. E.; Shah, M. (1999). Shape from Shading: A Survey. *IEEE Transaction on pattern analysis and machine intelligence*, vol. 21, No. 8, pp 690-706.

Section 4

Applications

Automatic Coin Classification and Identification

Reinhold Huber-Mörk[1], Michael Nölle[1], Michael Rubik[1],
Michael Hödlmoser[2], Martin Kampel[2] and Sebastian Zambanini[2]
[1]*Department Safety and Security, Austrian Institute of Technology*
[2]*Computer Vision Lab, Vienna University of Technology*
Austria

1. Introduction

We investigate object recognition and classification in a setting with a large number of classes as well as recognition and identification of individual objects of high similarity. Real-world data sets were obtained for the classification and identification tasks. The considered classification task is the discrimination of modern coins into several hundreds of different classes. Identification is investigated for hand-made ancient coins. Intra-class variance due to wear and abrasion vs. small inter-class variance makes the classification of modern coins challenging. For ancient coins the intra-class variance makes the identification task possible, as the appearance of individual hand-struck coins is unique. Figure 1 shows sample images for the considered collections of coins.

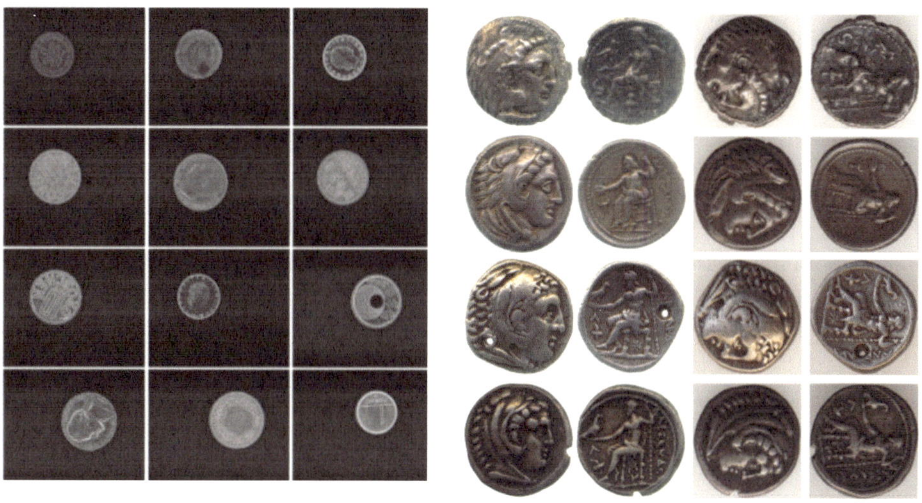

(a) Modern coins (b) Ancient coins

Fig. 1. Examples of images of modern and ancient coins

Modern coins were acquired by a high-speed machine vision system for coin sorting described in detail by Fürst et al. (2003). For ancient coins the setting is more general, images acquired by scanner and camera devices are considered. We will also discuss the use of a 3D acquisition device and 3D models for ancient coins (Zambanini et al., 2009).

The initial step of object recognition will be discussed as the problem of detection. i.e. foreground-background segmentation. Background knowledge on coins, i.e. the circular shape, which holds for most modern coins and is approximately true for ancient coins, is exploited in suggested segmentation methods (Zambanini & Kampel, 2009). Invariance with respect to translation is solved by segmentation, scaling is covered by normalization and rotation is handled in the suggested methods for invariant description, classification and identification.

We will compare two approaches for classification of coins, a method based on matching edge features in polar coordinates representation (Nölle et al., 2003) and a method for matching based on an Eigenspace representation (Huber et al., 2005). Discussion on the influence of dirt and abrasion will be included. Classification of modern coins makes additional use of geometric measurements and information extracted from obverse and reverse side of the coins. Incorporation of geometrical measurements and fusion of coin sides is realized by preselection and Bayesian fusion. In order to limit the number of coin classes to discriminate the concept of multiple Eigenspaces (Leonardis et al., 2002) is applied in the Eigenspace framework. Rejection of unknown coins and a discussion on false classification and false acceptance rates vs. false rejection is included.

For identification of coins we will consider an approach based on shape features describing the edge of an ancient coin (Huber-Mörk et al., 2008; Zaharieva et al., 2007). Features are derived from the Fourier domain representation of the coin contour. Comparison of two coins is done by matching the features derived from contour representations. Bayesian fusion of coin sides is studied. In order to discuss the identification performance a discussion on precision vs. recall is included (Huber-Mörk et al., 2010). Improvement by 3D modeling and analysis is also presented (Hödlmoser et al., 2010).

Results are presented for all considered data sets and methods. The data set for classification of coins consisted of approximately 12 000 coins with images of reverse and obverse sides. The data set contained 932 different coin classes. A derived data set was made publicly available as a benchmark by the EU MUSCLE network of excellence (Nölle & Hanbury, 2006; Nölle et al., 2006). Depending on the acceptable rejection rate correct decisions are taken in more than 92% for the Eigenspace approach. With the edge matching method approximately 86% of the coins are either correctly classified or correctly rejected. Considering only valid coins, i.e. coins in the database of 932 coins, the Eigenspace approach achieved a correct classification rate of 94.58%, whereas the direct edge matching approach scored 84.79%. Correct rejection of invalid coins was obtained at a rate of 78.45% for the Eigenspace approach and 98,29% were achieved in the direct edge matching approach.

The data set for identification of ancient coins was provided by the Fitzwilliam Museum, Cambridge, UK and was made publicly available by the EU COINS project (Kampel et al., 2009). The data set consists of 240 coins of the same class with 1200 images of obverse sides and 1200 images of reverse sides which were acquired by different acquisition devices. Results for identification based on shape matching are on the order of magnitude of 98%.

This contribution is organized as follows. Section 2 reviews the state of the art in automated coin image analysis. Section 3 describes coin detection and invariant preprocessing and Section 4 discusses matching based on various feature descriptors. Classification, identification and information fusion is described in Section 5. Results are presented in Section 6 and conclusions are drawn in Section 7.

2. State of the art in coin image analysis

For modern coins, i.e. machine struck coins, judging systems using electromechanical devices are wide-spread. Those systems are commonly based on measuring weight, diameter, thickness, permeability and conductivity (Davidsson, 1996), oscillating electromagnetic field characteristics (Neubarth et al., 1998), and photo- and piezoelectric properties (Shah et al., 1986). Typically, such systems are only capable to discriminate a small number of different coin denominations and are mostly limited to a specific currency.

Approaches towards classification of modern coins using image processing are described in various papers and patents. A neural network approach capable of discriminating between 500 Won and 500 Yen coins was published by Fukumi et al. (1992). A number of coin authentification methods employing optical means are described in patents, e.g. a system by which both sides of a coin are first imaged by cameras, followed by feature extraction from binarized images, and finally combined with a magnetic sensor measurement is described by Hibari & Arikawa (2001). The so called Dagobert coin recognition system was developed for high volumes of coins and a large number of currencies (Fürst et al., 2003; Nölle et al., 2003). Image binarization followed by area measurement and comparison of coin center and center of gravity was also suggested in a patent (Onodera & M., 2002). Another system based on the analysis of one side of a coin by transformation of its image into polar coordinates and matching of profiles taken along angle direction was described by Tsuji & Takahashi (1997). A special acquisition device for coins employing colored illumination from various angles was suggested by Hoßfeld et al. (2006). Methods based on matching gradient directions (Reisert et al., 2006; 2007) and color, shape and wavelet features (Vassilas & Skourlas, 2006) were suggested. An approach based on multiple Eigenspaces aims at classification for a large number of classes (Huber et al., 2005). This approach initially obtains a translationally and rotationally invariant description and secondly an illumination-invariant Eigenspace is selected from multiple Eigenspaces (Leonardis et al., 2002). Finally probabilities for coin classes are derived for the obverse and reverse sides of each coin and Bayesian fusion is performed.

For ancient coins, i.e. hand struck coins, some publications discussing approaches for classification appeared. Early approaches, which achieved a moderate classification performance, were based on matching of contour and texture features (Van Der Maaten & Postma, 2006) or make use of interest point extraction and matching of local features (Zaharieva et al., 2007). More recently, an approach based on interest points and improved feature description and matching was reported (Arandjelović, 2010). The inherent properties of hand struck coins result in individual features of each coin and a large intra-class variance. Therefore, object classification becomes challenging. However, in contrast to object classification, object identification relies on those unique features which distinguish a given object from all other members of the same class. Results on identification of ancient coins were reported by Huber-Mörk et al. (2008), where the combination of shape and local descriptors to capture the unique characteristics of the coin shape and die information was suggested. For ancient coin recognition features from the Scale-invariant feature transform (SIFT) (Lowe, 2004) was used and compared to algorithms based on shape matching i.e. a shape context description and a robust correlation algorithm (Zaharieva et al., 2007). Ancient coins are in general not of a perfect circular shape. From a numismatic point of view, the shape of a coin is a very specific feature. Thus, the shape described by the edge of a coin serves as a first clue in the process of coin identification and discrimination. A shape based method tuned to the properties of ancient coins was combined with matching of local features through Bayesian fusion (Huber-Mörk et al., 2010).

3. Coin image preprocessing

The appearance of coins in 2D images is highly influenced by the lighting conditions and the orientation of the imaged surface. Coins are characterized by a 3D surface and the reflected light into the camera direction is typically a mixture of strong specular and diffuse refections depending on the placement of camera and light sources, the type of light sources, the coin surface structure, dirt and abrasion. In order to diminish the influence induced by the lighting conditions a controlled acquisition setup is recommended. Controlled acquisition strongly improves recognition of objects of low intra-class surface variation, e.g. modern coins. Ancient coins are characterized by high surface variation even within a single class, therefore different type and direction of light sources make small patterns on the coin look very different which limits, for instance, the use of local image features for coin recognition. Best practice for acquisition of ancient coins was summarized by Kampel & Zambanini (2008) and Hoßfeld et al. (2006) described a sophisticated system for modern coin acquisition.

In this section, we will discuss preprocessing under controlled illumination for modern coins and slightly varying conditions for ancient coins. Since the shape of historical coins might not be as regular or flat as the shape of their present counterparts, it is a promising approach to calculate 3D models for higher coin matching rates. Therefore, we will also present acquisition of 3D data from stereo image pairs and stripe projection in this section.

3.1 Coin detection

The separation of an object of interest from background is commonly termed segmentation. Under controlled acquisition automatic intensity thresholding approaches (Sezgin & Sankur, 2004) are feasible for modern coins (Nölle et al., 2003). Due to textured background, presence of other objects in the image, inhomogeneous or poor illumination and low contrast, straightforward methods based on global image intensity thresholding tend to fail.

In situations, where explicit knowledge on the properties of objects is available, this knowledge can be used to steer segmentation parameters. For example, the compactness measure was used in a comparable application to find an intensity threshold in images showing circular spot welds by Ruisz et al. (2007). Similarly, ancient coins were localized by thresholding the local intensity range, i.e. the difference between maximum and minimum graylevel, in a local window and evaluation of the compactness measure (Zambanini & Kampel, 2008). Typically, the shape of modern coins is circular,

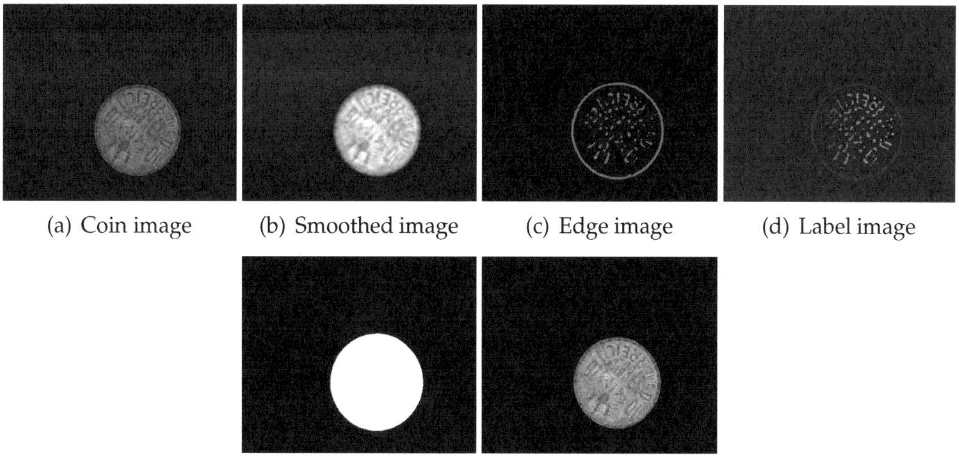

(a) Coin image (b) Smoothed image (c) Edge image (d) Label image

(e) Convex hull (f) Overlay image

Fig. 2. Image of a modern coin, intermediate detection results and segmentation.

whereas ancient coins deviate from this shape, but still stay close to a circular outline. Therefore, approaches based on edge detection and application of the Hough transform (Duda & Hart, 1972) were applied to modern coins (Reisert et al., 2006) as well as to ancient coins (Arandjelović, 2010), where a modified version of the Hough transform was used.

For a modern coin, such as shown in Fig.2 (a), we suggest an edge based technique to segment the coin from the background. The detection of the coin employs a common segmentation approach and works reliably for controlled lighting conditions and relatively clean background, e.g. a moderately dirty conveyor belt. Problems might be caused by very dark coins, i.e. coins which reflect only a small amount of light towards the camera. A multi-stage segmentation procedure is suggested. The outline of the suggested segmentation method is:

1. Smoothing of the image to suppress noise and background texture, see Fig.2(b).
2. Edge filtering using a Laplacian of Gaussian approach followed by zero-crossing detection (Marr & Hildreth, 1980), see Fig.2(c).
3. Labeling of the detected regions, see Fig.2(d), and selection of the region with largest bounding box as coin region candidate.
4. Form a blob by computing the convex hull of the coin region candidate, see Fig.2(e)

An example of an overlay of the extracted blob onto the input image is shown in Fig.2(f). Coin position and diameter are estimated from the detected blob, which directly delivers access to a translation invariant description.

For ancient coins we employ a measure of compactness c_t related to a threshold t defined as

$$c_t = 4\pi A_t / P_t^2 \tag{1}$$

where A_t is the area of the region covered by the coin and P_t is the perimeter of the coin. The measures A_t and P_t are obtained by connected components analysis (Sonka et al., 1998) applied to the binary image which is derived from thresholding the intensity range image. Figure 3 (a) shows an intensity image of an ancient coin, Fig. 3 (b) is the corresponding intensity range image and Figs. 3 (c)-(e) show thresholded images for different selections of t along with calculated values for compactness c_t. The image thresholded at the optimal level t_{opt} with highest compactness is given in Fig. 3 (f). A sudden decrease of the compactness measure occurs with oversegmentation of the coin into several small regions, e.g. compare to Fig. 3 (e).

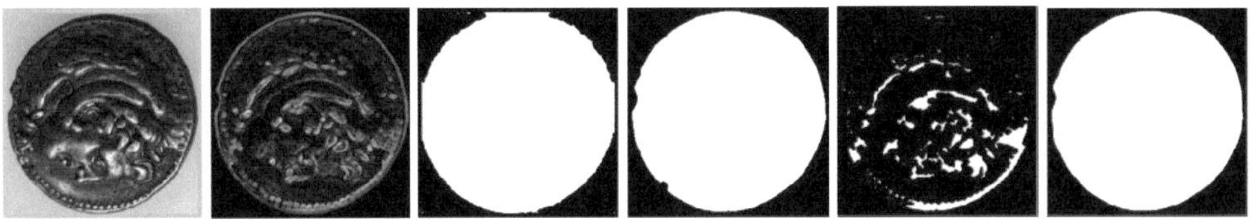

(a) Coin image (b) Intensity range (c) Binarized, $t = 5$, $c_5 = 0.096$ (d) Binarized, $t = 65$, $c_{65} = 0.859$ (e) Binarized, $t = 85$, $c_{85} = 0.018$ (f) Binarized, $t = 49$, $c_{49} = 0.888$

Fig. 3. Image of an ancient coin, intensity range image and different binary images with corresponding threshold and compactness.

3.2 Invariant preprocessing for 2D images

Apart from illumination dependency the appearance of a coin varies considerably with respect to its grey values depending on dirt and abrasion. These variations frequently are inhomogeneous. This suggests, even if illumination influence could be neglected, that for recognition purposes grey values by themselves will not give appropriate results. On the other hand, edge information remains more or less stable or at least degrades gracefully. Therefore, we based the feature extraction for coin recognition on edges. In principle any edge detector may be used for this purpose. From our experience the approaches suggested by Canny (1986), by Rothwell et al. (1995) and the Laplacian of Gaussian method (Marr & Hildreth, 1980) work satisfactorily.

For reliable matching of coins invariance with respect to rotation has to be taken into account. Invariance with respect to translation is already discussed and taken into account by an approach involving segmentation in Sec. 3.1. Scale variance is accounted for either by using a calibrated acquisition device or normalization of the segmented image.

In general, rotational invariance is either approached via the use of geometrical moments (Hu, 1962), radial coding of features (Torres-Mendez et al., 2000), or using a mapping from Cartesian to polar coordinate representation, e.g. log-polar mapping (Kurita et al., 1998). A method based on the construction of an Eigenspace from uniformly rotated images was published by Uenohara & Kanade (1997). The application of their approach works through locating of a specific small pattern in a larger image. In a later paper (Uenohara & Kanade, 1998) an improvement of the location method based on the discrete cosine transform (DCT) was suggested.

We obtain rotational invariance by estimation of the rotational angle followed by a rotation into a reference pose. Angle estimation is performed for images transformed into polar coordinates. In the polar image shift invariance, corresponding to rotational invariance when mapped back to Cartesian coordinates, is achieved through cross-correlation. Cross-correlation is efficiently implemented using the fast Fourier transform (FFT) (Cooley & Tukey, 1965).

Rotational invariance for a coin edge image involves cross-correlation with reference edge images. The edge image is mapped from Cartesian to polar coordinates, see Fig.4. The result of cross-correlation between the coin image to be classified and a set of reference images is used to derive class hypotheses. In detail, for both sides of a coin under investigation rotational invariant processing and hypothesis generation proceeds as follows:

1. Estimation of coin diameter from coin detection.
2. Selection of a set of reference images depending on thickness and diameter measure (if available). Each reference image is associated with a coin class.
3. Cross-correlation of the coin side edge image under investigation with all reference coin edge images in the selected reference set, resulting in a cross-correlation value and associated rotation angle estimation for each reference class.
4. Ranking of the reference set by the maximum correlation value and generation of a set of hypotheses for the highest-ranking classes.

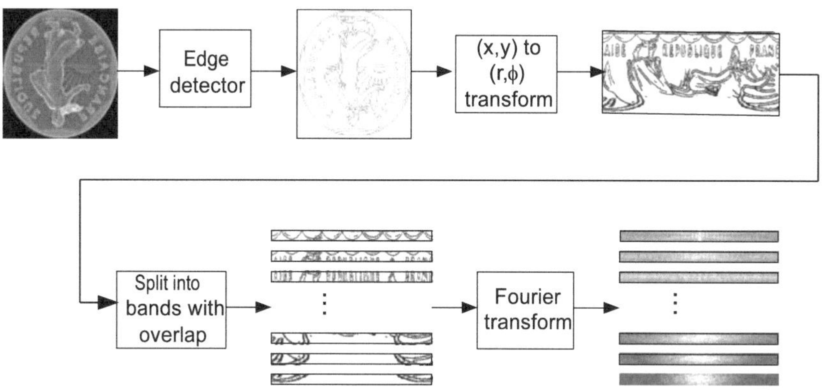

Fig. 4. Processing for rotational invariance

To obtain reliable estimates for cross-correlation and rotation angle the polar image is split into n bands along the radius coordinate, corresponding to concentric rings in Cartesian coordinates. The peak of the correlation value K_i for band i is determined for each band and the position of the peak is taken as an estimate for the rotation angle in band i. The sample mean angle direction $\bar{\alpha}$ is estimated via (Fisher, 1995):

$$\bar{\alpha} = \begin{cases} \arctan(S/C) & \text{if } S \geq 0 \text{ and } C > 0 \\ \arctan(S/C) + \pi & \text{if } C < 0 \\ \arctan(S/C) + 2\pi & \text{if } S < 0 \text{ and } C > 0 \end{cases} \tag{2}$$

with $C = \sum_{i=1}^{n} \delta_i \cos \alpha_i$, $S = \sum_{i=1}^{n} \delta_i \sin \alpha_i$. If band i contains a significant number of edge pixels in reference coin and coin under investigation $\delta_i = 1$, otherwise $\delta_i = 0$.

A cross-correlation estimate K for the coin under investigation is calculated using $K = 1/n' \sum_{i=1}^{n} \delta_i K_i$. The number of bands $n' \leq n$ used in cross-correlation and angle estimation varies between images and is simply obtained by $n' = \sum_{i=1}^{n} \delta_i$.

3.3 Surface analysis from 3D data

Analysis of coin images in 2D might lead to loss of important features, e.g. highlights due to specular reflections decrease the quality of the images and handicap automatic analysis. Especially ancient coin surfaces are reliefs visualizing inscriptions and symbols. Therefore, the appearance of coins in 2D images is highly influenced by the lighting conditions. Different lighting directions make small patterns on the coin look very different and limits, for instance, the use of local image features for coin recognition. Since the surface shape of historical coins might not be as regular or flat as the shape of their present counterparts, we suggest to calculate 3D reconstructions for higher coin matching rates. With 3D scans, detailed models of both coin sides are obtained which allow a more accurate analysis (Akca et al., 2007).

However, 3D acquisitions are more laborious and expensive and, to our knowledge, 3D vision approaches applied to 3D databases of coins do not exist at the moment. By using 3D coin models, various additional features can be obtained for object matching which are not available in 2D (e.g. changes on the coin's surface, thickness and volume measurements). The profile of an exemplary ancient coin is shown in Fig. 5 (a). Two coin cuts, which are obviously visible in the 3D reconstruction Figure 5 (a) can be seen in the profile plot in Fig. 5 (b).

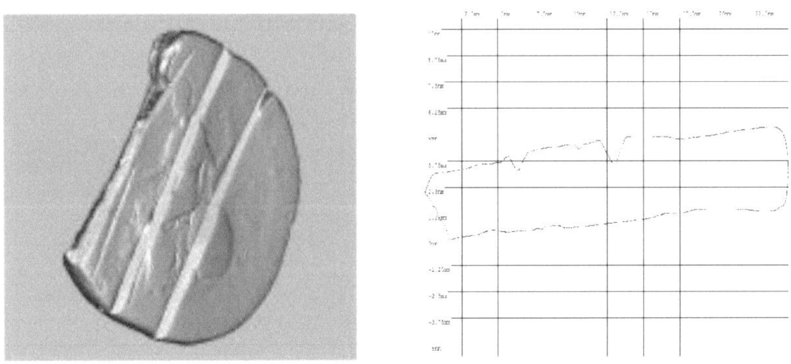

(a) 3D rendering (b) Profile plot

Fig. 5. 3D reconstruction of an ancient coin.

The Breuckmann stereoSCAN 3D system (`http://www.breuckmann.com/index.php?id=stereoscan`) was used for coin data acqusition (Zambanini et al., 2009). The scanner is an active stereo system consisting of a projector and two cameras serving as stereo camera pair and combines the shape from structured light and stereo vision approach (Stoykova et al., 2007). In order to evaluate the accuracy of the coin models acquired by the Breuckmann stereoSCAN 3D, real world coin data is compared to data gathered from their virtual 3D model counterparts.

A black and white stripe pattern is projected on the coin's surface. The stripes get deformed by the coin's shape and its surface structure. By using a stereo camera pair, 3D information can be obtained from two 2D images showing the same object at exactly the same time from different views. In active stereo vision, a light source projects artificial features. This features are easy to extract as their properties are known and they can be matched unambiguously. In the setup used for coin acquisition, the scanner provides a theoretical x-y resolution of 20 μm and a theoretical z-resolution limit of 1 μm.

The goal of stereo vision is to obtain depth information from 2D input data. Since the two cameras have a fixed relative orientation, the distance between them is not variable and the position of any point in 3D space can be obtained by triangulation. Therefore, the intersection between two lines of two images, where each line is passing through the projection of the point and the projection center, has to be determined. The setup can be described using epipolar geometry, which is the geometry between two views (Hartley & Zisserman, 2003). As an initial step, corresponding points must be found, which is performed using the projected and deformed stripe pattern on the object's surface. We fixed the coins on a rotation / tilt table in front of the active stereo system and the object was scanned from eight different but known viewing positions. For aligning the data from different viewpoints, the Iterative Closest Point (ICP) algorithm, which was presented by Besl & McKay (1992) and Chen & Medioni (1992), is used. Since the position of the rotation/tilt table is known, a preliminary alignment process can be performed first. All eight scans are finally aligned and merged into a polygon mesh.

3.4 Extraction of coin shape features

As the appearance of an ancient coin is often unique, e.g. due to variations in the hammering process, die, mint signs, shape, scratches, wearing, etc. its image contains important information for identification. The uniqueness in the appearance of coins results from variations in the coin blank material and application of the tools in minting, as well as from wear of the coin. Therefore, for numismatists the shape of the coin edge is regarded to be an important feature to characterize a coin.

Our approach of shape comparison is based on a description of the difference between the shape of a coin and the shape of a circle. Therefore, the suggested approach is called deviation from circular shape matching (DCSM). In order to represent the coin shape, a border tracing on the binary image resulting from segmentation is performed. A list of border pixels is obtained and resampled to l samples using equidistantly spaced intervals with respect to the arc length. Figures 6 (a)-(d) show this operation.

A one-dimensional descriptor, i.e. a curve describing the border, is obtained from fitting the coin edge to a circle and unrolling the polar distances between sample points and fitted circle into a vector. The center $s_c = (x_c, y_c)$ of the fitted circle is derived from the center of gravity and the radius r is the mean distance between the center and all sample points $s_i = (x_i, y_i)$ using

$$x_c = \frac{1}{l} \sum_{i=1,\ldots,l} x_i, \quad y_c = \frac{1}{l} \sum_{i=1,\ldots,l} y_i, \quad r = \frac{1}{l} \sum_{i=1,\ldots,l} \|s_i - s_c\| \tag{3}$$

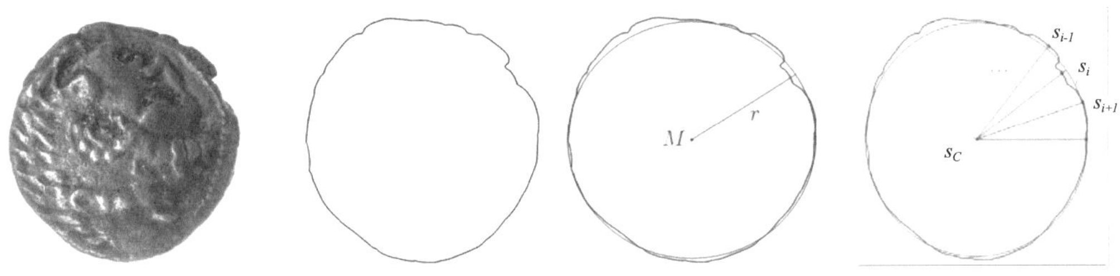

(a) Coin image (b) Coin edge (c) Fitted circle (d) Sampling along arc

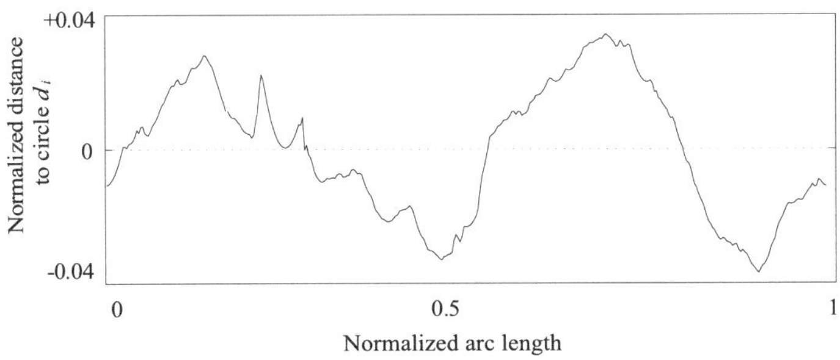

(e) normalized 1D description of coin shape

Fig. 6. Processing of coin contour.

where (x_i, y_i) are the coordinates of sample point s_i and $\|\cdot\|$ denotes the L_2-norm. The 1D representation is given by $D = (d_1, \ldots, d_l)$, where

$$d_i = (\|s_i - s_c\| - r)/r, i = 1, \ldots, l \tag{4}$$

The division by r makes the representation invariant with respect to scale. Figure 6 (e) shows the obtained 1D representation.

4. Matching for classification and identification

Matching for classification or identification is based on edge based features extracted as described in the previous section. In this section, we will discuss direct matching of edge features, Eigenspace matching and shape matching.

4.1 Direct matching of edges

In the direct matching approach for edge points we start with a binary edge image E derived from a coin image. Let $E^c = \{(x - x_m, y - y_m) | E(x, y) = 1\}$ be the list of cartesian edge point coordinates with the center of gravity (x_m, y_m) as origin. The polar coordinate representation of E^c is given by

$$E^p = \{(\theta, \rho) | (x, y) \in E^c\} \tag{5}$$

$$\theta = \arctan y/x, \quad \rho = \sqrt{x^2 + y^2}, \quad x = \rho \cos\theta, \quad y = \rho \sin\theta$$

Assume E_m is a reference image, or so called master edge image, and E_a is an edge image to be matched. Then in general there is an unknown rotation ϕ around the center of gravity that aligns both edge images. In polar coordinates this rotation transforms into a cyclic translation in the angular direction. To determine ϕ we may deploy a fast correlation method based on the edge images, see Subsec 3.2 Although correlation methods based on the fast Fourier transformation perform efficiently, there are some drawbacks using the edge images directly. First, to preserve the visual information the resolution of the edge image cannot be too small. Depending on the diameter of the coin we typically get coin image resolutions from 100×100 to 300×300 pixels and the correlation would add significantly to the overall computational costs. Secondly, the outer border, which in most cases contains a substantial part of the edge points, usually does not help to find ϕ as it comprises too many symmetries. To avoid both we suggest to calculate the correlation on a two dimensional edge density function restricted to the inner part of the coin. This is given by

$$H^d_{i,j} = |\{(\theta,\rho) \in E^p | \theta_{i-1} \leq \theta < \theta_i, \rho_{j-1} < \rho < \rho_j\}| \tag{6}$$

$$E^d_{i,j} = H^d_{i,j}/N, \quad i = 1,\ldots,n; j = 1,\ldots,l, \quad N = \sum_{i,j}^{n,l} H^d_{i,j}$$

The sets $\{\theta_0,\ldots,\theta_n\}$ and $\{\rho_0,\ldots,\rho_l\}$ are the discrete resolutions in angular and distance directions, respectively. Now, we may estimate ϕ by correlating E^d_m and E^d_a. By choosing a high resolution in the angular direction (i.e. $n \geq 512$) and a coarse resolution (i.e. $l \leq 16$) in the distance direction, omitting to include the coin borders, we found that ϕ usually may be determined up to $\pm 0.5°$. Once ϕ is known, we may align the actual coin image to the master. This is done efficiently by only calculating the rotated coordinates for the edge points in E^c_a resulting in the rotated actual coin edge image $E_{a\phi}$. From here we compute two distance measures

$$e_{\text{abrasion}} = \frac{1}{|E^c_m|} \sum_{(x,y)\in E^c_m} (1 - \bar{E}^d_{a\phi}(x,y)) \tag{7}$$

$$e_{\text{dirt}} = \frac{1}{|E^c_{a\phi}|} \sum_{(x,y)\in E^c_{a\phi}} (1 - \bar{E}^d_m(x,y)) \tag{8}$$

where $\bar{E}^d$ is the result of applying a morphological dilation operation to the binary edge image E in order to counteract the remaining uncertainty of the angular position. e_{abrasion} tells us how many expected (master) edge points are missing, whereas e_{dirt} sums the additional edge points in the actual edge image. If these errors are higher than given thresholds we have to dismiss the match. In general we cannot know which master coin corresponds to the actual coin image. Therefore, we have to calculate eqns. 7 and 8 for all master coin candidates.

4.2 Eigenimage representation and matching

The Eigenspace decomposition for image analysis was introduced by Sirovich & Kirby (1987) and found numerous applications over the last decades, most prominently in the field of face recognition (Turk & Pentland, 1991). We start with the description of the mathematical procedure of eigenspace construction employing principal components analysis (PCA). Subsequently, we discuss multiple Eigenspaces in the context of coin recognition.

In the Eigenspace approach, we consider a set of M images B_1 to B_M. Each image B_i is of size $N \times N$ pixels. The images are reformed into vectors Γ_1 to Γ_M, e.g. by scanning the image line by line. If all pixels of an image are used to produce a vector, each vector Γ_1 has length $L = N^2$. An average vector Ψ and difference vectors ψ_i are calculated by

$$\Psi = \frac{1}{M}\sum_{i=1}^{M}\Gamma_i, \quad \text{where} \quad \psi_i = \Gamma_i - \Psi, i = 1, \ldots, M \tag{9}$$

Principal axes are obtained by the Eigendecomposition of the covariance matrix C defined by

$$C = \frac{1}{M}\sum_{i=1}^{M}\psi_i\psi_i^T = AA^T, \quad \text{where} \quad A = (\psi_1, \psi_2, \ldots, \psi_M) \tag{10}$$

The Eigenvectors are sorted in non-increasing order depending on the corresponding Eigenvalue. A small number M' of significant Eigenvectors is retained from the ranked Eigenvalues, a common practice which leads to the most expressive features (Turk & Pentland, 1991). A weighting factor ω_k corresponding to the k-th Eigenimage for a new reformed image is obtained by projection onto the k-th Eigenspace component u_k using

$$\omega_i = u_k(\Gamma - \Psi), \quad K = 1, \ldots, M' \tag{11}$$

The weights ω_k are arranged in an vector $\Omega = (\omega_1, \ldots, \omega'_M)^T$. For the coin recognition task, not the full images are reformed into a vector, only the interior pixels of the coin are rearranged into the vector Γ, see Fig. 7.

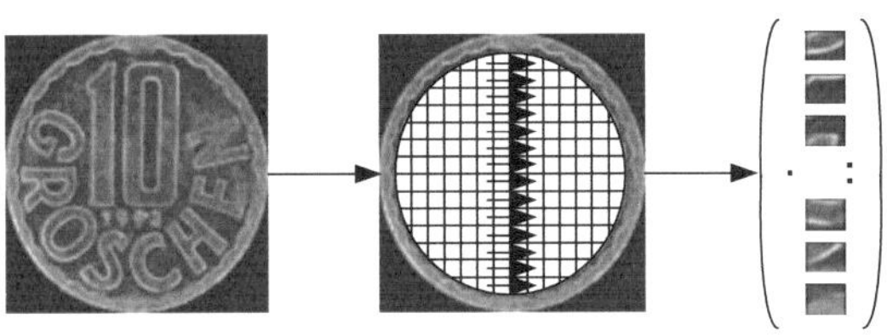

Fig. 7. Arrangement of inner coin pixels into a vector.

To overcome limitations regarding illumination variation in the Eigenspace approach a number of solutions were proposed, e.g. Murase & Nayar (1994) investigate the determination of the illumination which gives best discrimination. The PCA of edge images and smoothed edge images is suggested as an illumination invariant way of Eigenspace construction by Yilmaz & Gökmen (2000), gradient images are used as input to PCA by Venkatesh et al. (2002) and Bischof et al. (2001) use a set of gradient based filter banks applied to the Eigenimage representation.

Figure 8(a) shows the first 32 Eigenimages constructed from graylevel images, the top left image is the Eigenimage corresponding to the largest Eigenvalue. Histogram equalization is sometimes suggested as a way to achieve illumination invariance. Figure 8(b) shows the most expressive Eigenimages constructed from histogram equalized images. Figure 8(c) shows the most expressive Eigenimages constructed from edge images. Eigenhills have been suggested by Yilmaz & Gökmen (2000). There Eigenhills are derived from application of the PCA to edge images which are covered by a "membrane". We used a 2D Gaussian filter kernel with a s of 1.5 to smooth the edge images which are of size 128x128 pixels. Figure 8(d) shows the most expressive Eigenimages, i.e. Eigenhills, constructed from smoothed edge images.

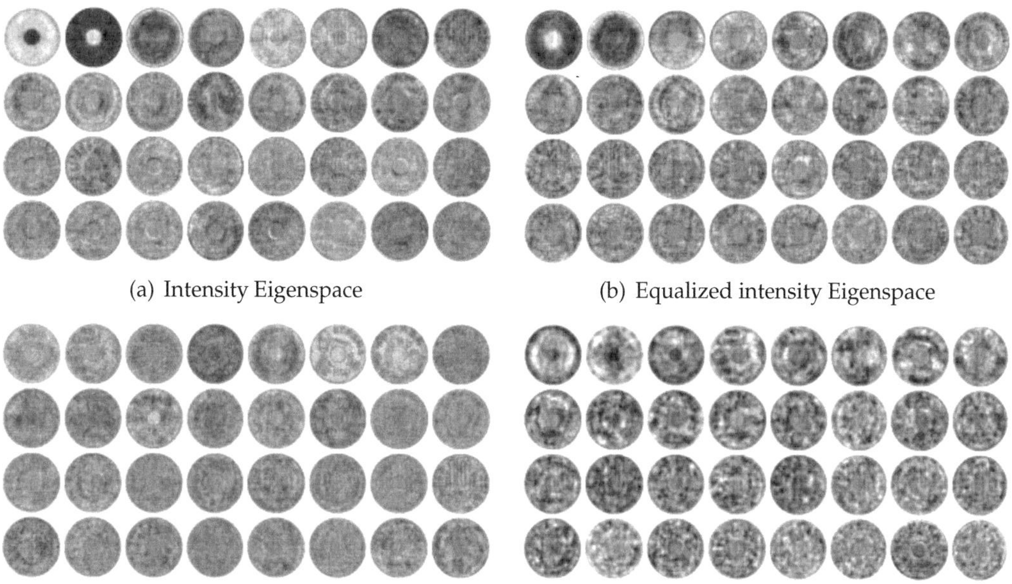

(a) Intensity Eigenspace

(b) Equalized intensity Eigenspace

(c) Edge Eigenspace

(d) Eigenhills

Fig. 8. First 32 Eigenimages ranked by corresponding Eigenvalues for different variants of Eigenspace representation.

Figure 9 gives the normalized cumulative sum of the sorted Eigenvalues for all the considered variants of Eigenspace representation. For intensity Eigenspace i.e. the first 32 Eigenimages retain approximately 78% of the variance present in the original set of intensity images. Approximately 60% of the variance present in the original set of histogram equalized intensity images is contained in the first 32 sorted Eigenimages. For edge Eigenspace, only about 42% of the variance present in the original set of edge images is contained in the first 32 sorted Eigenimages. Approximately 76% of the variance present in the original set of smoothed edge images is contained in the first 32 sorted Eigenhills. Therefore, the Eigenhills approach achieves a compact representation comparable to intensity Eigenspace, while also being illumination invariant.

4.3 Shape matching

The shape descriptions of two coins are compared by a linear combination of global and local shape matching. The local matching is derived from the difference of Fourier shape descriptors, whereas the correlation coefficient between the curves serves as global measure of shape similarity.

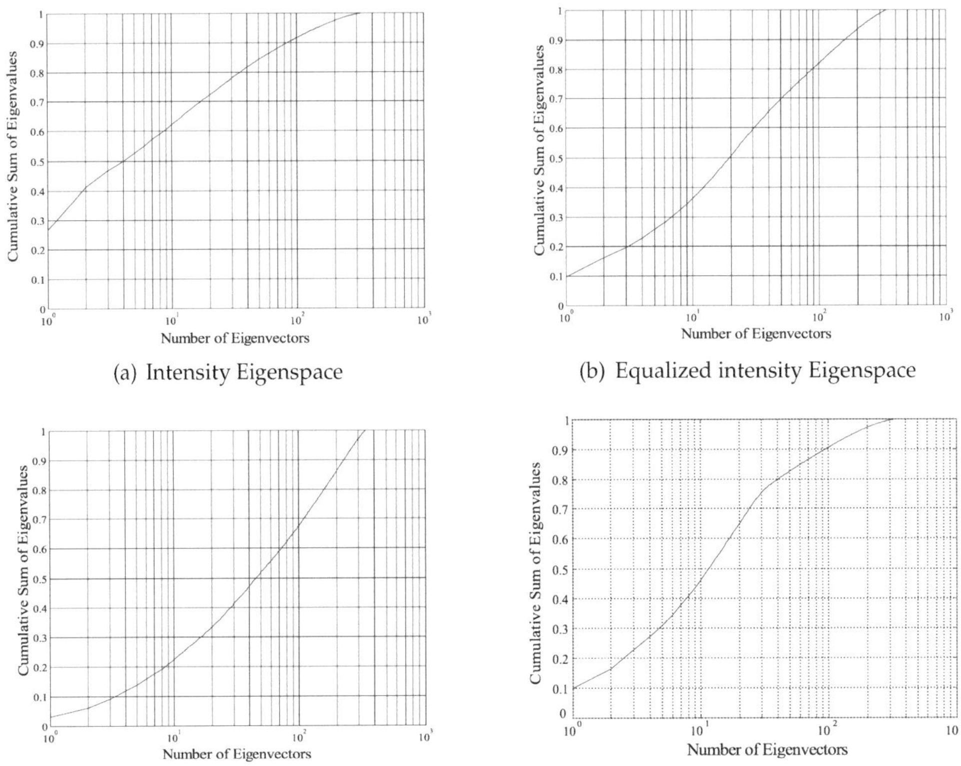

(a) Intensity Eigenspace

(b) Equalized intensity Eigenspace

(c) Edge Eigenspace

(d) Eigenhills

Fig. 9. Cumulative sum of Eigenvalues depending on the number of Eigenvectors for different variants of Eigenspace representation.

The mean absolute or squared distance between the magnitude values of the Fourier coefficients is used as local measure of dissimilarity, i.e.

$$D_L = \sum_{i=v,\dots,l-u} \frac{\|\mathrm{sd}_{\mathrm{A}}(i) - \mathrm{sd}_{\mathrm{B}}(i)\|_p}{l-u-v+1} \tag{12}$$

where $\|\cdot\|_p, p \in \{1,2\}$ is the L_p norm. The lower $v \geq 1$ and upper offsets $u \geq 0$ for the Fourier descriptors are small constants and used to limit errors stemming from imprecise circle fitting and quantization noise.

The global shape matching is obtained from a measure of dissimilarity or similarity, e.g. from the mean squared error (MSE) or the normalized cross correlation (NCC) coefficient $ncc(u)$ for a shift of u samples

$$\mathrm{ncc}(u) = \frac{\sum_{i=1,\dots,l} d_A(i) \cdot d_B(i+u)}{\sqrt{\sum_{i=1,\dots,l} d_A(i)^2 \cdot \sum_{i=1,\dots,l} d_B(i)^2}} \tag{13}$$

where $i + u$ might exceed l and modulo addition is applied. The maximum $D_G = (1 - \max_{i=1...,l} \mathrm{ncc}(i))/2$ is used as a measure of global shape match. Similarly, the MSE is given by

$$\mathrm{mse}(u) = \frac{1}{l} \sum_{i=1,...,l} (d_A(i) - d_B(i+u))^2 \quad (14)$$

In the case of MSE, the maximum $D_G = \max_{i=1...,l} \mathrm{mse}(i)$ is used as a measure of global dissimilarity. The position of the minimum of D_G is related to the rotation angle between the compared coins. While the MSE requires l shifts of the signal and l evaluations of eqn. 14, the NCC is efficiently computed in a more efficient way (Lewis, 1995).

The overall measure of shape dissimilarity becomes

$$\mathrm{D}_{AB} = \alpha D_L + (1 - \alpha) D_G \quad (15)$$

where the weighting factor $\alpha \in [0, 1]$ controls the influence of local and global dissimilarity terms.

In order to be invariant with respect to mirroring, the D_G is replaced by the minimum of global dissimilarity obtained from matching the signal and the reversed signal. Mirror invariance enables the matching of coins irrespective of which side is shown on the image.

5. Classification and information fusion

A framework for classification and identification based on preselection, classification and Bayesian fusion is presented. For modern coins preselection based on correlation, classification based on Eigenspace representation and prior information, and fusion of obverse and reverse class probabilites is discussed. For identification of ancient coins preselection on shape features and classification based on fusion of shape and a local features based representations is demonstrated.

5.1 Classification and information fusion of modern coins

In the Eigenspace approach, we consider a collection of reference coefficient vectors $\Omega_r = (\omega_{r1}, \ldots, \omega_{rD})^T$, $r = 1, \ldots, R$ and an observed coefficient vector $\Omega^s = (\omega_1^s, \ldots, \omega_D^s)^T$, corresponding to the coin side to be classified. Classification starts from two observation vectors together with a set of hypotheses, ranked by their corresponding correlation measure. We introduce the following notation with typical values of parameters given in brackets:

R number of reference coefficient vectors (typically $R = K \cdot 20$) ,

S number of coin sides (usually $S = 2$),

K number of classes (typically $K = 2 \ldots 113$),

H number of hypotheses (usually $H = 5$),

D dimension of coefficient vector (typically $D = 32$),

G_h^s hypothesis number h on side S,

d_r^s distance to r-th coefficient vector on side S,

l_r^s label of r-th coefficient vector on side S.

The selection of the parameter R is motivated by the balance between representing occurring variation within a coin and efficient construction of the Eigenspace. The Eigenproblem for general $R \times R$ matrices require on the order of R^3 arithmetic operations (Pan & Chen, 1999), accordingly a small R is preferred. The number of coin sides S is obviously equal to 2. The maximum number of classes per Eigenspace is determined by preselection of classes, usually based on measurements of diameter and thickness, if available. This means multiple Eigenspaces, each of which holding a limited number of classes to discriminate, are build and selected from geometric measurements (Huber et al., 2005). The number of hypotheses H generated from ranking of correlation values was limited to 5. This decision is motivated by observing the necessary number of hypotheses to ensure that the valid decision is included in the considered set of hypotheses. From a validated set of coins, it was observed, that the correct coin class is contained in 92.62, 95.15, 96.91, 98.04 or 98.88% of all cases when retaining the first 1,2,3,4 or 5 hypotheses, respectively. This means, a classification scheme considering the highest ranking result only would not do better than 92.62%. On the other hand, considering 5 hypotheses limits a classification and fusion system to 98.88%, which is a reasonable limit for practical application.

5.1.1 Classification of modern coins

The distance to the r-th coefficient vector on side s is calculated by the Euclidean distance

$$d_r^s = \sum_{i=1}^{D} (\omega_i^s - \omega_{ri})^2 \tag{16}$$

The class labels $l_r^s \in \{1, \ldots, K\}$ correspond to the distances d_r^s. The distance for hypothesis h on side s is derived as the average distance to coefficient vectors with class label $G_h^s \in \{1, \ldots, K\}$

$$D_h^s = \frac{1}{N_h} \sum_{r=1}^{R} d_r^s \delta_{rh}^s, \qquad \delta_{rh}^s = \begin{cases} 1 \text{ if } & l_r^s = G_h^s \\ 0 \text{ else} \end{cases} \tag{17}$$

where N_h is the number of training samples for class G_h^s. The conditional probability for observation Ω^s depending on hypothesis G_h^s on side s is estimated to be inversely proportional to the distance D_h^s

$$P^s(\Omega^s | G_h^s) = 1/(D_h^s \sum_{i=1}^{H} 1/D_i^s) \tag{18}$$

where the summation term in the denominator accounts for normalization.

5.1.2 Information fusion of modern coins

A-priori probabilities $P^s(G_h^s)$ are either set to equal probability, e.g. $P^1(G_h^1) = 1/H$ for side 1 and $P^1(G_h^1) = 1/H$ for side 2, respectively. If the coins are imaged in way that there is no rotation between obverse and reverse images, one can make use of this knowledge as modern coins are characterized by either 0 or 180 degrees of rotation between sides. In this case, the $P^s(G_h^s)$ are derived from the difference in rotation angle α_h for side 1 (e.g. obverse) and angle

α_j for side 2 (e.g. reverse) using

$$P^2(G_j^2) = P^2(G_h^1, G_j^2) = a + bP(\alpha_h^1, \alpha_j^2), \quad a + b = 1 \tag{19}$$

The weights a and b account for the fact that a number of coins exist which appear similar under rotation. The constant term is chosen relatively small, in our study $a = 0.08$ turned out to be a good choice.

The prior probability $P^2(G_h^1, G_j^2)$ is assumed normally distributed around zero angle difference for coins with same orientation on front and back side and around 180 degree angle difference for coins turned upside down between sides.

The fusion of probabilities estimated of both coin sides and prior information uses the Bayes formula

$$P^s(G_h^s|\Omega^s) = \frac{P^s(\Omega^s|G_h^s)P^s(G_h^s)}{\sum_{i=1}^{H} P^S(\Omega^s|G_i^s)P^s(G_i^s)} \tag{20}$$

We concentrate on the nominator since the denominator is a constant term. Combination of both sides is done by the product rule (Kittler et al., 1998)

$$P(G_k|\Omega) = P(G_h^1 = G_j^2|\Omega^1, \Omega^2) = P^1(G_h^1|\Omega^1) \cdot P^2(G_h^2|\Omega^2) \tag{21}$$

where probabilities are only derived for hypotheses present for both sides. The product rule of combination is equivalent to naive Bayes fusion of classifiers. Naive Bayes fusion of classifiers in turn coincides with Bayes classification over composite descriptors if the individual features are conditionally independent (Shi & Manduchi, 2003).

5.2 Classification and information fusion of ancient coins

Apart from shape features, descriptors based on local features were used for classification and identification of ancient coins in related papers (Huber-Mörk et al., 2008; Kampel et al., 2009; Zaharieva et al., 2007). Local features based on SIFT (Lowe, 2004) were used in preselection for shape feature matching. Probabilities are derived from ranked results from shape matching and fused with results from local features based matching. Fusion of ancient coins is performed similar to modern coins. In cases were images of both coin sides are available, fusion of coin side results is also possible.

5.2.1 Classification of ancient coins

Local features based approaches and shape descriptors deliver distance measures between the coin in question and all other images in the database. In this case, a two-stage rank based strategy is possible, i.e. a small subset is preselected based on shape comparison and further processed using local features based matching (Huber-Mörk et al., 2008). Here, we follow a strategy combining probabilities which are derived from distance measures through a rule of combination (Huber-Mörk et al., 2010), e.g. the product rule Kittler et al. (1998). Conditional independence between shape and local features, as well as between coin sides, can be assumed.

From ranking the shape dissimilarity D_{AB} for shapes given in eqn. 15 for shape B matched to shape A results in a preselection set $\mathcal{P}$. From an observed shape description A we derive a conditional probability for a coin side label $\mathcal{L}$ assigned to B. The conditional probability for a $P_{shape}(\mathcal{L}|A)$ is estimated to be inversely proportional to the dissimilarity given in eqn. 15 between coin A and coin B labelled $\mathcal{L}$:

$$P_{shape}(\mathcal{L}|A) = \frac{1}{\mathrm{D}_{AB} \sum_{C \in \mathcal{P}} 1/\mathrm{D}_{AC}} \tag{22}$$

where the summation term in the denominator accounts for normalization.

A similar argument is applied to derive a conditional probability for observed local descriptors X matched to local descriptors Y labeled $\mathcal{L}$ and corresponding to an image contained in the preselection set $\mathcal{P}$:

$$P_{local}(\mathcal{L}|X) = \frac{M_{XY}}{\sum_{Z \in \mathcal{P}} M_{XZ}} \tag{23}$$

where M_{XY} denotes the number of matches between the query image with local descriptors X and the coin side image with local descriptors Y and the denominator accounts for normalization.

5.2.2 Information fusion of ancient coins

As local and shape features describe different properties of a coin, it is reasonable to assume statistical independence between shape and local feature measurements. Thus, the combination is performed by the product rule Kittler et al. (1998):

$$\begin{aligned} P(\mathcal{L}|A,X) &= P(\mathcal{L}_{shape} = \mathcal{L}_{local}|A,X) \\ &= P_{shape}(\mathcal{L}|A) \cdot P_{local}(\mathcal{L}|X) \end{aligned} \tag{24}$$

where $\mathcal{L}_{shape}$ and $\mathcal{L}_{local}$ are labels derived from shape and local descriptions.

The idea of fusion of different descriptor outputs is extended to a fusion of more than one image of a coin. Typically, a coin is presented by images of the obverse and reverse side. Fusion of coin sides is obtained in a straightforward fashion. Eqn. 24 is extended to the following four terms

$$P(\mathcal{L}|A_i, X_i) = P_{shape}(\mathcal{L}|A_1) \cdot P_{local}(\mathcal{L}|X_1) \cdot P_{shape}(\mathcal{L}|A_2) \cdot P_{local}(\mathcal{L}|X_2) \tag{25}$$

where A_i and X_i corresponds to shape and local feature descriptions of the $i-$th coin side.

6. Results

In this section we summarize results for classification of modern coins and identification of ancient coins.

6.1 Results for modern coins

Image data of modern coins was acquired trough a coin collection which took place in the course of the implementation of the Euro currency in twelve European countries at the turn of the year 2001 to 2002. During this campaign 300 tons of coins coming from virtually all countries of the world but predominately from the twelve Euro member states have been collected by the Dagobert coin sorting system. Results are presented for two samples of 11 949 coins and 12 949 coins, respectively, taken randomly from the collected money. Those coins have been manually labeled into valid and invalid coins. Valid coins are coins from 30 countries including most European countries, the USA, Canada and Japan. The portion of valid coins in the sample was 91.6% or 94.15%, depending on the considered set. The remaining 8.4% or 5.85%, respectively, are dominated by coins from Asia, South-America, Africa and former socialist countries. Figure 1 (b) shows examples for these coin images.

6.1.1 Direct edge matching based approach

Apart from image sensors for obverse and reverse coin sides sensors for thickness and area measurements are present in the Dagobert system. Based on their measurements a first rough pre-selection of potential master coins is determined, in our case a set of 6 coins are preselected. This provides us with a set of master coins that have almost the same diameter and that have to be distinguished. A total number of 12949 coin images were validated manually as well as tested against 913 master coin patterns of all diameters in the recognition pattern set. Table1 shows the results. The set of incorrectly sorted coins is quite small.

	Acceptance		Rejection
Valid coins 94.15%	Correct classification 79.83%	False classification 0.10%	False Rejection 14.22%
Invalid coins 5.85%	False acceptance 0.10%		Correct rejection 5.75%
All coins 100%	Correct descisions 85.58%		

Table 1. Classification results for modern coins using edge based matching

The Dagobert system was used to sort several tons of coins and is able to meet the real-time conditions, i.e. to process 5 to 6 coins per second. Using the obverse and reverse face for the recognition task, approximately 85% of the material is either sorted into classes defined in the recognition pattern set, i.e. the set of valid coins, which contained around 1500 patterns of coin faces, or is correctly rejected. Random tests performed on classified sets of coins indicate that we seem to meet the goal of having less than 0.1% false classifications.

6.1.2 Edge Eigenspace based matching

We discuss results including rejection based on the a-posteriori probability $P(G_k|\Omega)$. A coin pattern Ω is accepted to be of class G_k if $P(G_k|\Omega) \geq t$, and rejected if $P(G_k|\Omega) < t$, where $t \in [0, 1]$ is the rejection threshold. The parameter t is used to tune the system towards the desired trade-off between false rejection and false acceptance. The trade-off between false acceptance rate (FAR) and false rejection rate (FRR) is an important performance measure in verification and recognition systems. False acceptance of invalid coins is measured by the

FAR, and false rejection for valid coins is measured by FRR. A classification method should maximize correct classification for valid coins and correct rejection for invalid coins. Apart from FAR and FRR the case of wrong classification of a valid coin is also an undesired event termed false classification rate (FCR).

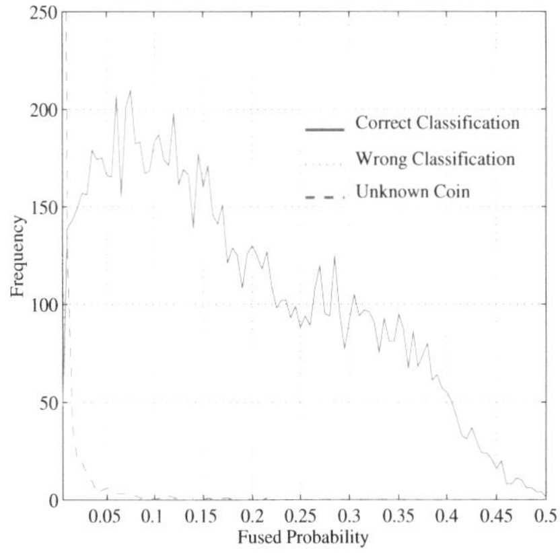

(a) Distribution with respect to fused classification result

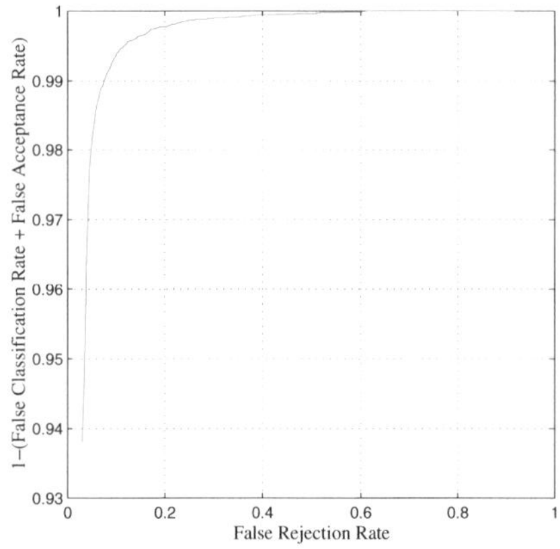

(b) Receiver operator curve

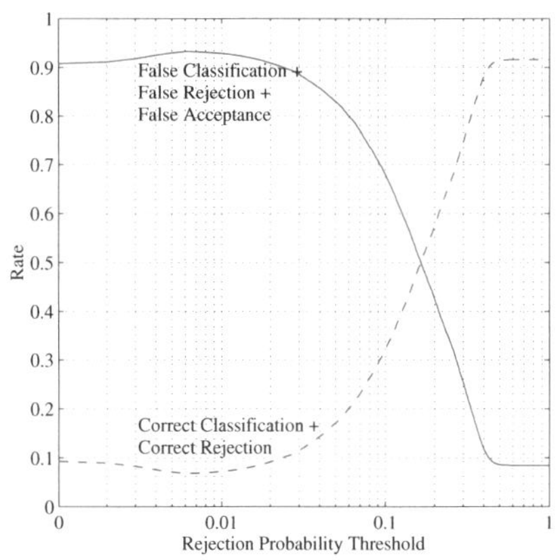

(c) Dependency of correct and false descision rates on rejection threshold

Fig. 10. Results for modern coin classification.

Figure 10 (a) shows the distribution of fused probabilities for correctly classified valid coins as the solid line. Incorrectly classified valid coins are shown by the dashed line. The fused probability distribution for invalid coins is represented by the dotted line. Selection of threshold t on governs FAR, FCR and FRR, e.g. increasing t reduces FAR and FCR and increases FRR. From a receiver operator characteristics (ROC) curve, as shown in Fig. 10 (b), the tradeoff between FCR plus FAR and FRR can be identified. An operating point, corresponding to a specific t, is found on the ROC curve, e.g. for perfect classification with FAR + FCR ≈ 0, a very high FRR has to be taken into account (i.e. FRR > 0.5). If the incorrect decisions FCR, FRR and FAR are equally weighted and we aim at minimization of the sum of false decisions FD=FCR+FAR+FAR. We find the optimum value for the rejection threshold t as the minimum of FD. This can be seen from Fig. 10 (c), in which the minimum of FD is found for t = 0.006. At the same time correct decisions, i.e. correct classification and correct rejection rates, are maximized.

Considering only valid coins, i.e. the 91.6% coins included in the 30 countries mentioned above, and using no rejection mechanism, correct classification was made for 98.27% of valid coins, which is close to the practical optimum of 98.88% mentioned in Section 5.1 With rejection at the chosen level of t=0.006, a percentage of correct classification of 94.54%, 0.53% false classification and 4.93% false rejection is achieved for valid coins. Considering only invalid coins, i.e. the 8.4% coins not included in the 30 countries mentioned above, and rejection at the chosen level of t=0.006 classification into any of the known coin classes happens for 20.47% of the unknown coins. Correct rejection of unknown coins is performed for 79.53% of invalid coins. Examining at the mixed sample, a correct decision, i.e. correct classification or rejection, was made for 93.23% of all coins. False decisions, i.e. either false classification, false rejection or false acceptance, took place for 6.77% of all coins. Table 2 summarizes the final results.

	Acceptance		Rejection
Valid coins 91.6%	Correct classification 86.64%	False classification 0.49%	False Rejection 4.52%
Invalid coins 8.4%	False acceptance 1.76%		Correct rejection 6.59%
All coins 100%	Correct descisions 92.23%		

Table 2. Classification results for modern coins using edge Eigenspace based matching.

6.2 Results for ancient coins

To evaluate our approach on coin data, we use an image database provided by the Fitzwilliam Museum, Cambridge, UK, which consists of 2400 images of 240 different ancient coins of the same class. Figure 1 (b) shows four of the coins contained in the data set. Each row shows the same coin acquired by different devices at varying conditions and different orientations. In particular, each coin side was acquired at three different angles of rotation using a scanner device and two acquisitions were made using a digital camera and varying illumination. At first sight, all coins bear the same characteristics. However, the coins shown in the different rows are produced by different dies. What makes this data set special and ideal to thoroughly test identification methods, is that all the coins are very similar. All the images are issued in the time of, or at least in the name of, Alexander the Great who came to power in Macedonia in 336 BCE and died as emperor in 323 BCE. Some of the coins are from much later and were minted in places around the Black Sea, in Egypt, in modern-day Turkey, Iran, etc. All coins follow the same basic standard: on the obverse side there is the head of Heracles in a lion-skin. The reverse side shows the god Zeus, seated left on a throne. Nevertheless, there is a huge range of detail in the minor variations that experts use to deduce the mint and date of the coin.

6.2.1 2D matching

It takes 0.006 seconds to compare two coins based on their shape description on a Intel Core 2 CPU with 2.5 GHz. Therefore, shape matching is suited as a preselection step to the less efficient matching based on local features which typically takes two orders of magnitude longer (Bay et al., 2006). The size of the preselection set is determined experimentally from Precision-Recall curves. Recall measures the ratio given by true positives divided by the sum of true positives and false negatives, i.e. $rec = TP/(TP + FN)$ and precision is given by $prec = TP/(TP + FP)$, where FP is the number of false positives. Figure 11 (a) shows plots of precision versus recall for the test set of 240 different images containing 10 images of each coin. Different settings of the shape matching weight parameter α show that a relatively large value of α, which directs the matching dissimilarity towards more local influence, performs best. In order to obtain a preselection set of moderate size and high quality, i.e. the coin in question should likely be contained, a high recall is aspired. This is obtained by selecting the set size corresponding to the sudden decrease in Fig. 11 (a). Figure 11 (b) shows that this sudden decrease in precision versus recall corresponds to a preselection set size of 9 to 10 images.

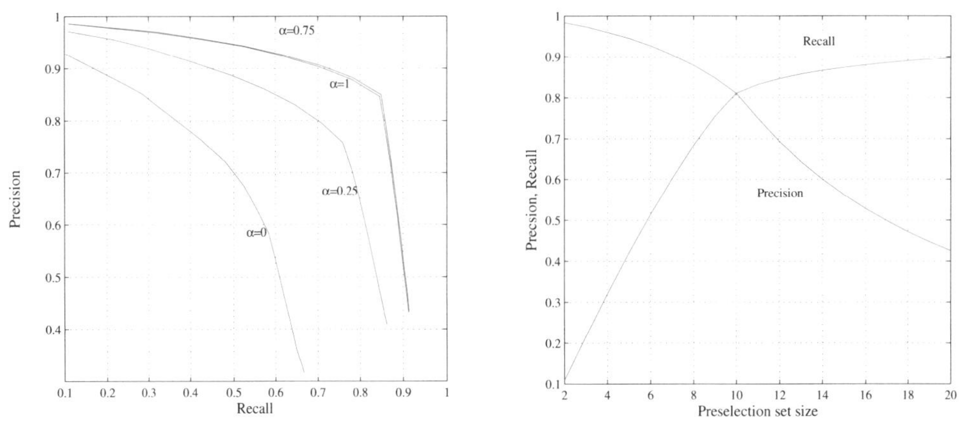

(a) Precision versus recall (b) Precision and recall versus preselection set size

Fig. 11. Results for ancient coin classification based on shape.

We combine shape and local descriptors to increase the identification rate. Preselection based on shape matching allows for the restriction of required comparisons for local features matching. As a result we achieve speed up of the identification process and higher accuracy rate. Since our shape descriptor is mirroring invariant, preselection can be performed either on the whole available coin data, i.e. the preselected set can contain images of the second coin side, or preselection can be performed on the relevant coin side directly.

As a conclusion the preselection size was set to 10. Therefore, for the experiments presented here, $P_{shape}(\mathcal{L}|A)$ is computed for the 10 images with lowest dissimilarity and $P_{local}(\mathcal{L}|X)$ for the same 10 images. The final decision is made according to the product rule given in Equ 24.

Table 3 shows the identification rates for the single descriptors and their combination with a leave-one-out evaluation scheme. The shape-based preselection of size 10 was performed accordingly to the given side of the test coin image. The DCSM alone gives an identification rate of 97.04% on the whole data set of 2400 images. For a preselection size of 10, there are only 13 cases (0.54%) where the correct coin is not contained in the preselected set. Consequently, local feature matching on the preselected set and fusion with the label probabilities from DCSM lead to an identification rate of 98.54%.

Descriptor	DCSM	SIFT	DCSM + SIFT
Accuracy	97.04%	71.77%	98.54%

Table 3. Identification rates derived from leave-one-out accuracy estimation.

6.2.2 3D extensions

Usually, a reference object, e.g. a cone, a square prism or a cylinder, is scanned and measured manually when the accuracy of the scanner needs to be calculated. After gathering all the dimensions, the values can be compared to the values determined from the 3D reconstruction. Additionally, scanner resolution evaluations can be made. Due to the fact that in our case the scanned object is small and both the surface and the shape of historical coins are not regular or flat, many dimensions cannot be measured precisely (e.g. coin profile details). Since we cannot provide the same accurate values for coins as we can provide for known objects, like cones or cylinders, our results will be based on a comparison between manually measured values from ancient coins and the values determined from the 3D model counterparts. As evaluation parameters, the maximal diameter and the volume of each coin are used.

The models are analyzed using Geomagic Studio, a commercial software for 3D data processing. The volumes of the original coins are calculated manually after computing the density by using the uplift of the coin in water and by measuring the weight of the coin. The compared diameter value represents the maximal existing value on the coin's surface. The maximal diameter from a real world coin is also determined manually. From a 3D model, the volume can be calculated using Geomagic Studio. The maximum diameter can be computed by segmenting one side of the coin and taking the largest distance between two border points. Because of the irregular shape of some coins, both the obverse and the reverse side of a coin must be taken into account.

In total, we scanned 22 coins: 14 ancient coins from the Roman era and 8 tornese silver coins from medieval age. Figure 12 (a) shows the volume of both the original ancient coins using the water volume calculation and their 3D model counterparts using Geomagic Studio. The maximum difference between manual and automatic measurements is 36.24 mm^3. The smallest difference between real-world data and the data gathered from 3D models is 0.57 mm^3. Figure 12 (b) shows the maximum diameter of both the real world manually measured one and the value calculated by using 3D models in Geomagic Studio. A maximum difference of 1.12 mm is measured, two coins have exactly the same diameter measured from 3D models and from real-world data. Table 4 shows maximum difference, minimum difference, and the mean variation coefficient of all volume and diameter measurements.

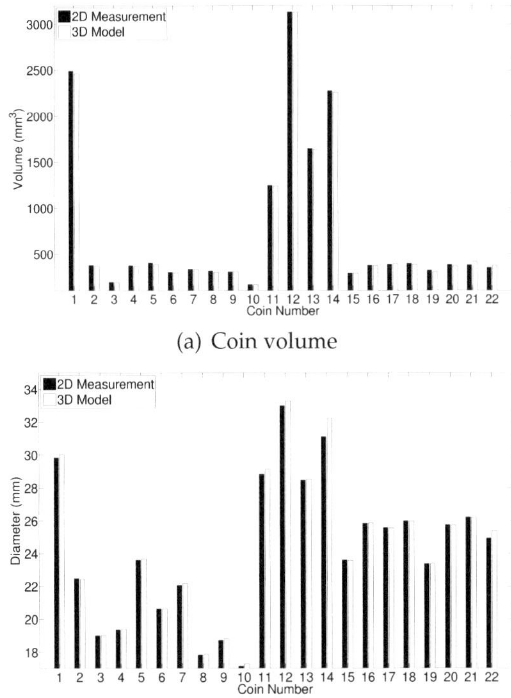

Fig. 12. Results for automatic 3D measurements and manual 2D measurements of ancient coin properties.

	Maximum difference	Minimum difference	Coefficient of variation
Volume	36.24 mm^3	0.57 mm^3	1.23%
Diameter	1.12 mm	0.00 mm	0.26%

Table 4. Maximum difference, minimum difference and coefficient of variation between automatic 3D measurements and manual 2D measurements of ancient coin properties.

7. Conclusion

We have presented methods for coin classification and identification applicable to coin collections comprising either a large number of coin classes, e.g. modern coins, or high intra-class variation, e.g. ancient coins.

Modern coins represent financial value only if the coins are sorted and returned to the respective national banks. A tunable system is required as national banks accept coins only if they are delivered with a high degree of purity. The rejection mechanism based on the probabilistic fusion result allows to adjust a tradeoff between rigorous classification (yielding high reliability against false acceptance but a higher rate of false rejections) versus tolerant classification (yielding more false acceptances but fewer false rejections). Coin class probabilities for both coin sides are combined through Bayesian fusion including a rejection mechanism. Correct decision into one of the 932 different coin classes and the rejection class, i.e. correct classification or rejection, was achieved for 93.23% of coins in a test sample containing 11 949 coins. False decisions, i.e. either false classification, false rejection or false acceptance, were obtained for 6.77% of the test coins.

In order to facilitate prevention and repression of illicit trade of stolen ancient coins technologies aimed at allowing permanent identification and traceability of coins become of interest. Since every individual coin has signs, caused by minting techniques for pre-industrial ones or by use-wear for more recent ones, that make it unique and recognizable to an expert's eye, traceability of pre-industrial coins can make use of visual inspection. We presented an approach for object identification based on the combination of shape and local descriptors and applied it to the task of ancient coins identification. Shape matching was used to match coin edges whereas the die of the coin was matched by means of local features. From the output of each of these two methods individual coin label probabilities were estimated and finally fused. On a data set of 2400 coin images the combination of shape and local features outperform the accuracy rate of the single features and achieved an identification rate of 98.83%.

The results for classification of modern coins and identification of ancient coins are regarded to be almost perfect. Due to large intra-class variance, the classification of ancient coins is still a challenging task, especially if attempted from single 2D images. Additional information, e.g. from 3D measurements, or complementary information, e.g. textual descriptions, is supposed to improve the classification task for ancient coins significantly.

8. Acknowledgements

The research was funded by the Austrian Science Fund (FWF): TRP140-N23-2010. The authors would also like to thank Dr. Mark Blackburn†(Fitzwilliam Museum, UK) for providing images for 2D image analysis and Mario Schlapke (Thüringisches Landesamt für Denkmalpflege und Archäologie, Weimar, Germany) for providing the coins for 3D scanning.

9. References

Akca, D., Gruen, B., Breuckmann, B. & Lahanier, C. (2007). High definition 3D-scanning of arts objects and paintings, *Optical 3-D Measurement Techniques VIII*, Vol. 2, pp. 50–58.

Arandjelović, O. (2010). Automatic attribution of ancient roman imperial coins, *Proc. of Conference on Computer Vision Pattern Recognition*, pp. 1728–1734.

Bay, H., Tuytelaars, T. & Gool, L. V. (2006). SURF: Speeded up robust features, *Proc. of Europ. Conf. on Comput. Vision*, Vol. 3951/2006 of *LNCS*, Springer, pp. 404–417.

Besl, P. & McKay, N. (1992). A method for registration of 3D shapes, *IEEE Trans. Patt. Anal. Mach. Intell.* 14(2): 239–256.

Bischof, H., Wildenauer, H. & Leonardis, A. (2001). Illumination insensitive eigenspaces, *Proc. of International Conference on Computer Vision*, pp. 233–238.

Canny, J. (1986). A computational approach to edge detection, *IEEE Trans. Patt. Anal. Mach. Intell.* 8(6): 679–698.

Chen, Y. & Medioni, G. (1992). Object modeling by registration of multiple range images, *Image and Vision Computing* 10(3): 145–155.

Cooley, J. W. & Tukey, J. W. (1965). An algorithm for the machine calculation of complex fourier series, *Math. Comput.* 19: 297–301.

Davidsson, P. (1996). Coin classification using a novel technique for learning characteristic decision trees by controlling the degree of generalization, *Proc. Conf. Industrial & Engineering Appl. of Artif. Intell. & Expert Syst.*, pp. 403–412.

Duda, R. & Hart, P. E. (1972). Use of the hough transformation to detect lines and curves in pictures, *Comm. ACM* 15: 11–15.

Fisher, N. (1995). *Statistical analysis of circular data*, Cambridge University Press, chapter 2: Descriptive methods, pp. 15–37.

Fukumi, M., Omatu, S., Takeda, F. & Kosaka, T. (1992). Rotation-invariant neural pattern recognition system with application to coin recognition, *IEEE Trans. Neural Netw.* 3: 272–279.

Fürst, M., Kronreif, G., Wögerer, C., Rubik, M., Holländer, I. & Penz, H. (2003). Development of a mechatronic device for high speed coin sorting, *Proc. Conf. Industrial Technology*, Vol. 1, pp. 185–189.

Hartley, R. & Zisserman, A. (2003). *Multiple View Geometry in Computer Vision*, Cambridge University Press.

Hibari, E. & Arikawa, J. (2001). Coin discriminating apparatus. European Patent EP1077434.

Hödlmoser, M., Zambanini, S., Kampel, M. & Schlapke, M. (2010). Evaluation of historical 3D coin models, *Proc. Conf. Computer Appl. and Quantitative Methods in Archaeology*.

Hoßfeld, M., Chu, W., Adameck, M. & Eich, M. (2006). Fast fast 3D-vision system to classify metallic coins by their embossed topography, *Elec. Let. on Comp. Vis. and Image Anal.* 5(4): 47–63.

Hu, M.-K. (1962). Visual pattern recognition by moment invariants, *IRE Transactions on Information Theory* 8: 179–187.

Huber-Mörk, R., Zaharieva, M. & Czedik-Eysenberg, H. (2008). Numismatic object identification using fusion of shape and local descriptors, *Proc. Symp. on Visual Computing*, pp. 368–379.

Huber-Mörk, R., Zambanini, S., Zaharieva, M. & Kampel, M. (2010). Identification of ancient coins based on fusion of shape and local features, *Machine Vision and Applications* (in press, published online July 11, 2010).

Huber, R., Ramoser, H., Mayer, K., Penz, H. & Rubik, M. (2005). Classification of coins using an Eigenspace approach, *Pattern Recogn. Lett.* 26(1): 61–75.

Kampel, M., Huber-Mörk, R. & Zaharieva, M. (2009). Image-based retrieval and identification of ancient coins, *IEEE Intell. Syst.* 24(2): 26–34.

Kampel, M. & Zambanini, S. (2008). Coin data acquisition for image recognition, *Proc. Conf. Computer Applications and Quantitative Methods in Archaeology*.

Kittler, J., Hatef, M., Duin, R. & Matas, J. (1998). On combining classifiers, *IEEE Trans. Patt. Anal. Mach. Intell.* 20(3): 226–239.

Kurita, T., Hotta, K. & Mishima, T. (1998). Scale and rotation invariant recognition method using higher-order local autocorrelation features of log-polar images, *Proc. Asian Conf. Comput. Vis.*, Vol. II, pp. 89–96.

Leonardis, A., Bischof, H. & Maver, J. (2002). Multiple eigenspaces, *Pattern Recognition* 35(11): 2613Ű2627.

Lewis, J. (1995). Fast normalized cross-correlation, *Proc. of Vision Interface*, pp. 120–123.

Lowe, D. G. (2004). Distinctive image features from scale-invariant keypoints, *Int. J. of Comput. Vision* 60(2): 91–110.

Marr, D. & Hildreth, E. (1980). Theory of edge detection, *Proc. of the Royal Society of London* B-207: 187–217.

Murase, H. & Nayar, S. (1994). Illumination planning for object recognition using parametric eigenspaces, *IEEE Trans. Patt. Anal. Mach. Intell.* 16(12): 1219–1227.

Neubarth, S., Gerrity, D., Waechter, M., Everhart, D. & Phillips, A. (1998). Coin discrimination apparatus. Canadian Patent CA2426293.

Nölle, M. & Hanbury, A. (2006). MUSCLE Coin Images Seibersdorf (CIS) Benchmark Competition 2006, *IAPR Newsletter* 28(2): 18–19.

Nölle, M., Penz, H., Rubik, M., Mayer, K. J., Holländer, I. & Granec, R. (2003). Dagobert – a new coin recognition and sorting system, *Proc of Int. Conf. on Digital Image Computing – Techniques and Applications*, pp. 329–338.

Nölle, M., Rubik, M. & Hanbury, A. (2006). Results of the muscle CIS coin competition 2006, *Proc. of the Muscle CIS Coin Competition Workshop*, Berlin, Germany.

Onodera, A. & M., S. (2002). Coin discrimination method and device. United States Patent US2002005329.

Pan, V. & Chen, Z. (1999). The complexity of the matrix eigenproblem, *Proc. of Annual ACM Symposium on Theory of Computing*, Atlanta, GA, USA, pp. 507–516.

Reisert, M., Ronneberger, O. & Burkhardt, H. (2006). An efficient gradient based registration technique for coin recognition, *Proc. Muscle CIS Coin Competition Workshop*, pp. 19–31.

Reisert, M., Ronneberger, O. & Burkhardt, H. (2007). A fast and reliable coin recognition system, *Proc. of DAGM*, pp. 415–424.

Rothwell, C., Mundy, J., Hoffman, W. & Nguyen, V. (1995). Driving vision by topology, *Proc. of International Symposium on Computer Vision*, pp. 395Ű–400.

Ruisz, J., Biber, J. & Loipetsberger, M. (2007). Quality evaluation in resistance spot welding by analysing the weld fingerprint on metal bands by computer vision, *Int. J. of Adv. Manuf. Tech.* 33(9-10): 952–960.

Sezgin, M. & Sankur, B. (2004). Survey over image thresholding techniques and quantitative performance evaluation, *J. Electron. Imaging* 13(1): 146–165.

Shah, G., Pester, A. & Stern, C. (1986). Low power coin discrimination apparatus. Canadian Patent CA1336782.

Shi, X. & Manduchi, R. (2003). A study on Bayes feature fusion for image classification, *Proc. Conf. Comput. Vis. Patt. Recogn. Workshop*, pp. 95–103.

Sirovich, L. & Kirby, M. (1987). Low-dimensional procedure for the characterization of human faces, *Journal of the Optical Society of America A* 4: 519–524.

Sonka, M., Hlavac, V. & Boyle, R. (1998). *Image Processing, Analysis, and Machine Vision*, 2nd edn, PWS - an Imprint of Brooks and Cole Publishing.

Stoykova, E., Alatan, A., Benzie, P., Grammalidis, N., Malassiotis, S., Ostermann, J., Piekh, S., Sainov, V., Theobalt, C. & Thevar, T. (2007). 3-D time-varying scene capture technologies - A survey, *IEEE Trans. Circuits and Systems for Video Tech.* 17(11): 1568–1586.

Torres-Mendez, L., Ruiz-Suarez, J., Sucar, L. & Gomez, G. (2000). Translation, rotation, and scale-invariant object recognition, *IEEE Trans. Syst., Man and Cybern.* 30(1): 125–130.

Tsuji, K. & Takahashi, M. (1997). Coin discriminating apparatus. European Patent EP0798669.

Turk, M. & Pentland, A. (1991). Eigenfaces for recognition, *J. Cogn. Neurosci.* 3(1): 71–86.

Uenohara, M. & Kanade, T. (1997). Use of Fourier and Karhunen-Loeve decomposition for fast pattern matching with a large set of templates, *IEEE Trans. Patt. Anal. Mach. Inell.* 19(8): 891–898.

Uenohara, M. & Kanade, T. (1998). Optimal approximation of uniformly rotated images: Relationship between Karhunen-Loeve expansion and discrete cosine transform, *IEEE Trans. Image Proc.* 7(1): 116–119.

Van Der Maaten, L. & Postma, E. (2006). Towards automatic coin classification, *Proc. of Conf. on Electronic Imaging and the Visual Arts*, Vienna, Austria, pp. 19–26.

Vassilas, N. & Skourlas, C. (2006). Content-based coin retrieval using invariant features and self-organizing maps, *Proc. of Int. Conf. on Artif. Neur. Netw.*, pp. 113–122.

Venkatesh, B., Palanivel, S. & Yegnanarayana, B. (2002). Face detection and recognition in an image sequence using eigenedginess, *Proc. Indian Conf. Vis., Graph. Image Proc.*

Yilmaz, A. & Gökmen, M. (2000). Eigenhills vs. eigenface and eigenedge, *Proc. of International Conference on Pattern Recognition*, Vol. 2, pp. 827–830.

Zaharieva, M., Huber-Mörk, R., Nölle, M. & Kampel, M. (2007). On ancient coin classification, *Proc. of Int. Symp. on Virtual Reality, Archaeology and Cultural Heritage*, pp. 55–62.

Zambanini, S. & Kampel, M. (2008). Segmentation of ancient coins based on local entropy and gray value range, *Proc. Comput. Vis. Winter Workshop*, pp. 9–16.

Zambanini, S. & Kampel, M. (2009). Robust automatic segmentation of ancient coins, *Proc. Conf. on Comp. Vision Theory and Appl.*, Vol. 2, pp. 273–276.

Zambanini, S., Schlapke, M., Kampel, M. & Müller, A. (2009). Historical coins in 3D: Acquisition and numismatic applications, *Proc. Symp. Virtual Reality, Archaeology and Cultural Heritage*, pp. 49–52.

8

Non-Rigid Objects Recognition: Automatic Human Action Recognition in Video Sequences

Mehrez Abdellaoui[1], Ali Douik[1] and Kamel Besbes[2]
[1]National Engineering School of Monastir,
[2]Faculty of Sciences of Monastir,
Tunisia

1. Introduction

Non-rigid objects recognition is an important problem in video analysis and understanding. It is nevertheless a challenging task to achieve due to the properties carried out by the non-rigid objects, and is more complicated by camera motion as well as background variation. Human body recognition in video sequences is the best application of the non-rigid objects recognition due to the large capacities of the human body in doing actions and poses. These difficulties prohibit practical attempts toward conceiving a robust global model for each action class. Human body recognition is highly interesting for a variety of applications: detecting relevant activities in surveillance video, summarizing and indexing video sequences. It relies, however, on the interpretation of the body movements and classifies them in different events.

A considerable amount of previous work has addressed the question of human action categorization and motion analysis. One line of work is based on the computation of correlation between volumes of video data (Efros et al., 2003). Another popular approach is to track body parts at first and then uses the obtained motion trajectories to perform action recognition (Ramanan & Forsyth, 2004). The robustness of the approach is highly dependent on the tracking system. Alternatively, researchers have considered the analysis of human actions by looking at video sequences as space-time intensity volumes (Bobick & Davis, 2001). Some researchers have also explored unsupervised methods for motion analysis such as hierarchical dynamic Bayesian network model (Hoey, 2001; Zhong et al., 2004). Another approach uses a video representation based on spatiotemporal interest points (STIPs). In spite of the existence of a fairly large variety of methods to extract interest points (IPs) from static images Harris corner detector (Harris & Stephens, 1988), Scale invariant feature transform (Lowe, 1999), Salient regions (Kadir & Brady, 2003) …, less work has been done on STIPs detection in videos. In 2005, Laptev (Laptev, 2005) present a STIPs detector based on the idea of the Harris IPs operators. They detect local structures in space-time where the image values have significant local variations in space and time dimension. IPs extracted with such methods had been used as features for human action classification. These points are particularly interesting because they focus the initial information contained in any image in a few specific points. The integration of the time component can perform filtering on the IP and keep only those who also have a temporal discontinuity.

We propose in this chapter a motion analysis and classification approach to learn and recognize human actions in video, taking advantage of the robustness of STIPs and the unsupervised learning approaches. Experimental results are validated on KTH human action database (Schuldt et al., 2004), and ATSI Human Action Database (see Figure 1). Results are compared to recent works on the human motion analysis and recognition.

Fig. 1. Samples from the KTH human action database

2. Spatio-temporal interest points

2.1 Presentation

Interest Points in a bitmap image are defined as pixels with maximum variations of the intensity in the local neighbourhood. These pixels represent corners, intersections, isolated points and specific points on image texture. This definition can describe the Spatio-temporal Interest Points (STIPs) when considering a video sequence instead of the image. Consequently, we deduce that STIPs can be defined as pixels with significant changes in space and time. It can represent irregular movements of the human body such as bending elbows or knees, moving limbs. Whereas, uniform movement such as moving a hard object does not generate any STIP. Video sequences are represented as a 3D function over two spatial dimensions (x, y) and one temporal dimension t. Many detectors can be used such as: Laptev et al. detector (Laptev & Lindeberg, 2004); Dollàr et al. detector (Dollár et al., 2005); FAST-3D detector (Koelstra et al., 2009); and Oikonomopoulos et al. detector (Oikonomopoulos et al., 2006).

2.2 Laptev et al. detector

The Laptev et al. theory (Laptev & Lindeberg, 2004) is based on the Harris operator (Harris & Stephens, 1988) that had shown good performances interest points detection in static images. The operator extension over the spatiotemporal domain makes the spatio-temporal interest points detection possible. This extension consists of a search of points that maximize the local variation of image values simultaneously over the spatial dimensions and the temporal dimension. According to Laptev et al., a video sequence can be represented as a function $f: R^2 \times R \rightarrow R$ over two spatial dimensions (x, y) and one temporal dimension t. The Local space time features are defined as 3D blocks of the sequence containing variations in space and time.

The scale-space representation $L: R^2 \times R \times R_+^2 \mapsto R$ is generated by the convolution of f with a separable Gaussian kernel g (p ; Σ) (1). Where p is spatiotemporal position vector $p=(x,y,t)^T$, the parameters σ^2 and τ^2 of the covariance matrix correspond to the spatial and temporal scale parameters respectively and define spatiotemporal extension of the neighbourhoods.

$$g(p;\Sigma)=\frac{1}{\sqrt{(2\pi)^3 \det(\Sigma)}} e^{-\frac{(p^T \Sigma^{-1} p)}{2}} \quad \text{and} \quad \Sigma=\begin{pmatrix} \sigma^2 & 0 & 0 \\ 0 & \sigma^2 & 0 \\ 0 & 0 & \tau^2 \end{pmatrix} \tag{1}$$

A spatiotemporal second-moment matrix (2) is defined in terms of spatiotemporal gradients and weighted with a Gaussian window function.

$$\begin{aligned} \mu(\cdot;\Sigma) &= g(\cdot;\Sigma) * \left(\nabla L(\cdot;\Sigma)(\nabla L(\cdot;\Sigma))^T \right) \\ &= g(\cdot;\Sigma) * \begin{pmatrix} L_x^2 & L_x L_y & L_x L_t \\ L_x L_y & L_y^2 & L_y L_t \\ L_x L_t & L_y L_t & L_t^2 \end{pmatrix} \end{aligned} \tag{2}$$

The spatiotemporal second-moment matrix μ, considered also as a structure tensor, is interpreted in terms of eigen values. This fact makes the distinguishing of image structures possible with variations over one, two and three dimensions. Three-dimensional variation of f corresponds to image points with non-constant motion. Such points can be detected by maximizing the three eigen values λ1, λ2, λ3 of μ over space and time.

STIP detection is realized by the extension of the Harris operator H into the spatiotemporal domain (3). Detection is based on points with high eigen values.

$$H=\det(\mu)-k \cdot \text{trace}^3(\mu)=\lambda_1 \cdot \lambda_2 \cdot \lambda_3 - k \cdot (\lambda_1+\lambda_2+\lambda_3)^3 \tag{3}$$

Local maxima of H correspond to points with high values λ1, λ2, λ3 (λ1 ≤ λ2 ≤ λ3). H can be written as equation (4), where α = λ2/λ1 and β = λ3/λ1.

$$H=\lambda_1^3 \left(\alpha\beta - k(1+\alpha+\beta)^3 \right) \tag{4}$$

From the requirement H ≥ 0, we get the condition represented by (5).

$$k \le \alpha\beta / (1+\alpha+\beta)^3 \tag{5}$$

And it follows that for perfectly isotropic image structures ($\alpha = \beta = 1$), k assumes its maximum possible value kmax = 1/27. For sufficiently large values of k ≤ kmax, positive local maxima of H will correspond to space-time points with similar eigen values $\lambda 1$, $\lambda 2$, $\lambda 3$. Consequently, such points indicate locations of image structures with high spatiotemporal variation and can be considered as positions of local spatiotemporal features. As k in (3) only controls the local shape of image structures and not their amplitude, the method for local features detection is invariant with respect to the affine variation of image brightness.

2.3 Dollàr et al. detector

Compared to Laptev detector, Dollàr et al. detector (Dollàr et al., 2005) it produces dense features that can significantly improve the recognition performance in most cases. It uses two separate filters in spatial and temporal directions: 2-D Gaussian filter in space components and 1-D Gabor filter in time component.

A response function of the form (6) is obtained, where g is the 2D Gaussian kernel applied along the spatial dimensions of the video and h_{ev} (7) and h_{od} (8) are a quadrature pair of 1D Gabor filters applied in the temporal dimension.

$$R = (I * g * h_{ev})^2 + (I * g * h_{od})^2 \tag{6}$$

$$h_{ev}(t; \tau, \omega) = -\cos(2\pi t\omega)\ e^{-t^2/\tau^2} \tag{7}$$

$$h_{od}(t; \tau, \omega) = -\sin(2\pi t\omega)\ e^{-t^2/\tau^2} \tag{8}$$

The detector responds best to complex motions made by regions that are distinguishable spatially, including spatio-temporal corners, but not to pure translational motion or motions involving areas that are not distinct in space. Local maxima of the response function R are selected as interest points, and cuboids are extracted, which are the windowed pixel values around the interest point in the spatial and temporal dimensions.

2.4 The FAST-3D detector

The FAST-3D spatio-temporal detector, developed by (Koelstra et al., 2009), is inspired from the FAST detector (Features from Accelerated Segment Test detector). Instead of using a circle around each pixel (x, y, t), Koelstra et al considered the set C of the 26 directly neighbouring pixels to (x, y, t) in a 3D space-time neighbourhood. STIPs detection is correctly done even when videos are transformed by zoom, rotation or MPEG compression.

2.5 Laptev detector Implementation

The algorithm was applied to sequences of different types of video sequences for detecting the STIP. The application of the algorithm is made through two executable files "stipdet.exe" and "stipshow.exe". The first file corresponds to the detection algorithm STIP and the second for showing the detected STIPs on the sequences.

The implementation of the first program generates a text file with space-time coordinates of the tracks (x, y, t). The second program displays STIPs detected on the images of the video sequence. Video sequences are processed using Matlab with a single variable representation. The three-dimensional tensors represent properly video sequences. Figure 2 shows the detected STIPs in different video frames' samples from the KTH human action database. The three components are x (height) y (widths) and t (time axis). This representation makes possible the STIPs neighborhood search in space-time domain.

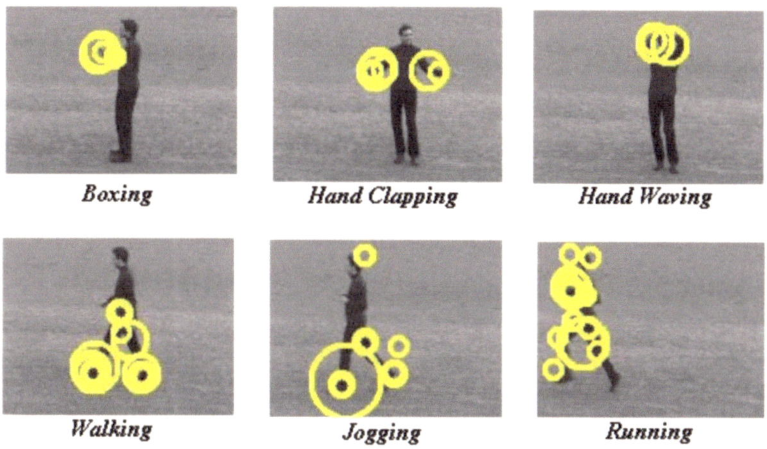

Fig. 2. Detected STIPs in different samples from the KTH human action database

Among all detected STIPs from video sequences, there are usually motion noises from the non uniform background that do not contribute to the action motion. In fact, those points normally make the modeling computation much harder and in some cases might completely distract the core parts of the action. In order to filter out these irrelevant elements, we consider only STIPs that coincide with the dilated shape of the human body.

The tensor elements contain gray level values of pixels in each frame of the video sequence. The criteria developed by Laptev et al. are applied on tensors and STIPs detected are pixels with maximum values in local neighborhoods and this by maximizing the criterion H. Figure 3 shows the structure of the tensor with the three axes.

The STIP detected by the Laptev algorithm have interesting properties including their stability to geometric transformations. Other robustness properties of the STIPs can be determined. These properties are related to noise from video sequences, such as impulse noise, contrast changes, quick movement of the camera and the MPEG compression effects. Several studies have been done in this area. Lejeune-Simac et al. (Lejeune-Simac et al., 2010) present a comprehensive study of the robustness of the detector STIPs various effects of noise from video sequences.

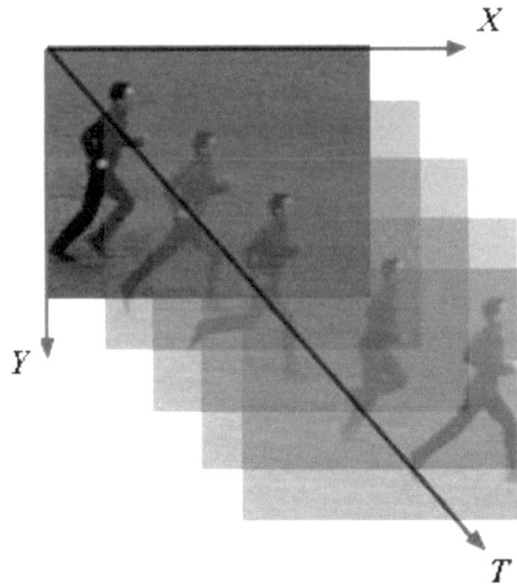

Fig. 3. Reference axes (x,y,t) representation on a video sequence from KTH human action database

3. Motion analysis approach

To analyse motion we defined different parameters based on STIP detection using Laptev detector. The first one calculates the number of STIP in the sequence, whereas the second is the "activity" function that evaluates the evolution of STIP during the sequence and the third parameter analyses the position of STIP points comparing to reference one associated to the body in movement.

3.1 Number of STIPs in a sequence

Human body movements can be differentiated by a quantitative survey on STIPs detected. Thus, an algorithm was developed with a purpose to calculate STIPs number for each sequence from different human body motion databases. This algorithm leads to interesting results. Indeed, STIPs number is high for fast movements like (running, jogging, jumping). Other movements made only by the arms (boxing, hand clapping or hand waving) lead to low STIPs number. Table 1 shows the evolution of the STIPs average number in 100 frames sequences (4 seconds of video) for each movement class. The algorithm was tested on 450 sequences from KTH database (75 for each movement).

Movement	STIPs average number per 100 frames
Running	685
Jogging	463,33
Walking	313,33
Hand waving	145
Hand clapping	114
Boxing	82

Table 1. Number of STIPs evolution for KTH human action database.

These statistics show that STIPs number depends directly of the movement realized. Indeed, running and jumping movements have high STIPs number however boxing and hand waving have a low STIPs number. Therefore we conclude that STIPs number in a sequence is an important parameter in human movements' recognition. To emphasize this study we present in the following section the evolution of STIPs in time by the "Activity" function.

3.2 Activity function

Evolution of the STIPs number in a sequence is an important factor in human motion recognition. To synthesize this criterion we have used the "Activity" function. This function was defined by Laganière et al. (Laganière et al., 2008) as the number of pixels that are modified between two consecutive frames in a video sequence. Hence, frames that correspond to local maxima of the "Activity" function are the scenes of major movements. We have changed the "Activity" to fit our research, so we defined it as STIPs number in each frame of the sequence. The evolution of this number can lead us to recognize the type of movement made by detecting its local maxima which are the locations of large amounts of movement and its distribution that indicates the positions of these quantities in time scale. In Figure 4, we present the activity function applied to samples of sequences from KTH database.

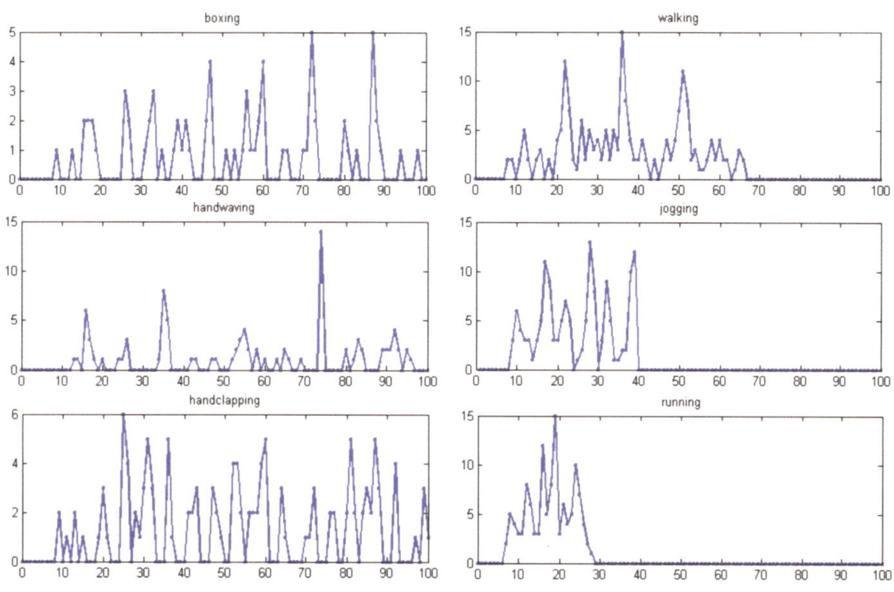

Fig. 4. Application of the Activity function on samples from KTH human action database.

The curves in Figure 4 have repetitive peaks. These peaks are local maxima of the activity function and can be regarded as major movement's events in each class. From this analysis we can extract important information about the class of the movement performed. The curves obtained are so noised. This is caused by non significant STIPs detected and which appear between local maxima. To resolve this problem we applied a smoothing algorithm on curves to accentuate the peaks and eliminate the STIPs values between the local maxima. The smoothing was done on segments of frames by adding the STIPs detected in an interval [n-2, n+2] where n is the time of the local maxima of the STIPs. Figure 5 shows the application of smoothing algorithm on the activity function curves for samples from the KTH human action database.

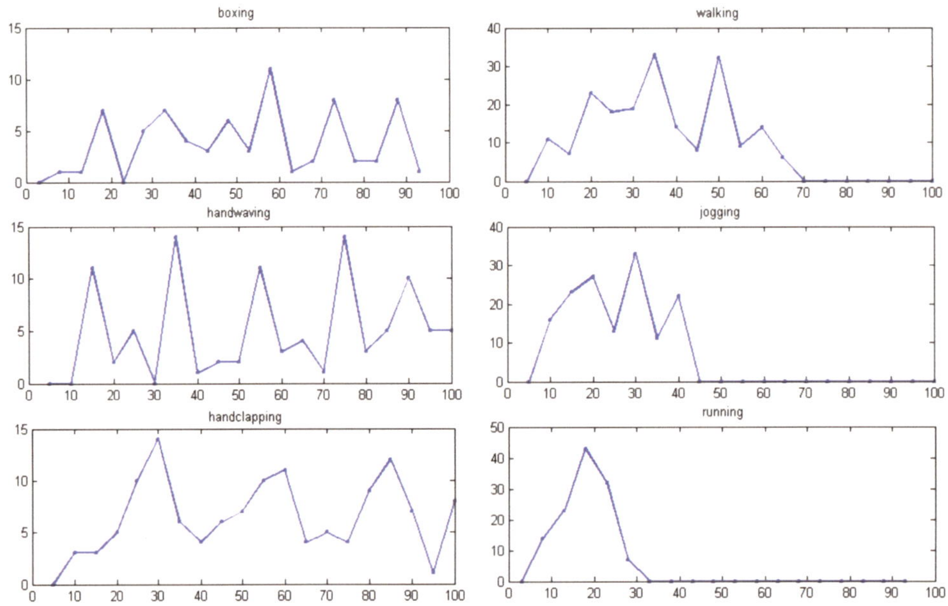

Fig. 5. Application of the smoothing algorithm on the activity function curves for samples from the KTH human action database.

We note that smoothing reduces the activity function noise and increases the local maxima values of the curves. To detect the locations of local maxima, a Gaussian model is fitted to the activity function. This model leads to the determination of the number of the local maxima and their time in a sequence. In addition, it contributes for motion recognition when considering the parameters of the used Gaussian model in the classification algorithm.

The value of the global maximum is deduced to detect movement with only one global maximum. Figure 6 shows the application of the Gaussian model to activity function on sequences taken from the KTH human action database (from left to right and row-wise of the Figure we have the actions of, boxing, walking, hands waving, jogging, hands clapping and running).

In Table 2, the number of local maxima is shown, their mean value and the global maximum value for different action classes taken from the KTH human action database. We note that the number of local maxima is the number of repetitions in a human movement such as walking or hand clapping. For fast movements such as running the smoothing algorithm reduces the number local maxima to one and extracts a single global maximum. The local maxima average value is a significant parameter in the classification of human movements. We note that the movements made only by arms such as: Boxing, Hand waving and Hand clapping have values lower than those achieved by the whole body such as: Running, Jogging and Walking. The global maximum can contribute to the classification since its values are different from one to another class of motion.

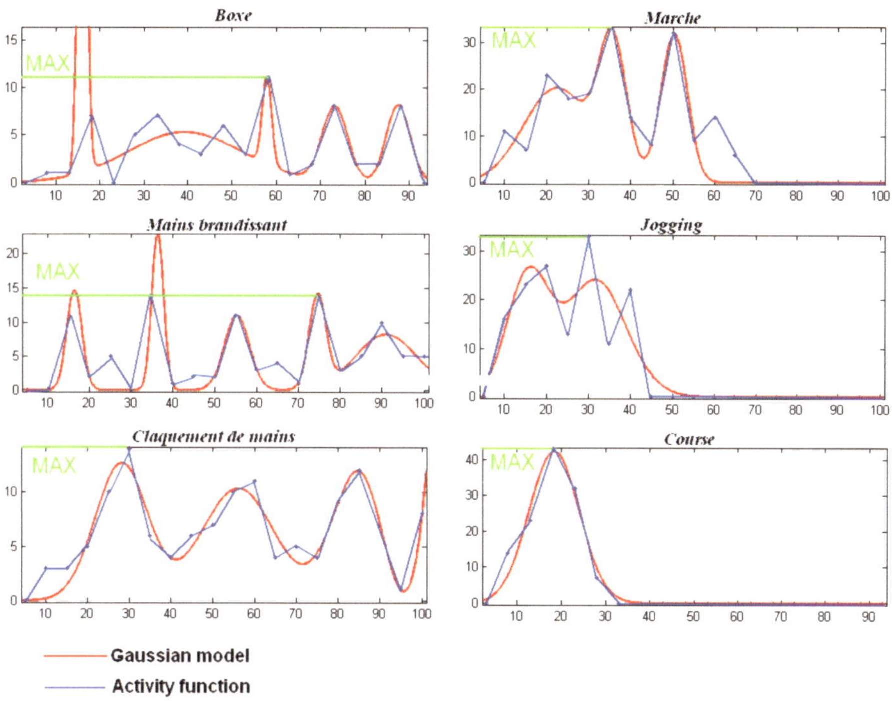

Fig. 6. Application of the Gaussian model to activity function on sequences taken from the KTH human action database

Action	Local maxima number	Local maxima mean value	Global maximum value
Running	1	42	43
Jogging	2	29	33
Walking	3	28	33
Hand waving	5	12	14
Hand clapping	3	12,33	14
Boxing	5	7,4	11

Table 2. Number of local maxima, mean value and the global maximum value for different action classes taken from the KTH human action database

The use of the activity function allows the tracking of the STIPs number in time. Its evolution has been modeled by a Gaussian model to extract its local maxima. This study can contribute to human motion recognition. Another important feature can be used. It consists on the spatiotemporal boxes associated to human body parts.

3.3 Spatiotemporal boxes

STIPs are the most significant motion locations in video sequences. Most of the STIPs are located at the most valuable human body parts such as knees, elbow joints, the moving limbs. Boxes containing STIPs called as "Spatiotemporal Boxes" can be considered as important information to describe the actions and to differentiate between them. Spatiotemporal boxes containing detected STIPs are the most shining regions to describe human motion. The boxes size can be effective information to differentiate between motion done only by hands and the full body motion (see Figure 7).

For all STIPs belonging to the same image, we determine their spatial coordinates (x1, y1) (x2, y2), ..., (xn, yn) in the image reference. The spatiotemporal boxes can be described by a rectangle between points (x_{Left}, y_{Top}) and (X_{Right}, y_{Bottom}) these coordinates are determined by reference to the following equations.

$$\begin{aligned} x_{Left} &= \min(x_1, x_2, ..., x_n) - r \\ y_{Top} &= \min(y_1, y_2, ..., y_n) - r \\ x_{Right} &= \max(x_1, x_2, ..., x_n) + r \\ x_{Bottom} &= \max(y_1, y_2, ..., y_n) + r \end{aligned} \tag{9}$$

r is the extension radius of the spatiotemporal boxes. Figure 7 shows spatiotemporal boxes detected on images taken from the KTH human action database.

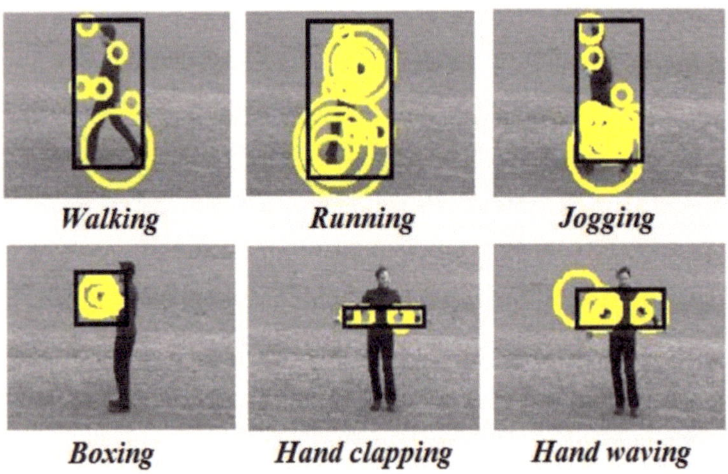

Fig. 7. Spatiotemporal boxes detected on images taken from the KTH human action database

Considering motion done using full body, we classified STIPs points in two parts, High body part STIPs (H-STIP) and Low body part STIPs (L-STIP). To achieve this classification we detected the centroid of the body silhouette in all frames of the sequence. Points located above centroid are classified in H-STIP and points below centroid are classified in L-STIP as shown in Figure 8.

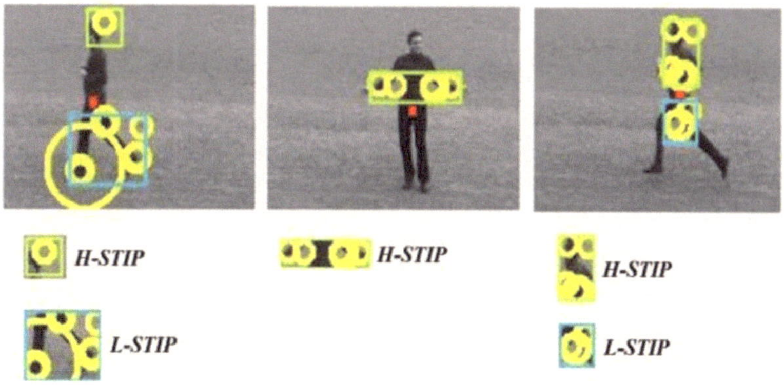

Fig. 8. Classification of H-STIP and L-STIP for action samples from KTH human action database

The evolution of H-STIP and L-STIP in time (see Figure 9) compared to centroid can be discriminative information to classify actions. In fact, actions containing H-STIP and L-STIP are Running, Jogging and Walking. On the other side, Boxing, Hand waving and Hand clapping contain only points of H-STIP type.

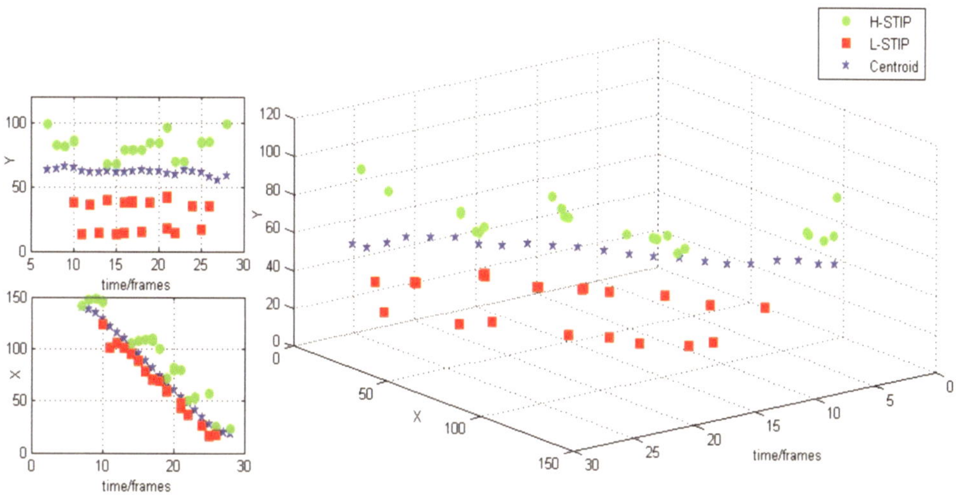

Fig. 9. An illustration of the evolution of H-STIP, L-STIP and Centroid in time for running action

4. Motion classification

To obtain fair judgement of the performances of the proposed approach, we compare our results with other human action recognition approaches using the same database. The performance of any approach is evaluated by measuring the accuracy of motion classification using a specified algorithm. Many algorithms can be used. The more used in will be described in the following subsections.

4.1 Probabilistic latent semantic analysis (pLSA)

It is a popular unsupervised method for learning object categories from interest point features and it was implemented based on Niebles et al. (Niebles et al., 2008). Histogram features of training or testing samples are concatenated to form a co-occurrence matrix which is an input of the pLSA algorithm.

4.2 Support Vector Machines (SVM)

Support Vector Machines (SVM) is one of the most popular classifier which has recently gained popularity within visual pattern recognition. In spatial recognition, local features have recently been combined with SVM in a robust classification approach. In a similar manner, Schuldt et al. (Schuldt et al., 2004) explored the combination of local space-time features and SVM and apply the resulting approach to the recognition of human actions.

4.3 Proposed algorithm

The classification algorithm is based on an unsupervised clustering algorithm K-MEANS The choice of this method is justified by the low running time and a priori knowledge of the number of classes K. The algorithm is based on a parameter vector V based on the criteria mentioned in previous sections. Table 3 shows the ranking of the parameters belonging to the vector V from the most to least significant paarameter.

Parameter	Feature
P1	Spatiotemporal box area
P2	Spatiotemporal box area/ Body bounding box area
P3	H-STIP existence (1 or 0)
P4	L-STIP existence (1 or 0)
P5	Distance between the spatiotemporal box centroid and the bounding box centroid
P6	STIPs Number /100 frames
P7	Global maximum value
P8	Local maxima number
P9	Mean value of local maxima
P10	Average value of the activity function variance
P11	Slope of the curve x=f(t) of the centroid

Table 3. List of parameters belonging to the vector V

The classification of movements is made in a hierarchical manner. Indeed a first algorithm classifies the movement into two classes. The first concerns the movements made by the whole body while the second represents the movements made only by hands. In this algorithm we used only five parameters {P2, P3, P4, P5 and P6}. The second algorithm achieves an overall classification and uses the entire set of parameters.

The clustering algorithm K-means (MacQueen, 1967) allows to partition the set of movements into k classes {C1, C2, ..., Ck}. U1 partition of the first algorithm contains two rows and n columns. While for the second algorithm U2 contains 6 rows and n columns where n is the number of video sequences. For each sequence a vector V is generated.

$$U1 = \begin{bmatrix} u_{1,1} & u_{1,2} & \cdots & u_{1,n} \\ u_{2,1} & u_{2,2} & \cdots & u_{2,n} \end{bmatrix}; \quad U2 = \begin{bmatrix} u_{1,1} & u_{1,2} & \cdots & u_{1,n} \\ u_{2,1} & u_{2,2} & \cdots & u_{2,n} \\ \vdots & \vdots & \ddots & \vdots \\ u_{6,1} & u_{6,2} & \cdots & u_{6,n} \end{bmatrix} \tag{10}$$

Where $u_{i,j} \in \{0,1\}$: means the belonging of the movement Pj to the class Ci.

$$\begin{cases} \text{if } P_j \in C_i \text{ then } u_{i,j} = 1 \\ \text{else } \quad u_{i,j} = 0 \end{cases} \tag{11}$$

In addition, we impose the following two constraints on each partition

$$\sum_{i=1}^{K} u_{i,j} = 1, \; j = 1,\dots,N \tag{12}$$

$$\sum_{i=1}^{N} u_{i,j} > 0, \; i = 1,\dots,K \tag{13}$$

With K is equal to 2 for the first algorithm and 6 for the second. The first specifies that any sample movement must belong to one and only one class of the partition, while the second specifies that a class must have at least one sample of movement.

5. Classification results

The KTH human action database is the largest database available. Each video contains a single action. The database contains six types of human movements (walking, jogging, running, boxing, hand waving and hand clapping). These movements are performed several times by 25 persons in different scenarios, in external or internal environment. The database contains a total of 600 long sequences, that can be divided to more than 10 short sequences of 4 seconds each one.

To test the results of our approach for the recognition task, we used 25% of samples from the video database for the learning task. The 75% remaining video samples are used in the validation task of the performance of the method developed. Figure 10 shows the confusion matrix of classification results for the KTH database.

The confusion matrix in Figure 10 shows the performance obtained for the KTH human action database. Indeed, 450 samples were used to obtain these results (75 for each class). Each column of the matrix represents the accuracy of a class estimated, while each row represents the accuracy of a real class.

	walking	jogging	running	hand clapping	hand waving	boxing
walking	0.97	0.02	0.01	0.00	0.00	0.00
jogging	0.02	0.91	0.07	0.00	0.00	0.00
running	0.01	0.10	0.89	0.00	0.00	0.00
hand clapping	0.00	0.00	0.00	0.98	0.02	0.00
hand waving	0.00	0.00	0.00	0.02	0.97	0.01
boxing	0.00	0.00	0.00	0.00	0.01	0.99

Fig. 10. Confusion matrix for KTH human action database

The best accuracy is obtained for running action while boxing action has the lowest accuracy. The overall recognition rate of our approach exceeds 95%.

The developed approach leads to interesting results compared to other algorithms for human action recognition. All these methods use STIPs to characterize movements without tracking algorithms or background segmentation. Our approach is also comparable to methods based on tracking or segmentation. In Table 4, we illustrate the classification of different approaches according to their accuracy.

Method	Year	Accuracy
Our Method	2011	95,17 %
Xunshi et al.	2010	90,30 %
Ikizler et al.	2009	89,40 %
Niebles et al.	2008	83,33 %
Dollár et al.	2005	81,17 %

Table 4. Classification of different approaches according to their accuracy

6. Conclusion

In this chapter we presented the approach developed for the human action recognition using spatiotemporal interest points STIPs. The STIPs were detected by the application of Laptev STIPs detector. Our classification approach is based on a parameter vector deduced from different studies. The first concerns STIPs number in 100 frames, the second studies the evolution of this number in each frame of the sequence while the third classifies the STIPs in spatiotemporal boxes associated to different parts of the body. For classification we used the k-means classifier. The approach developed has leaded to good performances compared to the well known methods for human action recognition.

As we have only considered K-means as the classification algorithm, we are actually implementing SVM and pLDA algorithms and we plane to make a comparative study between them. Additionally, other metrics will be used to evaluate the methods performances such as Precision, Recall, True Negative Rate (TNR) etc.

7. References

Bobick, A. F. & Davis, J. W. (2001). The recognition of human movement using temporal templates. *IEEE Transactions on Pattern Analysis and Machine Intelligence*, Vol.23, No.3, (Mars 2001), pp. 257 267, ISSN 0162 8828.

Dollár, P.; Rabaud, V.; Cottrell, G. & Belongie, S. (2005). Behavior recognition via sparse spatio-temporal features, *Proceedings of 2nd joint IEEE international workshop on visual surveillance and performance evaluation of tracking and surveillance*, pp. 65-72, ISBN 0-7803-9424-0, Beijing, China, October 15-16, 2005.

Efros, A. A., Berg, A. C., Mori, G., & Malik, J. (2003). Recognizing action at a distance. *Proceedings of the ninth IEEE international conference on computer vision*, Vol. 2, pp. 726–733, ISBN 0-7695-1950-4, Nice, France, October 13-16, 2003.

Harris, C., & Stephens, M. (1988). A combined corner and edge detector. *Proceedings of the fourth Alvey vision conference*, pp. 147- 152, University of Manchester, UK, August 31- September 2, 1988.

Hoey, J. (2001). Hierarchical unsupervised learning of facial expression categories. *Proceedings of IEEE workshop on detection and recognition of events in video*, pp. 99–106, ISBN 0-7695-1293-3, Vancouver, Canada, July 8, 2001.

Ikizler, N., & Duygulu, P., (2009). Histogram of oriented rectangles: A new pose descriptor for human action recognition. *Image and Vision Computing*, Vol.27, No.10, (September 2009), pp. 1515–1526, ISSN 0262-8856.

Kadir, T., & Brady, M., (2003). Scale saliency: a novel approach to salient feature and scale selection. *Proceedings of international Conference on Visual Information Engineering*, pp. 25–28, ISBN 1-55860-715-3, November, 2000.

Koelstra, S., & Patras, I., (2009). The fast-3D spatio-temporal interest region detector. *Proceedings of 10th Workshop on Image Analysis for Multimedia Interactive Services*, pp. 242-245, ISBN 978-1-4244-3609-5, London, UK, May 6-8, 2009.

Laganière, R., Bacco, R., Hocevar, A. Lambert, P. Païs, G. and Ionescu B.E., Video summarization from spatio-temporal features. ACM, 2008.

Laptev, I. (2005). On space-time interest points. *International Journal of Computer Vision*, Vol.64, No.2-3, (September 2005), pp. 107–123, ISSN 0920-5691

Laptev, I., & Lindeberg, T., (2004). Local descriptors for spatiotemporal recognition. Proceedings of First International Workshop "Spatial Coherence for Visual Motion Analysis" Springer LNCS Vol.3667, pp. 91-103, ISBN 3-540-32533-6. Prague, Czech Republic, May, 15, 2004.

Lowe, D., (1999). Object recognition from local scale-invariant features. *Proceedings of International Conference on Computer Vision*, pp. 1150–1157, ISBN 0-7695-0164-8, Kerkyra, Corfu, Greece, September, 20-25, 1999.

MacQueen, J. B. (1967). Some Methods for classification and Analysis of Multivariate Observations. *Proceedings of 5th Berkeley Symposium on Mathematical Statistics and Probability*, pp. 281–297, University of California, USA, June 21-July 18, 1965 and December 27, 1965-January 7, 1966

Niebles, J., Wang, H., & Fei-Fei, L., (2008). Unsupervised learning of human action categories using spatial-temporal words, *International Journal of Computer Vision* Vol.79, No.3 (September 2008), pp. 299-318, ISSN 0920-5691.

Oikonomopoulos, A., Patras, I., & Pantic, M., (2006). Spatiotemporal Salient Points for Visual Recognition of Human Actions, *IEEE Trans. Sys. Man. and Cybernetics,* Part B Vol.36, No.3, (June 2006), pp. 710-719, ISSN 1083-4419.

Ramanan, D., & Forsyth, D. A., (2004). Automatic annotation of everyday movements. In: *Advances in neural information processing systems,* Thrun, S.; Saul, L.; & Schölkopf, B., (Eds.), Vol.16, ISBN 0-262-20152-6 Cambridge: MIT Press.

Simac-Lejeune, A., Rombaut, M., & Lambert, P., (2010). Points d'intérêt spatio-temporels pour la détection de mouvements dans les vidéos. *Proceedings of MajecSTIC 2010,* Bordeaux, France, october, 13-15, 2010.

Schuldt, C., Laptev, I., & Caputo, B. (2004). Recognizing human actions: a local svm approach. *Proceedings of the 17th International Conference on Pattern Recognition,* pp. 32-36, ISBN 0-7695-2128-2, Cambridge, England, UK., August, 23-26, 2004.

Xunshi, Y., & Yupin, L. (2010). Making full use of spatial-temporal interest points: an ADABOOST approach for action recognition, *Proceedings of IEEE 17th International Conference on Image Processing,* pp. 4677- 4680, ISBN 978-1-4244-7992-4, Hong Kong, China, September, 26-29, 2010.

Zhong, H., Shi, J., & Visontai,M. (2004). Detecting unusual activity in video. *Proceedings of the 2004 IEEE computer society conference on computer vision and pattern recognition,* pp. 819-826, ISBN 0-7695-2158-4, Washington DC, USA, June 27-July 2, 2004.